After DOHA

THE CHANGING ATTITUDE & IDEAS OF THE NEW WTO ROUND

By Terence P. Stewart

Transnational Publishers, Inc.

Published and distributed by *Transnational Publishers, Inc.*
Ardsley Park
Science and Technology Center
410 Saw Mill River Road
Ardsley, NY 10502

Phone: 914–693–5100
Fax: 914–693–4430
E-mail: info@transnationalpubs.com
Web: www.transnationalpubs.com

Libraray of Congress Cataloging-in-Publication Data

Stewart, Terence P.
After Doha : the changing attitude and ideas of the new WTO round / by Terence P. Stewart.
p.cm.
ISBN 1–57105–261–5
1. World Trade Organization. 2. Foreign trade regulation. 3. Commercial treaties. 4. International economic relations. 5. Developing countries—Foreign economic relations. I. Title.

K3823 .S74 2002
341.7'54—dc21 2002024678

Manufactured in the United States of America

Contents

KEY DATES FOR THE NEGOTIATIONS

1. End of 2001	Completion of Rules of Origin Harmonization program
2. January 31, 2002	First meeting of Trade Negotiating Committee by now
3. June 30, 2002	(a) Services: initial requests for specific commitments due (b) Crosscutting issues: recommendations on S&D
4. July 31, 2002	(a) Textiles: whether to change quota growth rates (b) Subsidies: report on CVD investigations
5. End of 2002	(a) Implementation Issues: outstanding implementation issues for which there are not separate negotiating mandate (GATT 1994, SPS, TBT, TRIMS, Customs Valuation, Safeguards, Crosscutting issues) (b) Other reports and decisions on implementation due in other Negotiating Sectors
6. March 31, 2003	(a) Services: initial offers due (b) Agriculture: establish modalities for further commitments
7. May 2003	(a) Dispute Settlement Understanding: modifications to DSU to be adopted
8. Nov.-Dec. 2003	5th Ministerial - stocktaking, reports, negotiations on Singapore issues
9. January 1, 2005	Conclusion of all negotiations (other than DSU)

The WTO's Doha Development Round of Trade Negotiations
Launch: November 14, 2001
Target Completion Date: January 1, 2005

After Doha:
The Changing Attitude and Ideas of the New WTO Round

By: Terence P. Stewart, Esq.
Managing Partner

On Thursday, November 14, 2001, during the early evening, in Doha, Qatar, at the end of the WTO's 4th Ministerial meeting, 142 WTO member countries, including the US, agreed to the launch of a new round of trade negotiations (technically, India did not agree, simply did not block the launch of a new round). The first meeting of the negotiating committee will take place no later than January 2002* and the target for completion of negotiations is January 2005 (earlier for certain dispute settlement issues). Coming seven and a half years after the conclusion of the Uruguay Round negotiations in Marrakesh in 1994, the launch of the new round has a much heavier emphasis on issues of interest to developing countries and includes various modifications to existing WTO agreements in the name of addressing "implementation" issues. The new round includes the built-in agenda from existing WTO agreements (e.g., negotiations in agriculture and services) but adds many other issues which various members (developed and developing) sought to make future negotiations "balanced" and to address concerns of the public in various countries. Added to the negotiations is a substantial list of "outstanding implementation issues" in eleven categories which seek, *inter alia,* to rebalance the rights and obligations of nations assumed as part of the Uruguay Round package.**

The launch of a new round is being heralded by many as important considering the current global economic situation and the WTO's need to reestablish credibility after its inability to resolve issues two years ago at Seattle. For certain sectors of many economies, the launch and conclusion will undoubtedly be helpful, although the breadth of the new round and the delay in the start of negotiations on a host of issues renders it highly likely that negotiations will extend far beyond the January 1, 2005 announced conclusion. It is also true that the launch of the new round:

> will raise concerns within certain parts of the business community in various economies who perceive that the launch includes potentially damaging agreements on existing rights (e.g., pharmaceutical companies in a number of countries),
>
> reopens agreements where there has been strong industry and legislative opposition to inclusion (e.g., rules) in the US,

---

* The first TNC meeting is currently scheduled for January 28, 2002.

** During the 4th Ministerial, there were three other important events: admission of the People's Republic of China, and of Taiwan and the granting of a waiver to the EC in its ACP Program.

rebalances the rights and obligations in favor of developing countries in many areas,

reduces disciplines on trade distorting subsidies and trade related investment measures by developing countries,

deepens special and differential rights for developing countries, and

fails to include topics of importance to some, such as labor.

For a number of developing countries, there are also concerns that

the WTO Members have not addressed enough of the implementation issues raised to date,

the needs for capacity building and technical assistance are not being fully addressed, and

the system continues to favor developed countries.

This memorandum attempts to identify the major elements of the upcoming negotiations as well as reviewing the major decisions taken in Doha. Much of the language about particular provisions is taken from the documents listed below.

VIEW FROM THE WTO'S DIRECTOR-GENERAL

"By any standards, the 4th Ministerial conference of the WTO was an extraordinarily successful meeting. We tend to talk rather glibly about the historic importance of such events, but this time, for once, the claim is not exaggerated; the meeting at Doha will be remembered as a turning-point in the history of the WTO and the trading system and in relations between developed and developing countries within that system."

WTO Director-General Mike Moore, 28 November 2001, 14th general meeting of the Pacific Economic Cooperation Council
http://www.wto.org/english/news_e/spmm_e/spmmm73_e.htm

I. The package of documents coming out of Doha

The WTO has released the documents that were agreed to in Doha:

1. Ministerial Declaration, WT/MIN(01)/DEC/1, 20 November 2001 (adopted November 14, 2001);

2. Declaration on the TRIPS Agreement and Public Health, WT/MIN(01)/DEC/2, 20 November 2001 (adopted November 14, 2001);

3. Implementation-Related Issues and Concerns, Decision of 14 November 2001, WT/MIN(01)/17, 20 November 2001;

4. Compilation of Outstanding Implementation Issues Raised by Members, JOB(01)/152/Rev.1, 27 October 2001 (referenced in para. 13, footnote 2 of WT/MIN(01)/17 page 8)

5. Proposed Procedures for Extensions Under Article 27.4 for Certain Developing Country Members, G/SCM/39, 20 November 2001

INITIAL REACTIONS TO THE MINISTERIAL DECLARATION

Statement by Pascal Lamy, EC Trade Commissioner, Closing Press Conference, Doha, November 14, 2001: "we have now reached agreement on a Declaration that constitutes a extremely solid basis for a new set of WTO negotiations. * * *
A quick word on our objectives coming into this conference. We sought:
"Comprehensive trade liberalization, not least to restore business confidence;
"But not just a head long rush towards freer trade. We wanted legitimacy not just liberalization and a strengthening of the rules-based trade system.
"And most importantly, a Round which focuses on development. Not just the direct trade interests of developing countries, but sustainable development in the system.
"These have been the EU goals since before Seattle WTO train was all but derailed. The tracks were damaged and the locomotive had broken down. Many doubted that it could be repaired. Well we've proved them wrong. The WTO is back on track and the train has left the station. We'll be travelling at speeds that take account of the diversity of the 142 passengers who've climbed aboard and we're committed the single undertaking to pulling into the station together. * * * In short, we have made major strides towards realizing sustainable development; we have a proper balance between regulation and market access; and most of all, we have a negotiating equilibrium between systemic benefits to the WTO, EU interests, and the interests of developing countries." http://europa.eu.int/comm/trade/speeches_araticles/spla81_en.htm

INITIAL REACTIONS TO THE MINISTERIAL DECLARATION -- *CONTINUED*

"USTR Zoellick says world has chosen path of hope, openness, development and growth," USTR Press Release 01-100, November 14, 2001: "We've reached an agreement that affirms the commitment of 142 WTO members to work cooperatively to reduce the world's trade barriers. This signal of forward progress on trade gives an endorsement and very timely boost to the multilateral trading system. * * * Launching the negotiations with this declaration is a landmark achievement for U.S. agriculture. * * * Our work here can mark a new era in economic cooperation between developing and developed nations. On a range of issues, such as agricultural liberalization and reduction of tariffs on non-agricultural goods, we've shown how our interests can converge with the developing world. * * * The adoption of the landmark political declaration on the TRIPS Agreement and public health is a good example of developed and developing nations advancing common goals by working through issues together. I believe this declaration highlights that we have provisions in the TRIPS agreement that provide members with the flexibility to address public health emergencies, like HIV/AIDS and tuberculosis and malaria. And it also recognizes the importance of intellectual property protection for the development of new life saving medicines. * * * Through the declaration more than 140 members of the WTO members have expressed their strong support for the TRIPS Agreement and we believe this declaration affirms that TRIPS and the global trading system can help countries address pressing public health problems. In the area of rules, the text provides for a two-phase process of negotiations to clarify and improve the disciplines under the Agreements on Anti-dumping and Countervailing Measures, and on trade distorting practices that give rise to dumping and countervailing duties. The text notes that the negotiations should preserve the effectiveness of the Agreements and the instruments that we apply, thus recognizing that these instruments are legitimate means to counter unfair trade practices and should not be undermined. In services, the declaration sets the stage for the commencement of negotiations on new liberalization commitments, in sectors including telecommunications, financial services, energy, audio visual, and express delivery. * * * On environment, we have a number of excellent results. We have agreed to negotiate disciplines on fisheries subsidies * * * *. We have, for the first time, an agreement that calls for negotiations on the relationship between the WTO rules and the specific trade-related obligations of members of certain multilateral environmental agreements. * * * And we will negotiate to remove the barriers to environmental goods and services, a true win-win process."

II. The Ministerial Declaration and review of the Work Program identified therein

The Ministerial Declaration consists of three segments: (1) eleven introductory paragraphs which set the stage for the work program; (2) review of the work program agreed upon by the Members (33 paragraphs broken into 19 topics); and (3) organization and management of the work program.

A. Introductory paragraphs

Themes in the first 11 paragraphs include:

(1) role the multilateral trading system has played in economic growth;
(2) role international trade can play in economic development and need to place developing country "needs and interests at the heart of the Work Programme";
(3) need to address the marginalization of least developed countries and help them integrate into the multilateral trading system;
(4) role of WTO in global trade rule-making and liberalization and role of regional trade agreements;
(5) need to work with other "Bretton Woods institutions for greater coherence in global economic policy-making";
(6) reaffirmation of commitment to sustainable development;
(7) reaffirmation of right of Members to regulate the supply of services;
(8) reaffirmation of core labor standards; note ILO work on social dimension of globalization;
(9) welcome new members and accessions of China and Taiwan at Ministerial; importance to concluding remaining 28 accessions;
(10) commitment to internal transparency and effective participation by all members;
(11) in view of the above, "agree to undertake the broad and balanced Work Programme" included in the Declaration.

B. The Work Programme

There are **19** elements to the work program, the first of which "Implementation-Related Issues and Concerns" was of primary importance to developing countries, on the premise that there were many developing country rights not implemented by other countries despite the WTO being in existence for nearly seven years and certain rebalancing of the package needed to ensure developing and least developed countries participate reasonably in the benefits of trade expansion.

(1) Implementation-Related Issues and Concerns: Many developing countries have held the resolution of at least some of the many implementation issues raised as critical to gain their support for the launch of a new round. Paragraph 12 of the Ministerial Declaration has the Members (i) adopting the Decision on Implementation-Related Issues and Concerns (WT/MIN(01)/17), (ii) agreeing to make negotiations on outstanding implementation issues

INITIAL REACTIONS TO THE MINISTERIAL DECLARATION -- *CONTINUED*

Hwang Doo-yun, Minister for Trade, Republic of Korea, Nov. 27, 2001: "The agreement on the Doha Development Agenda sent a clear-cut message of optimism all over the world. Specifically, the Doha Declaration produced progress on three fronts. First of all, it has declared that the world is once more united behind the cause of further promoting free trade. Markets all around the world have been waiting in anticipation of this new momentum. Second, the declaration made it clear that the WTO's role will be further extended to encompass most areas of global economic activity, with many new rules being brought in under its umbrella. And, this extension of the WTO's presence in the global economy, of course, received an even greater boost with the participation of new members, China and Taiwan. Third, the Declaration made it very clear that the concerns of developing economies are not only being listened to but also being actively incorporated into the steps that the WTO is taking. Inclusion of the word development' in the name 'Doha Development Agenda' clearly reflects this, as does the separate ministerial declaration prepared on public health issues. Korea takes great satisfaction in being part of this gain; as we have been making very clear from the beginning that the development concerns have to be included as a key agenda in the WTO. Korea's efforts to put this belief into practice, in areas such as the implementations discussion, have paid off." http://www.mofat.go.kr/speech.nsf, "The WTO Doha Development Agenda and Korea's Trade Policy".

Statement by Minister Takeo Hiranuma, Minister of Economy, Trade and Industry, Japan, November 14, 2001: "The greatest achievement of this Ministerial Conference was the launching of the negotiations covering a broad agenda, which will enable us to respond to the challenges of the 21st century. I am delighted that we were able to deliver a strong message to the world precisely when the world economy is showing increased instability since September 11. * * * The Ministerial Declaration sets out a broad agenda for negotiations, including trade liberalization of industrial tariffs, improvement of existing WTO rules including strengthening of disciplines on anti-dumping measures, responding to the challenges in the 21st century such as the formulation of rules on investment and competition, the issue of trade and environment and electronic commerce. Furthermore, I commend the outcome for responding to the concerns of developing members, including the implementation-related issues and access to medicine. I would also like to highlight the inclusion of a specific commitment to begin anti-dumping negotiations and of the preparatory work for the negotiations on investment rules, which Japan has strongly insisted on." http://www.meti.go.jp/policy/trade_policy/wto/new_round/data/statement011114e.htm

INITIAL REACTIONS TO THE MINISTERIAL DECLARATION -- *CONTINUED*

"Major Gains for India at Doha Ministerial Conference," Press Information Bureau, Government of India, November 15, 2001: "India has made significant gains at the Doha Ministerial Conference of the World Trade Organization (WTO) with the Ministerial Declaration launching a work programme which takes on board India's concerns in the key areas of Agriculture, Implementation, TRIPs, Trade & Transfer of Technology and WTO Rules. India has also succeeded in warding off any commitments for negotiations in the important areas of Investment, Competition Policy and Transparency in Government Procurement. This has been made possible through extremely hard bargaining on India's part during the Doha Ministerial Conference." http://commin.nic.in/doc/nov01_release.htm

Hon. Mustafa Bello, Minister of Commerce, Nigeria, November 14, 2001, comments at closing event in Doha (transcribed from webbroadcast): "* * * I'm speaking on behalf of all of the countries of Africa. * * * from Seattle to Doha, the journey for Africa to this hour has not been an easy one. * * * our ministers arrived in Doha with an open mind to negotiate constructively in good faith because Africa believes in a rules-based multilateral trading system. * * * We had concerns in the areas of implementation and the Singapore issues. We also had reservations as to whether future negotiations in the area of trade and environment wouldn't be used as a trade barrier against our products in our market access efforts. Africa also had concerns then in the area of agriculture in terms of the need for some of our development partners to eliminate export subsidies that continued to have a negative impact on our agricultural production and marketing capacities. * * * Above all Africa has concerns about a declaration on TRIPS access to medicines and public health. * * * Unlike in Seattle, Africa has been satisfied with all the stages of consultations and negotiating processes throughout the negotiations in Doha. It is our hope and conviction that accepting the declaration will not only revive confidence in the multilateral trading system but also that we can build on the transparency achieved in the consultation process in Doha in order to safeguard the interests of African countries, the majority of which are least developed countries and need a functioning multilateral trading arrangement. We will hold our partners accountable for the full implementation of the Doha declaration which will come out of this conference. It is our hope that in making compromises and accepting the package which is the outcome of the Doha Ministerial Conference, the commitments that our development partners have made in respect of technical assistance and capacity building in order for our negotiators to enhance their understanding of the issues for negotiation will be kept."

an integral part of the work program: (A) folding issues into particular negotiating mandate where existent; (B) having all other outstanding implementation issues addressed by the various WTO Committees by the end of 2002.

The Compilation of Outstanding Implementation Issues Raised by Members (JOB(01)/152/Rev.1) has eleven categories of issues, only four of which appear to have their own negotiating mandate (dumping (13 issues), subsidies (20 issues), TRIPS (8 issues) and agriculture (1 issue)). Presumably, this means that negotiations will be undertaken during 2002 on the following seven areas:

A. General Agreement on Tariffs and Trade 1994 (balance of payments issues and Art. XVIII)(2 issues);
B. Agreement on the Application of Sanitary and Phytosanitary Measures (1 issue);
C. Agreement on Technical Barriers to Trade (2 issues);
D. Agreement on Trade-Related Investment Measures (4 issues);
E. Agreement on Implementation of Article VII of GATT 1994 (Customs Valuation)(5 issues);
F. Agreement on Safeguards (1 issue — increasing the level of imports of developing countries where exclusion from relief applies);
G. Crosscutting issues (preferential trading agreements between developing and developed countries; redistribution of negotiating rights in favor of small and medium-sized exporting members)(2 issues).

(2) **Agriculture**: This is one of the built-in agenda items and so, technically, negotiations have been ongoing since 2000. EU, Japan, Switzerland, Norway and others have wanted to factor non-trade concerns into the negotiations. EU was unwilling to accept language that requires elimination of export subsidies at least in this round. Paragraph 13 of the Ministerial Declaration outlines the objectives while recognizing that non-trade concerns will be reflected in the negotiations. Objectives include:

A. "substantial improvement in market access";
B. "reductions of, with a view to phasing out, all forms of export subsidies";
C. "substantial reductions in trade-distorting domestic support";
D. agreement that "special and differential treatment for developing countries shall be an integral part of all elements of the negotiations and shall be embodied in the Schedules of concessions and commitments and as appropriate in the rules and disciplines to be negotiated, so as to be operationally effective and to enable developing countries to effectively take account of their development needs, including food security and rural development";
E. taking into consideration non-trade concerns "as provided for in the Agreement on Agriculture"

INITIAL REACTION FROM MAJOR AGRICULTURAL EXPORTERS

Australian Minister for Trade Mark Vaile, Media release, November 15, 2001,"Vaile Welcomes New Trade Round" : "The launch of a new round has been the Coalition Government's key trade priority. This result in Doha is particularly satisfying following the disappointment in Seattle two years ago. The new negotiations will lead to new export opportunities and increased economic growth and job opportunities * * * * The Cairns Group of agricultural exporters, which Australia chairs, played a critical role at Doha in building support for an ambitious agricultural mandate. The Declaration's strong language to phase out export subsidies, achieve major reductions in domestic agricultural support levels and secure significant improvement in market access is a tremendous outcome for Australia. It will go a long way to ensuring agriculture and processed foods receive the long overdue attention they deserve in international trade negotiations." http://www.dfat.gov.au/media/releases/trade/2001/mvt151_01.html?forprint

"Minister says WTO meeting results will mean advantages for Brazil,' November 16, 2001: " Rio, 16 (Agencia Brasil - Abr) - In comments on the results of the World Trade Organization (WTO) meeting in Doha, Qatar, minister of Agriculture, Pratini de Morais, declared that decisions on export subsidies, market access and domestic support for farm produce will translate into a substantial increase in Brazilian agricultural exports over the next few years. The minister also pointed out that some products will now obtain better prices in dollars because prices will be set on the farm rather than at the Treasury, as they are nowadays." http://rvnews.radiobras.gov.br/ing-20011116-1812856-0085.htm

Canada's Department of Foreign Affairs and International Trade News Release, November 14, 2001,"WTO Members Launch Growth and Development Round": "'We have met our objectives,' said Minister Pettigrew. 'The agenda for the next round of negotiations will benefit Canadians and our economy. We are very proud that these negotiations will address the concerns of all WTO members - especially those from the developing world. This truly will be the growth and development round that Canada has been seeking.' 'We have achieved what we came to Doha for - the launch of broad-based negotiations that will allow us to get on with the job of negotiating a significant outcome in agriculture,' said Minister Vanclief. 'This is good news not only for Canada, but also for countries engaged in agricultural production around the world.'" http://webappsdfait-maeci.gc.ca/minpub/Publication.asp?FileSpec=/Min_Pub_Docs/104679.htm

Timetable for action:

(1) By March 31, 2003: establish modalities for further commitments by this date including special and differential treatment provisions;
(2) By Fifth Ministerial (end of 2003), submission of comprehensive draft schedules by each Member
(3) By January 1, 2005, negotiations, "including with respect to rules and disciplines and related legal texts," concluded

(3) **Services**: another part of the built in agenda, negotiations have been underway since 2000. Guidelines and Procedures for the Negotiations were adopted earlier in 2001 (March 28, 2001). "Initial requests for specific commitments" from trading partners are due by June 30, 2002 and initial offers are due by March 31, 2003.

(4) **Market access for nonagricultural products**: This has historically been the heart of GATT negotiations, reducing tariffs on industrial goods. Objectives identified in paragraph 16 of the Ministerial Declaration include the following:

A. Reduce or eliminate tariffs:

(i) including reducing or eliminating "tariff peaks, high tariffs and tariff escalation";
(ii) "as well as non-tariff barriers";
(iii) "in particular on products of export interest to developing countries".

B. Product coverage is "comprehensive and without *a priori* exclusions".

C. Take into account special needs of developing countries, "including through less than full reciprocity in reduction commitments".

D. Modalities for negotiation "will include appropriate studies and capacity-building measures to assist least-developed countries to participate effectively in the negotiations".

While market access improvement through reduced tariffs is welcome by many sectors, the objectives will pose challenges for sectors with above average existing tariff rates. Many developed country and export competitive developing country exporters will be disappointed with the lack of reciprocity in reduction commitments from developing countries.

(5) **Trade-Related Aspects of Intellectual Property Rights**: The work program under TRIPS has a number of elements:

A. establish a "system of notification and registration of geographical indications for wines and spirits" by the 5th Ministerial (end of 2003);

B. address other geographical indication issues under the implementation issue section (para. 12);

C. implement and interpret TRIPS "in a manner supportive of public health" (adopting a separate Declaration);

D. explore relationship between TRIPS and Convention on Biological Diversity and protection of traditional knowledge and folklore.

The Europeans have pushed hard for the first issue, various developing countries for the second - fourth. The pharmaceutical companies have concerns with the breadth of the third issue and presumably with the reach of the fourth as well.

(6) **Relationship between Trade and Investment**: One of the new areas pursued by the EU and Japan, language calls for negotiations to start after the

VIEWS ON WHETHER NEGOTIATIONS ON "THE SINGAPORE ISSUES" START AFTER THE FIFTH MINISTERIAL

I would like to note that some delegations have requested clarification concerning paragraphs 20, 23, 26 and 27 of the draft declaration. Let me say that with respect to the reference for an 'explicit consensus' being needed, in these paragraphs, for a decision to be taken at the Fifth Session of the Ministerial Conference, my understanding is that, at that session, a decision would indeed need to be taken by explicit consensus, before negotiations on trade and investment and trade and competition policy, transparency in government procurement, and trade facilitation could proceed.

In my view, this would also give each member the right to take a position on modalities that would prevent negotiations from proceeding after the Fifth Session of the Ministerial Conference until that member is prepared to join an explicit consensus.
Youssef Hussain Kamal, Qatari Finance, Economy and Trade Minister, Chairman of the Doha Ministerial. (emphasis added). http://www-heva.wto-ministerial.org/english/thewto_e/minist_e/min01_e/min01_chair_speaking_e.htm

"WTO Ministerial, Doha: Assessment of Results for EU," Memo, Doha, 14 November 2001: "* * * The Doha Declaration sets, for the first time ever, the objective of establishing a multilateral framework on competition policies. This should contribute towards a more effective application of domestic competition regimes and be of benefit for consumers worldwide. Even if negotiations will be preceded by a preparatory phase until 5th Ministerial, **there is a clear commitment to launch such negotiations at a certain date and the issue will fall within the single undertaking**" (emphasis added). http://trade-infor.cec.eu.int/europa/2001newround/p14.php

5th Ministerial conference (end of 2003) with ongoing work until then to seek clarification on a variety of issues on cross-border investment. Recognition of need for capacity building in and technical assistance to developing and least developed countries is included. There is some dispute whether language on this and the other Singapore issues (competition, government procurement transparency, trade facilitation) will be construed as requiring a new consensus at the 5th Ministerial on whether negotiations will take place. Issues to be further studied in the next two years include:

A. "scope and definition";
B. "transparency";
C. "nondiscrimination";
D. "modalities for pre-establishment commitments based on a GATS-type, positive list approach" (i.e., countries are only bound on sectors where they agree to be bound);
E. "development provisions";
F. "exceptions and balance-of-payments safeguards";
G. "consultation and the settlement of disputes between Members".

(7) **Interaction between Trade and Competition Policy**: a second new area pursued by the EU and Japan, with a timeline identical to Trade and Investment (negotiations starting after 5th Ministerial, etc.). Issues to be further studied:

A. "core principles, including":
(1) "transparency";
(2) "nondiscrimination";
(3) "procedural fairness";
B. "provisions on hard-core cartels";
C. "modalities for voluntary cooperation";
D. "support for progressive reinforcement of competition institutions in developing countries through capacity building".

(8) **Transparency in Government Procurement**: US and some other governments had hoped to get an agreement in this area at the Seattle Ministerial in 1999. Of great interest to developed countries, horizons have now been pushed back, with the area being treated like investment and competition policy and no negotiations until after the 5th Ministerial.

(9) **Trade facilitation** (release and clearance of goods, including goods in transit): same as investment, competition policy and transparency in government procurement. Negotiations will start after the 5th WTO Ministerial.

As many developing countries place great stock in expanded agricultural export opportunities (as do Canada, Australia and the US), **a program which prevents negotiations from starting until after the 5th Ministerial (end of 2003) virtually guarantees that there will be no further agricultural**

liberalization until well after January 2005. While transparency in government procurement and trade facilitation may be easy issues, both investment and competition policy will likely be very complex areas where progress will come slowly. Inclusion of these issues and the single undertaking aspect of much of the work strongly supports the conclusion that the Doha Development Round will take much longer than three years to conclude.

(10) **WTO Rules**: Paragraph 28 calls for negotiations on the Antidumping Agreement (Agreement on Implementation of Article VI of the GATT 1994) and the Agreement on Subsidies and Countervailing Measures. This paragraph was sought by a number of Members including Japan and Korea but presented major problems to the United States where Congress had repeatedly advised the Administration not to permit the weakening of US trade laws. The US sought modifications to the paragraph and was able to get the insertion of a few words "effectiveness" and "their instruments and objectives" into the final text (see B below). Rules are addressed not only in paragraph 28 of the Ministerial Declaration but also in the Decision on

VIEWS ON WTO RULES

Statement by Minister Takeo Hiranuma, Minister of Economy, Trade and Industry, Japan, November 14, 2001: "The Ministerial Declaration sets out a broad agenda for negotiations, including trade liberalization of industrial tariffs, improvement of existing WTO rules including strengthening of disciplines on anti-dumping measures, *** I would also like to highlight the inclusion of a specific commitment to begin anti-dumping negotiations and of the preparatory work for the negotiations on investment rules, which Japan has strongly insisted on." http://www.meti.go.jp/policy/trade_policy/wto/new_round/data/statement011114e.htm

"USTR Zoellick says world has chosen path of hope, openness, development and growth," USTR Press Release 01-100, November 14, 2001: "*** In the area of rules, the text provides for a two-phase process of negotiations to clarify and improve the disciplines under the Agreements on Anti-dumping and Countervailing Measures, and on trade distorting practices that give rise to dumping and countervailing duties. The text notes that the negotiations should preserve the effectiveness of the Agreements and the instruments that we apply, thus recognizing that these instruments are legitimate means to counter unfair trade practices and should not be undermined."

> Implementation-Related Issues and Concerns, Compilation of Outstanding Implementation Issues Raised by Members and the Proposed Procedures for Extensions Under Article 27.4 for Certain Developing Country Members. Objectives in para. 28 of the Ministerial Declaration are:
>
> A. "clarifying and improving disciplines under" the two agreements;
> B. "while preserving the basic concepts, principles and effectiveness of these Agreements and their instruments and objectives"
> C. "and taking into account the needs of developing and least-developed participants."
>
> There will be phases to the negotiations, although time lines are not identified in para. 28. The first phase will have parties indicating "the provisions, including disciplines on trade distorting practices, that they seek to clarify and improve in the subsequent phase." Fisheries subsidies are singled out as needing clarification and improved WTO disciplines.

As reviewed above, there are 33 issues (13 antidumping and 20 subsidies) that will be folded into the negotiations on rules that are identified in the Compilation of Outstanding Implementation Issues Raised by Members:

13 issues to be considered as part of negotiating mandate for antidumping:

1. whether to make the lesser duty rule mandatory (Art. 9.1 of AD Agreement);
2. whether "clarification" of Art. 2.2 (how to determine normal value when there aren't home market sales) is needed "in order to make appropriate comparison with respect to margin of dumping";
3. whether changes should be made to a wide variety of provisions "to prevent the imposition of arbitrary or primarily protectionist measures":
   (a) reviews,
   (b) product definition,
   (c) margin of dumping calculus;
   (d) imposition and collection of duties; and
   (e) cumulation of imports in injury determinations;
4. whether to raise the *de minimis* level of dumping for developing countries to 5%;
5. whether Members should apply the proposed *de minimis* in both investigations and reviews;
6. whether the Agreement should be modified to increase the threshold level of imports that are considered negligible from 3% (all countries) to 5 or 7% for developing countries;
7. whether the Agreement should be modified to change volume of sales that can be sold below cost without having them eliminated from home market sales base from 20% (current agreement) "to at least 40%";
8. whether the Agreement should be modified to add additional details "of dealing with foreign exchange rate fluctuations during the process of dumping" (Art. 2.4.1);

9. whether the Agreement should be modified to add to Article 3 (determination of injury) "a detailed provision dealing with the determination of material retardation of the establishment of a domestic industry" (no separate set of criteria for material retardation currently exist);
10. whether the Agreement should be modified to add a presumption of dumping by developed countries into developing countries where certain conditions are met;
11. whether the Agreement should be modified to eliminate special standard of review provided in Article 17 for dispute settlement (US had fought hard in Uruguay Round for a special standard);
12. whether the Agreement should be modified to develop simplified standards for bringing antidumping actions for least developed countries;
13. whether the Agreement should be modified to provide that imports from least developed countries should be deemed negligible unless at least 7% of total imports and to prohibit cumulation of imports from least developed countries.

20 issues raised on Agreement on Subsidies and Countervailing Measures (presumably a number flow from the commercial aircraft disputes between Canada and Brazil):

1. whether the Agreement should be modified so that prohibited subsidies are treated as non-actionable if provided by a developing country;
2. whether the Agreement should be modified so that developing country export credits are not viewed as subsidies if interest rates are above LIBOR;
3. whether the Agreement should be modified so that countervailing duties will be collected only to the extent the amounts exceed de minimis (i.e., if net subsidies are 5% and de minimis is 2%, government would only collect 3%);
4. whether the Agreement should be modified so that Annex VII (lists countries for whom prohibited subsidies are not prohibited based on income levels) covers more countries;
5. whether the Agreement should be modified so that the export subsidy prohibition becomes active under Art. 27.6, where country has achieved export competitiveness where country meets minimum share for five consecutive years vs. two years at present;
6. whether the Agreement should be modified to eliminate the prohibition on export subsidies by developing countries if "less than 5% of the fob value of the product";
7. whether the Agreement should be modified so that CVD cases are terminated where imports from a single developing country are less than 7% of total imports;
8. whether the Agreement should be modified to permit duty rate remission claims for developing countries even where they can't establish the source of inputs (i.e., eliminate subsidy finding where developing country can't supply required information);
9. whether the Agreement should be modified to permit developing countries to "neutralize the cost escalating effect of taxes";

10. whether the Agreement should be modified so that de minimis levels for developing countries is changed to 2.5% under Art. 11.9;
11. whether the Agreement should be modified so that CVD *de minimis* levels for developing countries is increased above current 3% level;
12. whether the Agreement should be modified to clarify that Art. 27.3 (subsidies contingent on use of domestic vs. imported goods) is "applicable not withstanding the provisions of any other agreements" (e.g., TRIMs Agreement)
13. whether the Agreement should be modified so that "inputs consumed in the production process" are expanded to include all inputs, not just physical inputs (major change to Annex II and indirect tax rebate schemes);
14. whether the Agreement should be modified to change Annex I (illustrative list of export subsidies) "to provide developing countries the flexibility to finance their exporters, consistent with their development needs";
15. whether Article 27 of the Agreement (special and differential treatment of developing country members) should be modified to address "the needs and specificities of developing countries concerning incentives and subsidies";
16. whether the illustrative list of export subsidies (specifically para. (k) of Annex I) contained in the Agreement should be modified "to permit developing countries to provide competitive export financing vis-à-vis conditions found in the international market or offered by the credit agencies of developed countries";
17. whether Annex VII of the Agreement should be modified to give greater flexibility to developing countries to qualify for use of export subsidies;
18. whether the Agreement should be modified so that "subsidies required for development, diversification and upgrading infant industries including freight rebate schemes in developing countries" are non-actionable;
19. whether the Agreement should be modified so that LDCs are exempt from cumulation, "exempt from competitiveness thresholds of subsidies" and so the threshold of imports under Art. 27.4 is increased to 10% from 4%;
20. whether the Agreement should be modified so that financial resources are "provided to LDCs to enable them to meet their special needs, in particular with respect to subsidies covered by Article 8.2(c)(green subsidies)"(environmental upgrading).

At the same time, the WTO Members adopted procedures for Extensions Under Article 27.4 for certain developing countries which essentially identifies steps that can be taken for developing countries who were phasing out export subsidies over the original 8 year period envisioned under 27.4.

Finally, in the Rules area, there are a number of "implementation-related" clarifications adopted which are reviewed separately.

Paragraph 29 of the Ministerial Declaration also calls for "negotiations aimed at clarifying and improving disciplines and procedures under the existing WTO provisions applying to regional trade agreements." The developmental aspect of RTAs are to be taken into account.

(11) **Dispute Settlement Understanding**: There has been an effort underway for a number of years to clarify a number of the provisions of the Dispute Settlement Understanding. There was a package that would likely have been adopted had events in Seattle resulted in the launch of a new round. Paragraph 30 permits "additional proposals by Members" to supplement the work that has been underway.

The target for agreement on improvements and clarifications is May 2003. It is envisioned that results of this exercise will be put into effect as quickly as possible after agreement.

(12) **Trade and Environment**: There has been a Trade and Environment Committee as part of the WTO since its inception, and the T&E Committee has had an agenda looking at a range of issues including the relationship between the WTO and multilateral environmental agreements (MEAs). Nonetheless, it was of great interest to the EU to have formal negotiations on Trade and Environment. Negotiations will take place on three topics:

A. "relationship between existing WTO rules and specific trade obligations set out in" the MEAs;
B. "procedures for regular information exchange between MEA Secretariats and the relevant WTO committees";
C. "the reduction, or, as appropriate, elimination of tariff and non-tariff barriers to environmental goods and services".

The ongoing work of the WTO Committee on Trade and Environment is to focus on market access issues (particularly for developing and LDCs), "the relevant provisions of" the TRIPS agreement, and "labelling requirements for environmental purposes".

The Committee will report at the 5th Ministerial (late 2003) and identify action that should be taken including additional negotiations.

As in most areas, capacity building for developing countries and technical assistance are identified as important in the T&E area.

(13) **Electronic Commerce:** the topic has been under review within the WTO since 1998 and will be continued. Customs duties are not to be imposed on electronic commerce until the 5th Ministerial; a report on progress in determining how to handle within the WTO will be made at the 5th Ministerial

(14) **Small Economies**: without creating a subcategory of WTO members, members will examine issues related to the trade of small economies for the fuller integration of such economies into the multilateral trading system. Recommendations for action shall be made to the 5th Ministerial (late 2003).

(15) **Trade, Debt and Finance**: An issue of significant importance to many developing and least developed countries, the work program on this topic is limited

to an examination of the relationship between trade, debt and finance and what, if any, steps the WTO can take to:

A. contribute to the solution of "external indebtedness of developing and least developed countries";
B. "strengthen the coherence of international trade and financial policies"

"with a view to safeguarding the multilateral trading system from the effects of financial and monetary instability" (e.g., Asian financial crisis of 1997)

The General Council will report to the 5th Ministerial on the progress of the examination undertaken (similar to programs adopted at the 1st Ministerial in Singapore).

(16) **Trade and Transfer of Technology**: a long-standing issue of interest to developing countries in all multilateral economic fora, this topic follows the trade, debt and finance model of calling for an examination of the linkages and what, if anything, the WTO can do to increase flows of technology to developing countries. A report at the 5th Ministerial is similarly mandated.

(17) **Technical cooperation and capacity building**: As is recognized by all of the members of the WTO, if the rights and obligations of WTO members are to be fully implemented and achieved, substantial technical cooperation and capacity building is needed in many member nations. Historically, the WTO and the GATT before it relied in large measure for voluntary contributions from member states for much of the technical cooperation activity. Efforts to bring countries into compliance with Customs Valuation requirements, TRIPS obligations and other obligations under the WTO have resulted in a need for substantial resources being provided by certain member states or other multilateral organization (e.g., WIPO on TRIPS capacity building).

The work program in this important area includes specific commitments in many of the areas reviewed above, stresses coordination with other groups in the delivery of technical cooperation and capacity building support and the elimination of uncertainty as to funding levels by making WTO technical assistance a budget issue within the organization. The Director-General will provide an interim report in December 2002 and a report at the 5th Ministerial on the implementation of the technical assistance promised.

(18) **Least-Developed Countries**: The WTO has been pursuing ways to better integrate LDCs into the multilateral system. Such countries in many cases continue to be marginalized in their participation in international trade.

Member nations are encouraged to provide improved market access with the objective being duty-free, quota-free market access for products from LDCs. The WTO is prioritizing the accession process of LDCs. It is also urging members to contribute to the trust funds for trade-related technical assistance to LDCs. The

Director-General will provide an interim report in December 2002 and a report at the 5th Ministerial on all issues affecting LDCs.

(19) **Special and Differential Treatment**: developing and least developed countries have obtained special and differential (S&D) treatment on many obligations and rights within the WTO and GATT before it. The work program agreed at Doha (para. 44) includes a review of all S&D treatment provisions for possible "strengthening" (i.e., giving greater latitude to developing and LDCs re obligations/rights within the WTO) and "making them more precise, effective and operational". Paragraph 12 of the Ministerial Declaration and the Compilation of Outstanding Implementation Issues Raised by Members are other areas where S&D issues are being pursued.

C. Organization and Management of the Work Programme

This section of the Ministerial Declaration:

1. outlines the date for conclusion of the negotiations (1 January 2005),
2. sets the 5th Ministerial as the time for stock taking of progress;
3. calls for the establishment of a Special Session of the Ministerial Conference once the negotiations are concluded "regarding the adoption and implementation of those results" (similar to Marrakesh meeting at the end of the Uruguay Round);
4. provides for supervision through a "Trade Negotiations Committee (TNC) under the authority of the General Council";
5. requires the first meeting of the TNC to occur by January 31, 2002 (currently scheduled for January 28, 2002);
6. calls for a single undertaking except for the DSU modifications reviewed above;
7. provides for provisional or definitive implementation of agreements reached before the conclusion of the negotiations;
8. makes negotiations open to all Members of the WTO and those in the accession process (although decisions on the outcomes of negotiations are taken by WTO Members only);
9. calls for negotiations to be transparent for all participants and to achieve an overall balance,
10. recognizes the principle of S&D treatment for developing and least developed countries;
11. has two committees (Committee on Trade and Development and Committee on Trade and Environment) "act as a forum to identify and debate developmental and environmental aspects of the negotiations, in order to help achieve the objective of having sustainable development appropriately reflected".

VIEWS ON TRIPs AGREEMENT

"**Minister commemorates Brazilian victory on patents," November 20, 2001** : "Brasilia, 20 (Agencia Brasil - Abr) - Minister of Development, Sergio Amarul, speaking at the seminar, '30 Years of Support for Technological Evolution,' declared that **Brazil obtained an extraordinary victory at the WTO meeting in Doha, Qatar, when a public health emergency situation was recognized as a reason to break patents on drugs**. 'The courageous, determined and innovative role of minister of Health, Jose Serra, deserves only praise,' said Amaral, pointing out that Serra led a movement which became worldwide against abusive economic power in the form of price setting and drug monopoly. '**We, and other countries, have a right to use and manufacture generic drugs every time the prices of name brand drugs are too high for public health needs,' concluded the minister.**" (emphasis added). http://rvnews.radiobras.gov.br/ing-20011120-162940-0153.htm

"**USTR Zoellick says world has chosen path of hope, openness, development and growth,"** USTR Press Release 01-100, November 14, 2001:
"*** The adoption of the landmark political declaration on the TRIPS Agreement and public health is a good example of developed and developing nations advancing common goals by working through issues together. I believe this declaration highlights that we have provisions in the TRIPS agreement that provide members with the flexibility to address public health emergencies, like HIV/AIDS and tuberculosis and malaria. And it also recognizes the importance of intellectual property protection for the development of new life saving medicines. * * * **Through the declaration more than 140 members of the WTO members have expressed their strong support for the TRIPS Agreement and we believe this declaration affirms that TRIPS and the global trading system can help countries address pressing public health problems."** (emphasis added).

Hon. Mustafa Bello, Minister of Commerce, Nigeria, November 14, 2001, comments at closing event in Doha (transcribed from webbroadcast): "* * * Above all Africa has concerns about a declaration on TRIPS access to medicines and public health. * * *"

III. Declaration on the TRIPS Agreement and Public Health

During the Uruguay Round consideration of Trade Related Aspects of Intellectual Property, a number of developing countries raised concerns about access to medicines and whether governments would be able to address national concerns under the agreement. Compulsory licensing is permitted under Article 31 of the TRIPS Agreement. Nonetheless, there have been some difficult situations which have developed in recent years where Sub-Saharan African nations, including some without sufficient manufacturing facilities in country to make use of compulsory licensing, have attempted to address medical crises from the spread of HIV/AIDS through importing unlicensed copies of patented drugs.

One of the objectives of many developing countries was to obtain a clarification at the start of any new negotiations that they were free to address public health problems without risk of WTO action. The Declaration on the TRIPS Agreement and Public Health is the document accepted by Members to address these concerns.

The Declaration attempts both to reinforce the importance of the TRIPS Agreement and to clarify rights of countries to protect public health (and indeed how the TRIPS Agreement contributes to the solution by developing medicines to address problems). An issue of potential importance is whether the Declaration will be used by panels or the Appellate Body in any forthcoming disputes to construe particular TRIPS provisions. The Declaration asserts no conflict and identifies various ways in which the agreement permits flexibility:

(1) "we affirm that the Agreement can and should be interpreted and implemented in a manner supportive of WTO Members' right to protect public health and, in particular, to promote access to medicines for all."

(2) "Each Member has the right to grant compulsory licenses and the freedom to determine the grounds upon which such licenses are granted".

(3) "Each Member has the right to determine what constitutes a national emergency or other circumstances of extreme urgency * * * *".

(4) "The effect of the provisions of the TRIPS Agreement that are relevant to the exhaustion of intellectual property rights is to leave each Member free to establish its own regime for such exhaustion without challenge, subject to the MFN and national treatment provisions of Article 3 and 4."

The Declaration calls on the Council for TRIPS within the WTO "to find an expeditious solution" to the problem of countries who have insufficient or no manufacturing capacities in the pharmaceutical sector to effectively invoke compulsory licensing rights. A report is due to the General Council by the end of 2002.

Technology transfer is encouraged to LDCs, and the Declaration extends the time for LDC compliance with certain provisions until 2016.

IV. Decision on Implementation-Related Issues and Concerns

This decision is an early deliverable for developing countries, addressing some four dozen issues (broken into fourteen areas) raised by developing countries in recent years "regarding the implementation of some WTO Agreements and Decisions, including the difficulties and resource constraints that have been encountered in the implementation of obligations in various areas". While many developed and some developing countries have been strong supporters of technical assistance and capacity building for developing countries to help them implement existing obligations and rights, the Decision in many areas goes far beyond these concerns whether by agreeing to extensions of time to implement obligations, by looking at broadening special and differential treatment provisions and in other ways.

(1) **GATT 1994**: two issues are raised: (a) reaffirmation that Art. XVIII is an S&D provision for developing countries and should be easier to use than Art. XII on Balance of payment issues; (b) clarification of the term "substantial interest" as used in Art. XIII.2(d) where quotas are being imposed by a Member (Member can negotiate with those countries with a "substantial interest") with recommendations to be made to the General Council by the end of 2002.

(2) **Agreement on Agriculture**: four issues are reviewed, one of which "urges" Members not to challenge green box subsidies notified by developing countries when the green box subsidies are to promote rural development or food security concerns. The other three issues involve the WTO taking note of a report from the Committee on Agriculture (G/AG/11) approving various recommendations on

(a) Implementation of the Decision on Measures Concerning the Possible Negative Effects of the Reform Programme on Least-Developed and Net Food -Importing Developing Countries:

(i) "food aid" — countries "are to review their food aid contributions with a view to better identifying and meeting the food aid needs of least-developed and WTO net food-importing developing countries", are to see that food aid is maintained during periods of high food prices, and is provided on a grant basis to LDCs and as possible to WTO net food-importing developing countries.

(ii) "technical and financial assistance in the context of aid programmes to improve agricultural productivity and infrastructure" — developed countries should provide such assistance to LDCs and "net food-importing developing countries to improve their agricultural productivity and infrastructure"; WTO's General Council should call upon the international development organizations to focus resources of the improvement of productivity and infrastructure.

(iii) "financing normal levels of commercial imports of basic foodstuffs" — differential treatment for ag export credits to

LDCs and WTO net food-importing developing countries and establishment of "an inter-agency panel of financial and commodity experts" to identify ways of improving access to multilateral programs in times of difficulty; report back on both areas to the General Council at the end of 2001 or mid-2002.

(iv) "review of follow-up" — a report on the progress on (i) - (iii) is due in the last third of 2002 (after September 2002 regular Committee on Agriculture meeting).

(b) Implementation of Art. 10.2 of the Agreement on Agriculture ("development of internationally agreed disciplines" re export credits, credit guarantees, etc.) — work is underway within the WTO Committee on Agriculture, Special Session negotiations within the WTO and in the OECD; the Committee on Agriculture is to report to the General Council after its September 2002 regular meeting.

(c) Tariff rate quotas and submission of addenda on their operation — obligations WTO members undertook to improve their reporting of the operation of TRQs are to be kept under review by the Committee on Agriculture

(3) **Agreement on the Application of Sanitary and Phytosanitary Measures**: there are six actions agreed to by the Members:

A. Clarifies length of time developing countries should be given under the S&D Treatment article of the SPS Agreement to continue to ship where phased introduction of new SPS protections are possible as being 6 months or longer.

B. Clarifies that when SPS regulations are proposed they will not take effect (absent urgent circumstances) before six months (unless the measure contributes to liberalization of trade).

C. Instructs the Committee on Sanitary and Phytosanitary Measures to further implement Article 4 on Equivalence, taking note of the October 26, 2001 SPS Committee Decision on implementing Article 4 which establishes procedures for exporting countries to obtain information on risk assessments and levels of protection being sought for particular products, provides timelines for consideration of requests for equivalence findings, encourages technical assistance, etc.

D. Clarifies Article 12.7 of the SPS Agreement by requiring the review of the operation and implementation of the SPS Agreement at least once every four years (12.7 required after 3 years and then as needed).

E. Encourages a continuation of cooperative efforts with standard setting bodies, to seek effective participation of LDCs and facilitating the provision of technical and financial assistance for their participation.

F. Urges Members to provide technical assistance to LDCs to help them respond to new SPS measures which could have significant negative effects on their trade and to see that technical assistance is provided to LDCs to help them implement the SPS Agreement.

(4) **Agreement on Textiles and Clothing**: With just a little over three years remaining before the full integration of textiles and clothing into the WTO, the Decision presents agreement on three matters and instructs an examination of two proposals. Members agreed that:

A. on early integration of products and the elimination of quota restrictions, the existing provisions of the Agreement "should be effectively utilized";

B. Members will exercise "particular consideration" before investigations under antidumping laws are initiated on textile and apparel imports within the first two years of the importing country's eliminating of quota

C. Rules of origin changes in textiles and apparel shall be notified to the Committee on Rules of Origin

Members also requested that the following proposals for expanded market access commitments be examined with recommendations to be made to the General Council by July 31, 2002 for action:

A. for small suppliers and least-developed countries, calculate quota levels using the most favorable methodology and largest growth rates "and, where possible eliminate quota restrictions on imports" from such countries.

B. For other countries, calculate quotas as if the growth-on-growth provision for stage 3 had been advanced two years to January 1, 2000.

Should such proposals be accepted they would constitute a significant increase in market access for textile and apparel products still subject to quota.

(5) **Agreement on Technical Barriers to Trade**: agreements reached in this area parallel those in the SPS agreement and focus on (a) technical assistance being provided particularly to LDCs to implement obligations and to meet new TBT measures that could effect their trade significantly, (b) adoption of minimum time frames (6 months) for countries to comply with new TBT measures (subject to exceptions), (c) facilitate increased participation in the standards setting bodies.

(6) **Agreement on Trade-Related Investment Measures**: the two actions taken in this section (a) take note of actions for certain developing countries to extend the time frame for eliminating certain TRIMs and (b) urges positive consideration for extensions for LDCs if having trouble implementing the agreement.

(7) **Agreement on the Implementation of Article VI of the General Agreement on Tariffs and Trade 1994**: Four matters are addressed in this part of the Decision, three of which require action by the end of 2002:

A. agreement that "special care" will be taken in looking at petitions for initiation of an antidumping case on the same product from the same country where a prior investigation ended in a negative finding within 365 days prior to the new filing.

B. Committee on Anti-Dumping Practices is instructed to develop guidelines within 12 months on making the Special and Differential provision of Article 15 of the agreement "operational". [Article 15 instructs: "Possibilities of constructive remedies provided for by this Agreement shall be explored before applying anti-dumping duties where they would affect the essential interests of developing country Members."]

C. Committee on Anti-Dumping Practices is instructed to develop a recommendation within 12 months on the amount of time importing countries should be using to determine if imports from a country are negligible under Art. 5.8 and hence justify the termination of an investigation. Objective is "predictability and objectivity."

D. Committee on Anti-Dumping Practices is instructed to develop guidelines within 12 months for the improvement of the annual reviews of the implementation and operation of the Agreement.

(8) **Agreement on the Implementation of Article VII of the General Agreement on Tariffs and Trade 1994**: The Customs Valuation agreement is important for predictability for exporters and importers as to the treatment of their products. The Decision mirrors, in part, the TRIMs Agreement elements reviewed above — noting actions taken for certain developing countries to extend the time for implementing the agreement and urging positive consideration to requests from LDCs for extensions.

In addition, cooperation between customs authorities is urged to help developing countries cope with concerns over the truth or accuracy of declared values. Sharing of information is called for subject to national law limitations. The Committee on Customs Valuation is directed to identify practical means that developing country Members can use to address concerns on the accuracy of declared values. Its report is due by the end of 2002.

(9) **Agreement on Rules of Origin**: The Decision urges the Committee to complete its harmonization work program by the end of 2001 and for Members to conform any interim arrangements to the Agreement and indicates such arrangements may be reviewed by the Committee.

(10) **Agreement on Subsidies and Countervailing Measures**: The Decision includes six issues involving the SCM Agreement:

A. Converts Annex VII(b) country exception to export subsidy disciplines to a 1990 constant dollars basis; countries on the list are eligible for exception until they exceed $1000 per capita GNP for three consecutive years. Decision takes effect when Committee adopts an agreed methodology for calculating constant 1990 dollars or on January 1,

2003.

B. While negotiations proceed on whether developing countries should have certain subsidies treated as non-actionable (subsidies to promote "regional growth, technology research and development funding, production diversification, development and implementation of environmentally sound methods of production"), Members are urged to "exercise due restraint" on whether to challenge such measures.

C. Committee on Subsidies and Countervailing Measures are to continue its review of the Agreement regarding countervailing duty investigations and provide a report by July 31, 2002.

D. Agreement to permit countries to requalify for export subsidy exception if the per capita GNP drops below $1000

E. Reaffirm general exception for LDCs from export subsidy prohibition (subject to being export competitive as defined in Art. 27.5 and 27.6) and clarifies that LDCs will have 8 years to phase out export subsidies after reaching export competitiveness.

F. Directs the Committee on Subsidies and Countervailing Measures to extend the transition period for certain Developing Countries (not identified in the Decision) pursuant to procedures reviewed in G/SCM/W/471/Rev.1 that is part of the final package of Doha documents and to treat similarly situation developing countries the same re extensions.

(11) **Agreement on Trade-Related Aspects of Intellectual Property Rights (TRIPS)**: Members agree not to request panels for non-violation nullification claims while the TRIPS Council examines the "scope and modalities" for such cases under TRIPS.

Article 66 of the TRIPS Agreement deals with least-developed country members. Paragraph 2 provides that "Developed country Members shall provide incentives to enterprises and institutions in their territories for the purpose of promoting and encouraging technology transfer to least-developed country Members in order to enable them to create a sound and viable technological base." The Doha Decision reaffirms that this paragraph is mandatory and calls for the creation of a mechanism to monitor implementation of developed country obligations. Developed country members agree to provide "detailed reports on the functioning in practice of the incentives provided to their enterprises for the transfer of technology" by the end of 2002. Information will be updated annually.

(12) **Cross-cutting Issues**: This section of the Decision sets up a series of action requests for the Committee on Trade and Development which appear aimed at expanding Special and Differential Treatment for developing countries and LDCs, including:

A. to make recommendations by July 2002 of those special and differential provisions in existing agreements that are discretionary now but should be converted to mandatory provisions;

B. to make recommendations by July 2002 on how to make existing S&D provisions more effective and ways developing countries and LDCs can be assisted to make the best use of existing S&D treatment provisions;

C. to consider how special and differential treatment can be "incorporated into the architecture of WTO rules". No time limit is provided here other than as part of the work program of the Doha Round.

The Decision also reaffirms that preferences granted to developing countries (e.g., GSP) "should be generalized, non-reciprocal and non-discriminatory".

(13) **Outstanding Implementation Issues**: As reviewed above, paragraph 12 of the Ministerial Declaration calls for outstanding implementation issues (which are defined in paragraph 13 of the Decision on Implementation-Related Issues and Concerns as those compiled in document "Job(01)/152/Rev.1") to be handled within the negotiating mandate where provided or to be handled by relevant WTO bodies with a report due by the end of 2002 "for appropriate action". Most of the outstanding implementation issues fit into the second category and will be considered during 2002. The "implementation" issues raised by developing countries are listed below.

(14) **Final Provisions**: This section of the Decision focuses on ensuring that technical assistance from the WTO will be prioritized to assist developing countries implement existing WTO obligations and increase their capacity to participate in multilateral negotiations. The WTO is to cooperate with other organizations to increase efficiency and avoid duplication.

V. Compilation of Outstanding Implementation Issues Raised by Members

The document reflects issues that had been contained in the draft Ministerial Text of 19 October 1999 or that were raised in the last two years by Members and that are not otherwise addressed in the Decision on Implementation-Related Issues and Concerns. As noted earlier, four of the eleven areas included are subject to specific negotiating mandates under the Doha Ministerial Declaration and the outstanding implementation issues for those areas will be addressed as part of those negotiations. The issues raised on antidumping and subsidies/countervailing measures were listed in the discussion of the Ministerial Declaration sections on these subjects. The other two areas where there are negotiating mandates are agriculture and TRIPS. Implementation issues that will be included in the negotiations to take place on those topics include the following:

A. Agreement on Agriculture: one implementation issue will be taken up — whether when calculating the aggregate measure of support, Members who have a "negative product specific support" amount because domestic support prices are lower than the external reference price ("to ensure access to basis foodstuffs by poor households") should "be allowed to increase their non-product specific support by an equivalent amount."

B. Agreement on Trade-Related Aspects of Intellectual Property Rights: Eight (8) implementation issues will be taken up as part of the TRIPS negotiating mandate:

(1) whether to extend "additional protection for geographical indications * * *for products other than wines and spirits";

(2) whether Members will agree that "patents inconsistent with Article 15 of the Convention on Biological Diversity shall not be granted."

(3) whether Members should adopt as a period for implementation of Art. 27.3(b)(where Members exclude from patentability "plants and animals other than micro-organisms, and essentially biological processes for the production of plants or animals other than non-biological and microbiological processes" they must provide for the protection of plant varieties either by patents or by an effective *sui generis* system"), five years from the date the review called for in the provision is completed (Agreement called for the review to be completed by the beginning of 1999);

(4) whether the transitional period for developing countries to bring themselves into compliance with the TRIPS Agreement should be extended beyond the period contained in Art. 65.2;

(5) whether the transition period for LDCs should be extended for as long as the Member remains an LDC;

(6) whether Articles 7 and 8 should be construed to require the transfer of technology "on fair and mutually advantageous terms" [Art. 7 describes the objectives of the TRIPS Agreement while Art. 8 identifies "principles"];

(7) whether Article 27.3(b) of the TRIPS Agreement should be modified to take into account the Convention on Biological Diversity and the

International Undertaking on Plant Genetic Resources, amongst other matters;

(8) whether there should be clarification that "all living organisms, including plants, animals and parts of plants and animals, including gene sequences, and biological and other natural processes for the production of plants, animals and their parts, shall not be granted patents."

The other seven areas will be taken up by appropriate WTO bodies and be the subject of a report/recommendation by the end of 2002 in accordance with paragraph 12 of the Ministerial Declaration. The following implementation issues are included in the Compilation:

C. GATT 1994:

(1) Whether only the BOP Committee "shall have the authority to examine the overall justification of BOP measures" (i.e., whether BOP actions can be challenged by Members through the dispute settlement system);

(2) Whether a review of Art. XVIII of GATT 1994 should be undertaken "to ensure that it subserves the original objective of facilitating the progressive development of economies in developing countries and to allow them to implement programmes and policies of economic development designed to raise the general standard of living of their people".

D. Agreement on the Application of Sanitary and Phytosanitary Measures: when SPS measures may have a significant effect on trade opportunities for developing countries, whether Members should notify the WTO and the concerned country(ies) prior to application and notify final rules or later decisions about earlier notifications. [These requested notifications go beyond existing transparency and notification requirements contained in the SPS agreement].

E. Agreement on Technical Barriers to Trade: whether Article 11 of the agreement dealing with technical assistance to other members should be amended to make the current obligation to provide "technical assistance on mutually agreed terms" mandatory so "technical assistance and cooperation is provided to developing countries" in standard setting.

F. Agreement on Trade-Related Investment Measures: The TRIMS Agreement addresses trade distorting investment measures (trade balancing, use of domestic over imported goods, etc.). The Compilation has four issues for consideration by the end of 2002:

(1) whether developing countries should have a second "opportunity to notify existing TRIMs measures" and have a transition period for phasing such notified measures out. [This would be a major modification to Art. 5.2 of the TRIMs Agreement which required notification within 90 days of entry into force of the WTO and a 2, 5 or 7 year phase-out of notified measures].

(2) Whether Art. 5.3 should be modified to make extension of the phase out time period mandatory where a developing or least-developed country demonstrates difficulties in implementing the obligations.
(3) Whether developing countries should be exempt from the disciplines on the application of domestic content requirements.
(4) Whether the Agreement should be modified "to provide developing countries the necessary flexibility to implement development policies (intended to address, among others, social, regional, economic, and technological concerns) that may help reduce the disparities they face *vis-à-vis* developed countries."

G. **Agreement on Implementation of Article VII of GATT 1994 (Customs Valuation)**: The Compilation contains four issues that will be considered by the end of 2002:

(1) Whether the cost of services "which are supplied directly or indirectly by the buyer free of charge or at reduced cost for production of" imported goods should be included in Art. 8:1(b)(iv) of the Agreement [**NOTE:** this proposal is aimed at eliminating from Art. 8.1(b) the language which prevents adding those costs where the value of the services has been included in the price actually paid or payable].
(2) Whether the "residual method of determining customs value" in Article 7 should be modified to permit resort to valuing based on domestic market prices or export prices in third countries (currently not permitted under Art. 7.2(a) and (e)).
(3) Whether the Agreement should be amended to permit the use of the highest value for valuation purposes when more than one transaction value is identified for identical or similar goods.
(4) Whether "buying commissions should be taken into account in determining customs value of imported goods as it forms a legitimate component of the landed cost of imported goods".
(5) Whether parties should automatically be viewed as "related" under the Agreement where there is an exclusive relationship (e.g., sole agent, sole distributor, sole concessionaire).

NOTE: Each of the above proposals if accepted would subject exporters to greater uncertainty in the valuation of their products in foreign markets, essentially changing the effective duty rate which for many countries would mean violations of their tariff bindings absent agreement on the above.

H. **Agreement on Safeguards**: Currently the Agreement on Safeguards provides that developing countries who individually account for less than 3 percent of total imports and where total imports of such developing countries do not exceed 9 percent are to be excluded from any remedy provided. The proposal for consideration is whether such numbers should be changed to 7 percent and 15 percent respectively.

I. **Cross-cutting issues**: two issues are identified: (1) whether preferential trading agreements between developed and developing countries should be subject to continued waivers to Art. I of GATT 1994 (MFN treatment) and (2) whether there should be "a redistribution of negotiating rights in favor of small and medium-sized exporting Members in trade negotiations".

VI. Timelines for action

1. End of 2001 — (a) Completion of Rules of Origin Harmonization program

2. January 31, 2002 — (a) Doha Development Round: first meeting of Trade Negotiating Committee by now

3. June 30, 2002 — (a) Services: initial requests for specific commitments due
(b) Cross-cutting issues: recommendations on S&D

4. July 31, 2002 — (a) Textiles: whether to change quota growth rates
(b) Subsidies: report on CVD investigations

5. End of 2002
(a) Implementation Issues: outstanding implementation issues for which there are not separate negotiating mandate (GATT 1994, SPS, TBT, TRIMS, Customs Valuation, Safeguards, Cross-cutting issues)
(b) Technology cooperation and capacity building: interim report
(c) Least-Developed Countries: interim report
(d) TRIPS: report on proposed solution for countries with limited or no manufacturing unable to invoke compulsory licensing
(e) GATT 1994 (Decision on Implementation): recommendations re countries with a substantial interest under Art. XIII:2(d)
(f) Antidumping: 3 issues from Decision on Implementation
(g) Customs Valuation: concerns re accuracy of declared values
(h) Subsidies: latest for decision on how to calculated constant 1990 dollars for Annex VII
(i) TRIPS: first report by developed countries on technology transfer program
(j) Electronic Commerce: no customs duty until; report on progress in evaluation

VI. Timelines for action (continued)

6. March 31, 2003 — (a) Services: initial offers due
   (b) Agriculture: establish modalities for further commitments

7. May 2003 — (a) Dispute Settlement Understanding: modifications to DSU to be adopted

8. 5th Ministerial (Nov.-Dec. 2003):

   (a) Agriculture: submission of comprehensive draft schedules
   (b) TRIPS: system of notification and registration of geographical indications for wines and spirits
   (c) Trade and Investment: start negotiations
   (d) Trade and Competition Policy: start negotiations
   (e) Transparency in Gov't Procurement: start negotiations
   (f) Trade facilitation: start negotiations
   (g) Trade and Environment: report on issues
   (h) Small Economies: recommendations for action
   (i) Trade, Debt and Finance: report on progress
   (j) Trade and Transfer of Technology: report on progress
   (k) Technical cooperation and capacity building: report on implementation
   (l) Least-Developed Countries: report on all issues affecting
   (m) Doha Development Round (overall): stocktaking

9. January 1, 2005 — Conclusion of all negotiations (other than DSU)

Appendix 1
Comparison of Draft Ministerial Declarations

Comparison of Draft Ministerial Declarations from WTO Doha Ministerial

Draft Ministerial Declaration 28 September 2001	Draft Ministerial Declaration 27 October 2001	Draft Ministerial Declaration 13 November 2001	Ministerial Declaration 14 November 2001

Methodological Notes

All comparisons have been made to thOctober 27, 2001 Draft Ministerial Declaration. In the September 28 Draft text which has been removed from the October 27 draft appears in ~~strikethru~~.

Text in the November 13 draft, which represents an addition to or change from the October 27 draft appears in under-line.

Text in the November 14 draft, which represents an addition to or change from the October 27 draft appears in under-line.

Text in the November 13 or 14 draft which has been moved within a paragraph appears in *italics.*

In all columns the language has been lined up as closely as possible to the October 27 draft, by adding spaces and lines, and breaking up paragraphs where necessary.

~~removed text~~ as compared to 27 October Draft
added text as compared to 27 October Draft
text moved within a paragraph for purposes of comparing to 27 October Draft

Comparison of Draft Ministerial Declarations from WTO Doha Ministerial

Draft Ministerial Declaration 28 September 2001	Draft Ministerial Declaration 27 October 2001	Draft Ministerial Declaration 13 November 2001	Ministerial Declaration 14 November 2001
	27 October 2001	13 November 2001	**WORLD TRADE ORGANIZATION** **WT/MIN(01)/DEC/1** **20 November 2001** **(01-5859)**
General Council Preparations for the Fourth Session of the Ministerial Conference Draft Ministerial Declaration	**General CouncilPreparations for the Fourth Session of the Ministerial Conference Draft Ministerial Declaration**	**Draft Ministerial Declaration**	**MINISTERIAL CONFERENCE** **Fourth Session** **Doha, 9 - 14 November 2001**
	Revision	**Revision**	**MINISTERIAL DECLARATION** <u>Adopted on 14 November 2001</u>
The attached draft Ministerial Declaration is submitted for the consideration of delegations by the Chairman of the General Council in co-operation with the Director-General. It represents what they judge to be the best possible basis at the present time for reaching an eventual consensus on a balanced text to be put before Ministers in Doha. This draft does not of course purport to be agreed in any part, and it is understood that agreement must be reached on the text as a whole. The present draft presents options in certain areas, and in other areas text remains to be developed. These are indicated by notes in italics which are not to be read as part of the text proper. Further intensive consultations based on this draft are envisaged, with the aim of resolving outstanding differences before a revision is issued. This text is issued at the same time as the Draft Elements for Decision on Implementation-Related Issues and Concerns (Job(01)/139). The	The attached draft Ministerial Declaration has been prepared by the Chairman of the General Council, in cooperation with the Director-General, for transmission to the Fourth Session of the Ministerial Conference. This draft does not purport to be agreed in any part at this stage.		

~~removed text~~ as compared to 27 October Draft
<u>added text</u> as compared to 27 October Draft
text moved within a paragraph for purposes of comparing to 27 October Draft

5

Comparison of Draft Ministerial Declarations from WTO Doha Ministerial

Draft Ministerial Declaration 28 September 2001	Draft Ministerial Declaration 27 October 2001	Draft Ministerial Declaration 13 November 2001	Ministerial Declaration 14 November 2001
relationship between these two texts will need to be further developed as consultations on both proceed, in line with the indications in the texts.			
General Council	**General Council**		
Preparations for the Fourth Session of the Ministerial Conference	**Preparations for the Fourth Session of the Ministerial Conference**		
Draft Ministerial Declaration	**Draft Ministerial Declaration**		
1. The multilateral trading system embodied in the World Trade Organization has ~~promoted~~ economic growth, development and employment throughout the past fifty years. We are determined, particularly in the light of the global economic slowdown, to maintain the process of reform and liberalization of trade policies, thus ensuring that the system plays its full part in promoting recovery and growth. We therefore strongly reaffirm the principles and objectives set out in the Marrakesh Agreement Establishing the World Trade Organization, and pledge to reject the use of protectionist ~~measures~~.	1. The multilateral trading system embodied in the World Trade Organization has contributed significantly to economic growth, development and employment throughout the past fifty years. We are determined, particularly in the light of the global economic slowdown, to maintain the process of reform and liberalization of trade policies, thus ensuring that the system plays its full part in promoting recovery, growth and development. We therefore strongly reaffirm the principles and objectives set out in the Marrakesh Agreement Establishing the World Trade Organization, and pledge to reject the use of protectionism.	1. The multilateral trading system embodied in the World Trade Organization has contributed significantly to economic growth, development and employment throughout the past fifty years. We are determined, particularly in the light of the global economic slowdown, to maintain the process of reform and liberalization of trade policies, thus ensuring that the system plays its full part in promoting recovery, growth and development. We therefore strongly reaffirm the principles and objectives set out in the Marrakesh Agreement Establishing the World Trade Organization, and pledge to reject the use of protectionism.	1. The multilateral trading system embodied in the World Trade Organization has contributed significantly to economic growth, development and employment throughout the past fifty years. We are determined, particularly in the light of the global economic slowdown, to maintain the process of reform and liberalization of trade policies, thus ensuring that the system plays its full part in promoting recovery, growth and development. We therefore strongly reaffirm the principles and objectives set out in the Marrakesh Agreement Establishing the World Trade Organization, and pledge to reject the use of protectionism.
2. International trade ~~plays a key~~ role in the alleviation of poverty. We recognize the ~~obligation to ensure that~~ all our peoples ~~may~~ benefit from the increased opportunities and welfare gains generated by the multilateral	2. International trade can play a major role in the promotion of economic development and the alleviation of poverty. We recognize the need for all our peoples to benefit from the increased opportunities and welfare gains that the multilateral trading system	2. International trade can play a major role in the promotion of economic development and the alleviation of poverty. We recognize the need for all our peoples to benefit from the increased opportunities and welfare gains that the multilateral trading system	2. International trade can play a major role in the promotion of economic development and the alleviation of poverty. Werecognize the need for all our peoples to benefit from the increased opportunities and welfare gains that the multilateral trading system

~~removed text~~ as compared to 27 October Draft
<u>added text</u> as compared to 27 October Draft
text moved within a paragraph for purposes of comparing to 27 October Draft

6

Comparison of Draft Ministerial Declarations from WTO Doha Ministerial

Draft Ministerial Declaration 28 September 2001	Draft Ministerial Declaration 27 October 2001	Draft Ministerial Declaration 13 November 2001	Ministerial Declaration 14 November 2001
trading system, and in the Work Programme adopted ~~through~~ this Declaration ~~we seek to place the interests and needs of~~ developing and least-developed countries ~~at the heart of the WTO's work.~~	generates. The majority of WTO Members are developing countries. We seek to place their needs and interests at the heart of the Work Programme adopted in this Declaration. Recalling the Preamble to the Marrakesh Agreement, we shall continue to make positive efforts designed to ensure that developing countries, and especially the least-developed among them, secure a share in the growth of world trade commensurate with the needs of their economic development. In this context, enhanced market access, balanced rules, and well targeted, sustainably financed technical assistance and capacity-building programmes have important roles to play.	generates. The majority of WTO Members are developing countries. We seek to place their needs and interests at the heart of the Work Programme adopted in this Declaration. Recalling the Preamble to the Marrakesh Agreement, we shall continue to make positive efforts designed to ensure that developing countries, and especially the least-developed among them, secure a share in the growth of world trade commensurate with the needs of their economic development. In this context, enhanced market access, balanced rules, and well targeted, sustainably financed technical assistance and capacity-building programmes have important roles to play.	generates. The majority of WTO Members are developing countries. We seek to place their needs and interests at the heart of the Work Programme adopted in this Declaration. Recalling the Preamble to the Marrakesh Agreement, we shall continue to make positive efforts designed to ensure that developing countries, and especially the least-developed among them, secure a share in the growth of world trade commensurate with the needs of their economic development. In this context, enhanced market access, balanced rules, and well targeted, ustainably financed technical assistance and capacity-building programmes have important roles to play.
	3. We recognize the particular vulnerability of the least-developed countries and the special structural difficulties they face in the global economy. We are committed to addressing the marginalization of least-developed countries in international trade and to improving their effective participation in the multilateral trading system. We recall the commitments made by Ministers at our meetings in Marrakesh, Singapore and Geneva, and by the international community at the Third UN Conference on Least-Developed Countries in Brussels, to help least-developed countries secure beneficial and meaningful integration into the multilateral trading system and the global economy. We are deter-	3. We recognize the particular vulnerability of the least-developed countries and the special structural difficulties they face in the global economy. We are committed to addressing the marginalization of least-developed countries in international trade and to improving their effective participation in the multilateral trading system. We recall the commitments made by Ministers at our meetings in Marrakesh, Singapore and Geneva, and by the international community at the Third UN Conference on Least-Developed Countries in Brussels, to help least-developed countries secure beneficial and meaningful integration into the multilateral trading system and the global economy. We are deter-	3. We recognize the particular vulnerability of the least-developed countries and the special structural difficulties they face in the global economy. We are committed to addressing the marginalization of least-developed countries in international trade and to improving their effective participation in the multilateral trading system. We recall the commitments made by Ministers at our meetings in Marrakesh, Singapore and Geneva, and by the international community at the Third UN Conference on Least-Developed Countries in Brussels, to help least-developed countries secure beneficial and meaningful integration into the multilateral trading system and the global economy. We are deter-

~~removed text~~ as compared to 27 October Draft
added text as compared to 27 October Draft
text moved within a paragraph for purposes of comparing to 27 October Draft

Comparison of Draft Ministerial Declarations from WTO Doha Ministerial

Draft Ministerial Declaration 28 September 2001	Draft Ministerial Declaration 27 October 2001	Draft Ministerial Declaration 13 November 2001	Ministerial Declaration 14 November 2001
	mined that the WTO will play its part in building effectively on these commitments under the Work Programme we are establishing.	mined that the WTO will play its part in building effectively on these commitments under the Work Programme we are establishing.	mined that the WTO will play its part in building effectively on these commitments under the Work Programme we are establishing.
3. We stress our commitment to the WTO as the unique forum for global trade rule-making and liberalization, while also recognizing that regional trade agreements can play an important role in promoting the liberalization and expansion of trade.	4. We stress our commitment to the WTO as the unique forum for global trade rule -making and liberalization, while also recognizing that regional trade agreements can play an important role in promoting the liberalization and expansion of trade and in fostering development.	4. We stress our commitment to the WTO as the unique forum for global trade rule -making and liberalization, while also recognizing that regional trade agreements can play an important role in promoting the liberalization and expansion of trade and in fostering development.	4. We stress our commitment to the WTO as the unique forum for global trade rule-making and liberalization, while also recognizing that regional trade agreements can play an important role in promoting the liberalization and expansion of trade and in fostering development.
4. We are aware that the challenges Members face in a rapidly changing international environment cannot be addressed through measures taken in the trade field alone. We shall continue to work with the Bretton Woods institutions for greater coherence in global economic policy-making, ~~and for effective cooperation with other intergovernmental organizations that have responsibilities related to those of the WTO.~~	5. We are aware that the challenges Members face in a rapidly changing international environment cannot be addressed through measures taken in the trade field alone. We shall continue to work with the Bretton Woods institutions for greater coherence in global economic policy-making.	5. We are aware that the challenges Members face in a rapidly changing international environment cannot be addressed through measures taken in the trade field alone. We shall continue to work with the Bretton Woods institutions for greater coherence in global economic policy-making.	5. We are aware that the challenges Members face in a rapidly changing international environment cannot be addressed through measures taken in the trade field alone. We shall continue to work with the Bretton Woods institutions for greater coherence in global economic policy-making.
5. We are convinced that the aims of upholding and safeguarding an open and non-discriminatory multilateral trading system, and acting for the protection of the environment and the promotion of sustainable development can and must be mutually supportive.	6. We strongly reaffirm our commitment to the objective of sustainable development, as stated in the Preamble to the Marrakesh Agreement. We are convinced that the aims of upholding and safeguarding an open and non-discriminatory multilateral trading system, and acting for the protection of the environment and the promotion of sustainable development can and must be mutually supportive.	6. We strongly reaffirm our commitment to the objective of sustainable development, as stated in the Preamble to the Marrakesh Agreement. We are convinced that the aims of upholding and safeguarding an open and non-discriminatory multilateral trading system, and acting for the protection of the environment and the promotion of sustainable development can and must be mutually supportive.	6. We strongly reaffirm our commitment to the objective of sustainable development, as stated in the Preamble to the Marrakesh Agreement. We are convinced that the aims of upholding and safeguarding an open and non-discriminatory multilateral trading system, and acting for the protection of the environment and the promotion of sustainable development can and must be mutually supportive.

~~removed text~~ as compared to 27 October Draft
added text as compared to 27 October Draft
text moved within a paragraph for purposes of comparing to 27 October Draft

Comparison of Draft Ministerial Declarations from WTO Doha Ministerial

Draft Ministerial Declaration 28 September 2001	Draft Ministerial Declaration 27 October 2001	Draft Ministerial Declaration 13 November 2001	Ministerial Declaration 14 November 2001
		[We **take note of the efforts by Members to conduct national environmental** assessments of trade policies on a voluntary basis.]	We take note of the efforts by Members to conduct national environmental assessments of trade policies on a voluntary basis.
We recognize the right of Members under ~~the multilateral~~ rules to take measures to uphold and enforce the levels of health, safety and environmental protection they deem appropriate, ~~including the right to regulate, and to introduce new regulations on, the supply of services~~. We agree to ensure that measures taken to address such concerns shall not be used for protectionist purposes.	We recognize the right of Members under WTO rules to take measures to uphold and enforce the levels of health, safety and environmental protection they deem appropriate. We agree to ensure that measures taken to address such concerns shall not be used for protectionist purposes.	[We recognize that under WTO rules no country should be prevented from taking measures for the protection of human, animal or plant life or health, or of the environment at the levels it considers appropriate, subject to the requirement that they are not applied in a manner which would constitute a means of arbitrary or unjustifiable discrimination between countries where the same conditions prevail, or a disguised restriction on international trade, and are otherwise in accordance with the provisions of the WTO Agreements. We welcome the WTO's continued cooperation with the United Nations Environment Programme and other intergovernmental environmental organizations. We encourage efforts to promote cooperation between the WTO and relevant international environmental and developmental organizations, especially in the lead up to the World Summit on Sustainable Development to be held in Johannesburg, South Africa, In September 2002.]	We recognize that under WTO rules no country should be prevented from taking measures for the protection of human, animal or plant life or health, or of the environment at the levels it considers appropriate, subject to the requirement that they are not applied in a manner which would constitute a means of arbitrary or unjustifiable discrimination between countries where the same conditions prevail, or a disguised restriction on international trade, and are otherwise in accordance with the provisions of the WTO Agreements. We welcome the WTO´s continued cooperation with UNEP and other inter-governmental environmental organizations. We encourage efforts to promote cooperation between the WTO and relevant international environmental and developmental organizations, especially in the lead-up to the World Summit on Sustainable Development to be held in Johannesburg, South Africa, in September 2002.
	7. We reaffirm the right of Members under the General Agreement on Trade in Services to regulate, and to introduce new regulations on, the supply of services.	7. We reaffirm the right of Members under the General Agreement on Trade in Services to regulate, and to introduce new regulations on, the supply of services.	7. We reaffirm the right of Members under the General Agreement on Trade in Services to regulate, and to introduce new regulations on, the supply of services.

~~removed text~~ as compared to 27 October Draft
added text as compared to 27 October Draft
text moved within a paragraph for purposes of comparing to 27 October Draft

9

Comparison of Draft Ministerial Declarations from WTO Doha Ministerial

Draft Ministerial Declaration 28 September 2001	Draft Ministerial Declaration 27 October 2001	Draft Ministerial Declaration 13 November 2001	Ministerial Declaration 14 November 2001
6. We reaffirm our declaration made at the Singapore Ministerial Conference regarding internationally recognized core labour standards. We take note of work under way in the International Labour Organization on the social dimensions of globalization.	8. We reaffirm our declaration made at the Singapore Ministerial Conference regarding internationally recognized core labour standards. We take note of work under way in the International Labour Organization (ILO) on the social dimension of globalization. The ILO provides the appropriate forum for a substantive dialogue on various aspects of this issue.	8. We reaffirm our declaration made at the Singapore Ministerial Conference regarding internationally recognized core labour standards. We take note of work under way in the International Labour Organization (ILO) on the social dimension of globalization.	8. We reaffirm our declaration made at the Singapore Ministerial Conference regarding internationally recognized core labour standards. We take note of work under way in the International Labour Organization (ILO) on the social dimension of globalization.
7. We note with particular satisfaction that this Conference has completed the WTO accession procedures for China and Chinese Taipei. We also welcome the accession as new members, since our last Session, of Albania, Croatia, Georgia, Jordan, Lithuania, Moldova and Oman.	9. We note with particular satisfaction that this Conference has completed the WTO accession procedures for China and Chinese Taipei. We also welcome the accession as new Members, since our last Session, of Albania, Croatia, Georgia, Jordan, Lithuania, Moldova and Oman.	9. We note with particular satisfaction that this Conference has completed the WTO accession procedures for China and Chinese Taipei. We also welcome the accession as new Members, since our last Session, of Albania, Croatia, Georgia, Jordan, Lithuania, Moldova and Oman.	9. We note with particular satisfaction that this Conference has completed the WTO accession procedures for China and Chinese Taipei. We also welcome the accession as new Members, since our last Session, of Albania, Croatia, Georgia, Jordan, Lithuania, Moldova and Oman, and note the extensive market-access commitments already made by these countries on accession.
These accessions will greatly strengthen the multilateral trading system, as will those of the 28 countries now negotiating their accession. We therefore attach great importance to concluding accession proceedings as quickly as possible, especially for least-developed countries.	These accessions will greatly strengthen the multilateral trading system, as will those of the 28 countries now negotiating their accession. We therefore attach great importance to concluding accession proceedings as quickly as possible. In particular, we are committed to accelerating the accession of least-developed countries.	These accessions will greatly strengthen the multilateral trading system, as will those of the 28 countries now negotiating their accession. We therefore attach great importance to concluding accession proceedings as quickly as possible. In particular, we are committed to accelerating the accession of least-developed countries.	These accessions will greatly strengthen the multilateral trading system, as will those of the 28 countries now negotiating their accession. We therefore attach great importance to concluding accession proceedings as quickly as possible. In particular, we are committed to accelerating the accession of least-developed countries.
8. Recognizing the challenges posed by expanding WTO membership, we confirm our collective responsibility to ensure internal transparency and the effective participation of all Mem-	10. Recognizing the challenges posed by an expanding WTO membership, we confirm our collective responsibility to ensure internal transparency and the effective participation of all Mem-	10. Recognizing the challenges posed by an expanding WTO membership, we confirm our collective responsibility to ensure internal transparency and the effective participation of all Mem-	10. Recognizing the challenges posed by an expanding WTO membership, we confirm our collective responsibility to ensure internal transparency and the effective participation of all Mem-

~~removed text~~ as compared to 27 October Draft
added text as compared to 27 October Draft
text moved within a paragraph for purposes of comparing to 27 October Draft

10

Comparison of Draft Ministerial Declarations from WTO Doha Ministerial

Draft Ministerial Declaration 28 September 2001	Draft Ministerial Declaration 27 October 2001	Draft Ministerial Declaration 13 November 2001	Ministerial Declaration 14 November 2001
bers. Emphasizing the intergovernmental character of the organization, we will continue to promote a better public understanding of the WTO and to communicate the benefits of a liberal, rules-based multilateral trading system, particularly through the more effective dissemination of information and improved dialogue with the public.	bers. Emphasizing the intergovernmental character of the organization, we will continue to promote a better public understanding of the WTO and to communicate the benefits of a liberal, rules-based multilateral trading system, particularly through the more effective dissemination of information and improved dialogue with the public.	bers. While emphasizing the intergovernmental character of the organization, we are committed to making the WTO's operations more transparent, including through more effective and prompt dissemination of information, and to improve dialogue with the public. We shall therefore at the national and multilateral levels continue to promote a better public understanding of the WTO and to communicate the benefits of a liberal, rules-based multilateral trading system.	bers. While emphasizing the intergovernmental character of the organization, we are committed to making the WTO's operations more transparent, including through more effective and prompt dissemination of information, and to improve dialogue with the public. We shall therefore at the national and multilateral levels continue to promote a better public understanding of the WTO and to communicate the benefits of a liberal, rules-based multilateral trading system.
9. In view of these considerations, we hereby agree to undertake the broad and balanced Work Programme set out below. This incorporates both an expanded negotiating agenda and other important decisions and activities necessary to address the challenges facing the multilateral trading system.	11. In view of these considerations, we hereby agree to undertake the broad and balanced Work Programme set out below. This incorporates both an expanded negotiating agenda and other important decisions and activities necessary to address the challenges facing the multilateral trading system.	11. In view of these considerations, we hereby agree to undertake the broad and balanced Work Programme set out below. This incorporates both an expanded negotiating agenda and other important decisions and activities necessary to address the challenges facing the multilateral trading system.	11.In view of these considerations, we hereby agree to undertake the broad and balanced Work Programme set out below. This incorporates both an expanded negotiating agenda and other important decisions and activities necessary to address the challenges facing the multilateral trading system.
	WORK PROGRAMME	**WORK PROGRAMME**	**WORK PROGRAMME**
IMPLEMENTATION-RELATED ISSUES AND CONCERNS	IMPLEMENTATION-RELATED ISSUES AND CONCERNS	IMPLEMENTATION-RELATED ISSUES AND CONCERNS	IMPLEMENTATION-RELATED ISSUES AND CONCERNS
10. We attach the utmost importance to the implementation issues and related concerns raised by Members and are determined to resolve them. Taking note of the General Council	12. We attach the utmost importance to the implementation-related issues and concerns raised by Members and are determined to find appropriate solutions to them. In this connection, and having regard to the General Council	12. We attach the utmost importance to the implementation-related issues and concerns raised by Members and are determined to find appropriate solutions to them. In this connection, and having regard to the General Council	12. We attach the utmost importance to the implementation-related issues and concerns raised by Members and are determined to find appropriate solutions to them. In this connection, and having regard to the General Council

~~removed text~~ as compared to 27 October Draft
added text as compared to 27 October Draft
text moved within a paragraph for purposes of comparing to 27 October Draft

11

Comparison of Draft Ministerial Declarations from WTO Doha Ministerial

Draft Ministerial Declaration 28 September 2001	Draft Ministerial Declaration 27 October 2001	Draft Ministerial Declaration 13 November 2001	Ministerial Declaration 14 November 2001
Decisions of 15 December 2000 ~~[and 3 October 2001], we adopt the further Decision contained in document …~~ ~~to address other outstanding issues. We agree that remaining implementation issues should be fully addressed, in accordance with appropriate guidelines to be developed, under the Work Programme we are establishing.~~	Decisions of 3 May and 15 December 2000, we further adopt the Decision on Implementation-Related Issues and Concerns in document Job(01)/139/Rev.1 to address a number of implementation problems faced by Members. We agree that negotiations on outstanding implementation issues shall be an integral part of the Work Programme we are establishing, and that agreements reached at an early stage in these negotiations shall be treated in accordance with the provisions of paragraph 40 below. In this regard, we shall proceed as follows: (a) where we provide a specific negotiating mandate in this Declaration, the relevant implementation issues shall be addressed under that mandate; (b) the other outstanding implementation issues shall be addressed as a matter of priority by the relevant WTO bodies, which shall report to the Trade Negotiations Committee, established under paragraph 39 below, by the end of 2002 for appropriate action.	Decisions of 3 May and 15 December 2000, we further adopt the Decision on Implementation-Related Issues and Concerns in document Job(01)/139/Rev.2 to address a number of implementation problems faced by Members. We agree that negotiations on outstanding implementation issues shall be an integral part of the Work Programme we are establishing, and that agreements reached at an early stage in these negotiations shall be treated in accordance with the provisions of paragraph 47 below. In this regard, we shall proceed as follows: (a) where we provide a specific negotiating mandate in this Declaration, the relevant implementation issues shall be addressed under that mandate; (b) the other outstanding implementation issues shall be addressed as a matter of priority by the relevant WTO bodies, which shall report to the Trade Negotiations Committee, established under paragraph 46 below, by the end of 2002 for appropriate action.	Decisions of 3 May and 15 December 2000, we further adopt the Decision on Implementation-Related Issues and Concerns in document WT/MIN(01)/17 to address a number of implementation problems faced by Members. We agree that negotiations on outstanding implementation issues shall be an integral part of the Work Programme we are establishing, and that agreements reached at an early stage in these negotiations shall be treated in accordance with the provisions of paragraph 47 below. In this regard, we shall proceed as follows: (a) where we provide a specific negotiating mandate in this Declaration, the relevant implementation issues shall be addressed under that mandate; (b) the other outstanding implementation issues shall be addressed as a matter of priority by the relevant WTO bodies, which shall report to the Trade Negotiations Committee, established under paragraph 46 below, by the end of 2002 for appropriate action.
FUTURE WORK PROGRAMME			
AGRICULTURE	AGRICULTURE	AGRICULTURE	AGRICULTURE
11. ~~Text to be elaborated through further consultations based on the following elements:~~ ~~* Reference to the ongoing negotiations, including a reference to the active participation of developing countries.~~	13. We recognize the work already undertaken in the negotiations initiated in early 2000 under Article 20 of the Agreement on Agriculture, including the large number of negotiating proposals	13. We recognize the work already undertaken in the negotiations initiated in early 2000 under Article 20 of the Agreement on Agriculture, including the large number of negotiating proposals	13. We recognize the work already undertaken in the negotiations initiated in early 2000 under Article 20 of the Agreement on Agriculture, including the large number of negotiating proposals

~~removed text~~ as compared to 27 October Draft
added text as compared to 27 October Draft
text moved within a paragraph for purposes of comparing to 27 October Draft

12

Comparison of Draft Ministerial Declarations from WTO Doha Ministerial

Draft Ministerial Declaration 28 September 2001	Draft Ministerial Declaration 27 October 2001	Draft Ministerial Declaration 13 November 2001	Ministerial Declaration 14 November 2001
* ~~Reference~~ to the long-term objective ~~of reform in agriculture.~~	submitted on behalf of a total of 121 Members. We recall the long-term objective referred to in the Agreement to establish a fair and market-oriented trading system through a programme of fundamental reform encompassing strengthened rules and specific commitments on support and protection in order to correct and prevent restrictions and distortions in world agricultural markets. We reconfirm our commitment to this programme. Building on the work carried out to date,	submitted on behalf of a total of 121 Members. We recall the long-term objective referred to in the Agreement to establish a fair and market-oriented trading system through a programme of fundamental reform encompassing strengthened rules and specific commitments on support and protection in order to correct and prevent restrictions and distortions in world agricultural markets. We reconfirm our commitment to this programme. Building on the work carried out to date,	submitted on behalf of a total of 121 Members. We recall the long-term objective referred to in the Agreement to establish a fair and market-oriented trading system through a programme of fundamental reform encompassing strengthened rules and specific commitments on support and protection in order to correct and prevent restrictions and distortions in world agricultural markets. We reconfirm our commitment to this programme. Building on the work carried out to date and without prejudging the outcome of the negotiations we commit ourselves
* ~~Reference to the direction or aims of reform in the areas of~~ market access, domestic support and export competition. *Reference to special and differential treatment.	we commit ourselves to comprehensive negotiations aimed at: substantial improvements in market access; reductions of, with a view to phasing out, all forms of export subsidies; and substantial reductions in trade-distorting domestic support. We agree that special and differential treatment for developing countries shall be an integral part of all elements of the negotiations and shall be embodied in the Schedules of concessions and commitments and as appropriate in the rules and disciplines to be negotiated, so as to be operationally effective and to enable developing countries to effectively take account of their development needs, including food security and rural development.	we commit ourselves to comprehensive negotiations aimed at: substantial improvements in market access; reductions of [, with a view to phasing out,] all forms of export subsidies; and substantial reductions in trade-distorting domestic support. We agree that special and differential treatment for developing countries shall be an integral part of all elements of the negotiations and shall be embodied in the Schedules of concessions and commitments and as appropriate in the rules and disciplines to be negotiated, so as to be operationally effective and to enable developing countries to effectively take account of their development needs, including food security and rural development.	to comprehensive negotiations aimed at: substantial improvements in market access; reductions of, with a view to phasing out, all forms of export subsidies; and substantial reductions in trade-distorting domestic support. We agree that special and differential treatment for developing countries shall be an integral part of all elements of the negotiations and shall be embodied in the Schedules of concessions and commitments and as appropriate in the rules and disciplines to be negotiated, so as to be operationally effective and to enable developing countries to effectively take account of their development needs, including food security and rural development.
* Reference to non-trade concerns.	We take note of the non-trade concerns reflected in the negotiating proposals submitted by Members and confirm that non-trade concerns will be taken into account	We take note of the non-trade concerns reflected in the negotiating proposals submitted by Members and confirm that non-trade concerns will be taken into account	We take note of the non-trade concerns reflected in the negotiating proposals submitted by Members and confirm that non-trade concerns will be taken into account

~~removed text~~ as compared to 27 October Draft
added text as compared to 27 October Draft
text moved within a paragraph for purposes of comparing to 27 October Draft

13

Comparison of Draft Ministerial Declarations from WTO Doha Ministerial

Draft Ministerial Declaration 28 September 2001	Draft Ministerial Declaration 27 October 2001	Draft Ministerial Declaration 13 November 2001	Ministerial Declaration 14 November 2001
	in the negotiations as provided for in the Agreement on Agriculture.	in the negotiations as provided for in the Agreement on Agriculture.	in the negotiations as provided for in the Agreement on Agriculture.
* ~~Benchmarks and time frames:~~	14. Modalities for the further commitments, including provisions for special and differential treatment, shall be established no later than … . Partici-pants shall submit their comprehen-sive draft Schedules based on these modalities no later than … .	14. Modalities for the further commitments, including provisions for special and differential treatment, shall be established no later than 31 March 2003. Partici-pants shall submit their comprehen-sive draft Schedules based on these modalities no later than the date of the Fifth Session of the Ministerial Conference. The nego-tiations, including with respect to rules and disciplines and related legal texts, shall be concluded as part and at the date of conclusion of the negotiating agenda as a whole.	14. Modalities for the further commitments, including provisions for special and differential treatment, shall be established no later than 31 March 2003. Partici-pants shall submit their comprehen-sive draft Schedules based on these modalities no later than the date of the Fifth Session of the Ministerial Conference. The nego-tiations, including with respect to rules and disciplines and related legal texts, shall be concluded as part and at the date of conclusion of the negotiating agenda as a whole.
* ~~Negotiating body:~~	The nego-tiations, including with respect to rules and disciplines and related legal texts, shall be concluded as part and at the date of conclusion of the negotiating agenda as a whole.		
SERVICES	SERVICES	SERVICES	SERVICES
12. The ~~mandated~~ negotiations on trade in services ~~are an important means~~ of promoting the economic growth of all trading partners and the development of developing countries. We ~~note with satisfaction the progress which has been made in these negotiations since their inception in~~ January 2000, and the large number of proposals submitted by Members on a wide range of sectors and several horizontal issues, as well as on movement of natural per-sons. We reaffirm the Guidelines and Procedures for the Negotia-tions adopted by the Council for Trade in Services on 28 March	15. The negotiations on trade in services shall be conducted with a view to promoting the economic growth of all trading partners and the development of developing countries. We recognize the work already under-taken in the negotiations, initiated in January 2000 under Article XIX of the General Agreement on Trade in Services, and the large number of proposals submitted by Members on a wide range of sectors and several horizontal issues, as well as on movement of natural per-sons. We reaffirm the Guidelines and Procedures for the Negotia-tions adopted by the Council for Trade in Services on 28 March	15. The negotiations on trade in services shall be conducted with a view to promoting the economic growth of all trading partners and the development of developing countries. We recognize the work already under-taken in the negotiations, initiated in January 2000 under Article XIX of the General Agreement on Trade in Services, and the large number of proposals submitted by Members on a wide range of sectors and several horizontal issues, as well as on movement of natural per-sons. We reaffirm the Guidelines and Procedures for the Negotia-tions adopted by the Council for Trade in Services on 28 March	15. The negotiations on trade in services shall be conducted with a view to promoting the economic growth of all trading partners and the development of developing and least-developed countries. We recognize the work already undertaken in the negotiations, initiated in January 2000 under Article XIX of the General Agreement on Trade in Services, and the large number of proposals submitted by Members on a wide range of sectors and several horizontal issues, as well as on movement of natural per-sons. We reaffirm the Guidelines and Procedures for the Negotia-tions adopted by the Council for Trade in Services on 28 March

~~removed text~~ as compared to 27 October Draft
added text as compared to 27 October Draft
text moved within a paragraph for purposes of comparing to 27 October Draft

Comparison of Draft Ministerial Declarations from WTO Doha Ministerial

Draft Ministerial Declaration 28 September 2001	Draft Ministerial Declaration 27 October 2001	Draft Ministerial Declaration 13 November 2001	Ministerial Declaration 14 November 2001
2001 as the basis for continuing the negotiations with a view to achieving the objectives of the General Agreement on Trade in Services, as stipulated in the Preamble, Article IV and Article XIX of that Agreement.	2001 as the basis for continuing the negotiations, with a view to achieving the objectives of the General Agreement on Trade in Services, as stipulated in the Preamble, Article IV and Article XIX of that Agreement. Participants shall submit initial requests for specific commitments by ... and initial offers by	2001 as the basis for continuing the negotiations, with a view to achieving the objectives of the General Agreement on Trade in Services, as stipulated in the Preamble, Article IV and Article XIX of that Agreement. Participants shall submit initial requests for specific commitments by 30 June 2002 and initial offers by 31 March 2003.	2001 as the basis for continuing the negotiations, with a view to achieving the objectives of the General Agreement on Trade in Services, as stipulated in the Preamble, Article IV and Article XIX of that Agreement. Participants shall submit initial requests for specific commitments by 30 June 2002 and initial offers by 31 March 2003.
MARKET ACCESS FOR NON-AGRICULTURAL PRODUCTS	MARKET ACCESS FOR NON-AGRICULTURAL PRODUCTS	MARKET ACCESS FOR NON-AGRICULTURAL PRODUCTS	MARKET ACCESS FOR NON-AGRICULTURAL PRODUCTS
13. We agree to negotiations which shall aim, by modalities to be agreed, to reduce or as appropriate eliminate tariffs, including the reduction or elimination of tariff peaks and tariff escalation, as well as non-tariff barriers. Product coverage shall be comprehensive and without a priori exclusions. The negotiations shall take into account the special needs and interests of developing and least-developed country participants, ~~including through less than full reciprocity in reduction commitments.~~	16. We agree to negotiations which shall aim, by modalities to be agreed, to reduce or as appropriate eliminate tariffs, including the reduction or elimination of tariff peaks, high tariffs, and tariff escalation, in particular on products of export interest to developing countries, as well as non-tariff barriers. Product coverage shall be comprehensive and without *a priori* exclusions. The negotiations shall take fully into account the special needs and interests of developing and least-developed country participants, in accordance with the relevant provisions of Article XXVIII *bis* of GATT 1994 and the provisions cited in paragraph 43 below.	16. We agree to negotiations which shall aim, by modalities to be agreed, to reduce or as appropriate eliminate tariffs, including the reduction or elimination of tariff peaks, high tariffs, and tariff escalation, as well as non-tariff barriers, in particular on products of export interest to developing countries. Product coverage shall be comprehensive and without *a priori* exclusions. The negotiations shall take fully into account the special needs and interests of developing and least-developed country participants, including through less than full reciprocity in reduction commitments, in accordance with the relevant provisions of Article XXVIII *bis* of GATT 1994 and the provisions cited in paragraph 50 below. To this end, the modalities to be agreed will include appropriate studies and capacity-building measures to assist least-developed countries to participate effectively in the negotiations.	16. We agree to negotiations which shall aim, by modalities to be agreed, to reduce or as appropriate eliminate tariffs, including the reduction or elimination of tariff peaks, high tariffs, and tariff escalation, as well as non-tariff barriers, in particular on products of export interest to developing countries. Product coverage shall be comprehensive and without *a priori* exclusions. The negotiations shall take fully into account the special needs and interests of developing and least-developed country participants, including through less than full reciprocity in reduction commitments, in accordance with the relevant provisions of Article XXVIII *bis* of GATT 1994 and the provisions cited in paragraph 50 below. To this end, the modalities to be agreed will include appropriate studies and capacity-building measures to assist least-developed countries to participate effectively in the negotiations.

~~removed text~~ as compared to 27 October Draft
added text as compared to 27 October Draft
text moved within a paragraph for purposes of comparing to 27 October Draft

15

Comparison of Draft Ministerial Declarations from WTO Doha Ministerial

Draft Ministerial Declaration 28 September 2001	Draft Ministerial Declaration 27 October 2001	Draft Ministerial Declaration 13 November 2001	Ministerial Declaration 14 November 2001
TRADE-RELATED ASPECTS OF INTELLECTUAL PROPERTY RIGHTS1	TRADE-RELATED ASPECTS OF INTELLECTUAL PROPERTY RIGHTS	TRADE-RELATED ASPECTS OF INTELLECTUAL PROPERTY RIGHTS	TRADE-RELATED ASPECTS OF INTELLECTUAL PROPERTY RIGHTS
	17. We stress the importance we attach to implementation and interpretation of the Agreement on Trade-Related Aspects of Intellectual Property Rights (TRIPS Agreement) in a manner supportive of public health, by promoting both access to existing medicines and research and development into new medicines and, in this connection, have adopted a separate Declaration.	17. We stress the importance we attach to implementation and interpretation of the Agreement on Trade-Related Aspects of Intellectual Property Rights (TRIPS Agreement) in a manner supportive of public health, by promoting both access to existing medicines and research and development into new medicines and, in this connection, have adopted a separate Declaration.	17. We stress the importance we attach to implementation and interpretation of the Agreement on Trade-Related Aspects of Intellectual Property Rights (TRIPS Agreement) in a manner supportive of public health, by promoting both access to existing medicines and research and development into new medicines and, in this connection, are adopting a separate Declaration.
14. We agree to ~~complete negotiations on~~ the establishment of a multilateral system of notification and registration of geographical indications for wines and spirits.	18. With a view to completing the work started in the Council for Trade-Related Aspects of Intellectual Property Rights (Council for TRIPS) on the implementation of Article 23.4, we agree to negotiate the establishment of a multilateral system of notification and registration of geographical indications for wines and spirits by the Fifth Session of the Ministerial Conference. We note that issues related to	18. With a view to completing the work started in the Council for Trade-Related Aspects of Intellectual Property Rights (Council for TRIPS) on the implementation of Article 23.4, we agree to negotiate the establishment of a multilateral system of notification and registration of geographical indications for wines and spirits by the Fifth Session of the Ministerial Conference. We note that issues related to	18. With a view to completing the work started in the Council for Trade-Related Aspects of Intellectual Property Rights (Council for TRIPS) on the implementation of Article 23.4, we agree to negotiate the establishment of a multilateral system of notification and registration of geographical indications for wines and spirits by the Fifth Session of the Ministerial Conference. We note that issues related to
15. ~~We agree [that the Council for Trade-Related Aspects of Intellectual Property Rights (TRIPS Council) shall examine issues related to possible negotiations on] [to negotiate]~~ the extension of the protection of geographical indications provided for in Article 23 to additional product areas.	the extension of the protection of geographical indications provided for in Article 23 to products other than wines and	the extension of the protection of geographical indications provided for in Article 23 to products other than wines and	the extension of the protection of geographical indications provided for in Article 23 to products other than wines and

~~removed text~~ as compared to 27 October Draft
added text as compared to 27 October Draft
text moved within a paragraph for purposes of comparing to 27 October Draft

16

Comparison of Draft Ministerial Declarations from WTO Doha Ministerial

Draft Ministerial Declaration 28 September 2001	Draft Ministerial Declaration 27 October 2001	Draft Ministerial Declaration 13 November 2001	Ministerial Declaration 14 November 2001
	spirits will be addressed in the Council for TRIPS pursuant to paragraph 12 of this Declaration.	spirits will be addressed in the Council for TRIPS pursuant to paragraph 12 of this Declaration.	spirits will be addressed in the Council for TRIPS pursuant to paragraph 12 of this Declaration.
16. We instruct the TRIPS Council, in pursuing its work programme, ~~to give due attention to~~ the relationship between the Agreement on Trade-Related Aspects of Intellectual Property Rights (TRIPS Agreement) and the Convention on Biological Diversity, the protection of traditional knowledge, ~~non-violation complaints, and keeping the TRIPS Agreement abreast of new technological and other developments~~. In undertaking this work, the TRIPS Council shall be guided by the objectives and principles of the TRIPS Agreement and shall take fully into account the development dimension.	19. We instruct the Council for TRIPS, in pursuing its work programme including under the review of Article 27.3(b), the review of the implementation of the TRIPS Agreement under Article 71.1 and the work foreseen pursuant to paragraph 12 of this Declaration, to examine, *inter alia*, the relationship between the TRIPS Agreement and the Convention on Biological Diversity, the protection of traditional knowledge and folklore, and other relevant new developments raised by Members pursuant to Article 71.1. In undertaking this work, the TRIPS Council shall be guided by the objectives and principles set out in Articles 7 and 8 of the TRIPS Agreement and shall take fully into account the development dimension.	19. We instruct the Council for TRIPS, in pursuing its work programme including under the review of Article 27.3(b), the review of the implementation of the TRIPS Agreement under Article 71.1 and the work foreseen pursuant to paragraph 12 of this Declaration, to examine, *inter alia*, the relationship between the TRIPS Agreement and the Convention on Biological Diversity, the protection of traditional knowledge and folklore, and other relevant new developments raised by Members pursuant to Article 71.1. In undertaking this work, the TRIPS Council shall be guided by the objectives and principles set out in Articles 7 and 8 of the TRIPS Agreement and shall take fully into account the development dimension.	19. We instruct the Council for TRIPS, in pursuing its work programme including under the review of Article 27.3(b), the review of the implementation of the TRIPS Agreement under Article 71.1 and the work foreseen pursuant to paragraph 12 of this Declaration, to examine, *inter alia*, the relationship between the TRIPS Agreement and the Convention on Biological Diversity, the protection of traditional knowledge and folklore, and other relevant new developments raised by Members pursuant to Article 71.1. In undertaking this work, the TRIPS Council shall be guided by the objectives and principles set out in Articles 7 and 8 of the TRIPS Agreement and shall take fully into account the development dimension.
17. ~~The TRIPS Council shall report on the progress of its work set out above to the General Council at the end of 2002 and submit a final report to the Fifth Session of the Ministerial Conference, which shall decide on further action~~.			

~~removed text~~ as compared to 27 October Draft
added text as compared to 27 October Draft
text moved within a paragraph for purposes of comparing to 27 October Draft

Comparison of Draft Ministerial Declarations from WTO Doha Ministerial

Draft Ministerial Declaration 28 September 2001	Draft Ministerial Declaration 27 October 2001	Draft Ministerial Declaration 13 November 2001	Ministerial Declaration 14 November 2001
RELATIONSHIP BETWEEN TRADE AND INVESTMENT	RELATIONSHIP BETWEEN TRADE AND INVESTMENT	RELATIONSHIP BETWEEN TRADE AND INVESTMENT	RELATIONSHIP BETWEEN TRADE AND INVESTMENT
		20. [Recognizing the case for a multilateral framework to secure transparent, stable and predictable conditions for long-term cross-border investment, particularly foreign direct investment, that will contribute to the expansion of trade.] we agree that the Fifth Session of the Ministerial Conference a decision will be taken on whether to launch negotiations in this area.	20. Recognizing the case for a multilateral framework to secure transparent, stable and predictable conditions for long-term cross-border investment, particularly foreign direct investment, that will contribute to the expansion of trade, and the need for enhanced technical assistance and capacity-building in this area as referred to in paragraph 21, we agree that negotiations will take place after the Fifth Session of the Ministerial Conference on the basis of a decision to be taken, by explicit consensus, at that Session on modalities of negotiations.
		25. We recognize the needs of developing and least-developed countries for enhanced support for technical assistance and capacity building in this area, including policy analysis and development so that they may better evaluate the implications of closer multilateral cooperation for their development policies and objectives, and human and institutional development. To this end, we shall work in coopera-tion with other relevant intergovern-mental organizations, including UNCTAD, and through appropriate	21. We recognize the needs of developing and least-developed countries for enhanced support for technical assistance and capacity building in this area, including policy analysis and development so that they may better evaluate the implications of closer multilateral cooperation for their development policies and objectives, and human and institutional development. To this end, we shall work in coopera-tion with other relevant intergovern-mental organisations, including UNCTAD, and through appropriate

~~removed text~~ as compared to 27 October Draft
added text as compared to 27 October Draft
text moved within a paragraph for purposes of comparing to 27 October Draft

18

Comparison of Draft Ministerial Declarations from WTO Doha Ministerial

Draft Ministerial Declaration 28 September 2001	Draft Ministerial Declaration 27 October 2001	Draft Ministerial Declaration 13 November 2001	Ministerial Declaration 14 November 2001
		regional and bilateral channels, to provide strengthened and adequately resourced assistance to respond to these needs.	regional and bilateral channels, to provide strengthened and adequately resourced assistance to respond to these needs.
18. ~~We agree to negotiations which shall aim to establish~~ a multilateral framework of rules to secure transparent, stable and predictable conditions for long-term cross-border investment, particularly foreign direct investment.	20. In the period until the Fifth Session of the Ministerial Conference, work will focus on the clarification of elements of a possible multilateral framework to secure transparent, stable and predictable conditions for long-term cross-border investment, particularly foreign direct investment, and to contribute to the expansion of trade. Core elements are:	21. In the period until the Fifth Session, further work in the Working Group on the Relationship Between Trade and Investment will focus on the clarification of:	22. In the period until the Fifth Session, further work in the Working Group on the Relationship Between Trade and Investment will focus on the clarification of:
It shall include as core elements provisions on scope and definition, transparency, non-discrimination, pre-establishment commitments based on a GATS-type approach, *and the settlement of disputes of governments.*	scope and definition; transparency; non-discrimination; modalities for pre-establishment commitments based on a GATS-type, positive list approach; development provisions; exceptions and safeguards; consultation and the settlement of disputes between Members; and negotiating modalities, including the question of participation.	scope and definition; transparency; non-discrimination; modalities for pre-establishment commitments based on a GATS-type, positive list approach; development provisions; exceptions and balance-of-payments safeguards; consultation and the settlement of disputes between Members.	scope and definition; transparency; non-discrimination; modalities for pre-establishment commitments based on a GATS-type, positive list approach; development provisions; exceptions and balance-of-payments safeguards; consultation and the settlement of disputes between Members.
The framework shall reflect in a balanced manner the interests of home and host countries, and take due account of ~~governments' regulatory responsibilities and economic~~ *development objectives.*	The framework should reflect in a balanced manner the interests of home and host countries, and take due account of the development policies and objectives of host governments as well as their right to regulate in the public interest.	Any framework should reflect in a balanced manner the interests of home and host countries, and take due account of the development policies and objectives of host governments as well as their right to regulate in the public interest.	Any framework should reflect in a balanced manner the interests of home and host countries, and take due account of the development policies and objectives of host governments as well as their right to regulate in the public interest.
The special development, trade and financial needs of developing and least-developed country participants shall be taken into account as an integral part of	The special development, trade and financial needs of developing and least-developed countries should be taken into account as an integral part of the	The special development, trade and financial needs of developing and least-developed countries should be taken into account as an integral part of any	The special development, trade and financial needs of developing and least-developed countries should be taken into account as an integral part of any

~~removed text~~ as compared to 27 October Draft
added text as compared to 27 October Draft
text moved within a paragraph for purposes of comparing to 27 October Draft

19

Comparison of Draft Ministerial Declarations from WTO Doha Ministerial

Draft Ministerial Declaration 28 September 2001	Draft Ministerial Declaration 27 October 2001	Draft Ministerial Declaration 13 November 2001	Ministerial Declaration 14 November 2001
the framework, which shall enable Members to undertake obligations commensurate with their individual needs and circumstances. ~~The negotiations shall pay due regard to other relevant WTO provisions and to existing bilateral and regional arrangements on investment.~~	framework, which should enable Members to undertake obligations and commitments commensurate with their individual needs and circumstances.	framework, which should enable Members to undertake obligations and commitments commensurate with their individual needs and circumstances.	framework, which should enable Members to undertake obligations and commitments commensurate with their individual needs and circumstances.
We commit ourselves to ensure that appropriate arrangements are made for the provision of technical assistance ~~and support for~~ capacity building ~~both during the negotiations and as an element of the agreement to be negotiated.~~ OR 19. ~~The Working Group on the Relationship between Trade and Investment shall undertake further focused analytical work, based on proposals by members. A report on this work shall be presented to the Fifth Session of the Ministerial Conference.~~	Due regard should be paid to other relevant WTO provisions. Account should be taken, as appropriate, of existing bilateral and regional arrangements on investment. At the Fifth Session, a decision will be taken on modalities of negotiations in this area. We commit ourselves to ensuring that appropriate arrangements are made for the provision of technical assistance and capacity building throughout, and as an element of the outcome.	Due regard should be paid to other relevant WTO provisions. Account should be taken, as appropriate, of existing bilateral and regional arrangements on investment.	Due regard should be paid to other relevant WTO provisions. Account should be taken, as appropriate, of existing bilateral and regional arrangements on investment.
INTERACTION BETWEEN TRADE AND COMPETITION POLICY	INTERACTION BETWEEN TRADE AND COMPETITION POLICY	INTERACTION BETWEEN TRADE AND COMPETITION POLICY	INTERACTION BETWEEN TRADE AND COMPETITION POLICY
		23. <u>[Recognizing the case for a multilateral framework to enhance the contribution of competition policy to international trade and</u>	23. <u>Recognizing the case for a multilateral framework to enhance the contribution of competition policy to international trade and</u>

~~removed text~~ as compared to 27 October Draft
<u>added text</u> as compared to 27 October Draft
text moved within a paragraph for purposes of comparing to 27 October Draft

20

Comparison of Draft Ministerial Declarations from WTO Doha Ministerial

Draft Ministerial Declaration 28 September 2001	Draft Ministerial Declaration 27 October 2001	Draft Ministerial Declaration 13 November 2001	Ministerial Declaration 14 November 2001
		development.]	development, and the need for enhanced technical assistance and capacity-building in this area as referred to in paragraph 24, we agree that negotiations will take
		we agree that the Fifth Session of the Ministerial Conference a decision will be taken on whether to launch negotiations in this area.	place after the Fifth Session of the Ministerial Conference on the basis of a decision to be taken, by explicit consensus, at that Session on modalities of negotiations.
		22. We recognize the needs of developing and least-developed countries for enhanced support for technical assistance and capacity building in this area, including policy analysis and development so that they may better evaluate the implications of closer multilateral cooperation for their development policies and objectives, and human and institutional development. To this end, we shall work in cooperation with other relevant intergovernmental organizations, including UNCTAD, and through appropriate regional and bilateral channels, to provide strengthened and adequately resourced assistance to respond to these needs.	24. We recognize the needs of developing and least-developed countries for enhanced support for technical assistance and capacity building in this area, including policy analysis and development so that they may better evaluate the implications of closer multilateral cooperation for their development policies and objectives, and human and institutional development. To this end, we shall work in cooperation with other relevant intergovernmental organisations, including UNCTAD, and through appropriate regional and bilateral channels, to provide strengthened and adequately resourced assistance to respond to these needs.
20. We agree to negotiations aimed at enhancing the contribution of competition policy to international trade and development. ~~To this end, the negotiations should establish a framework to address the following elements~~:	21. In the period until the Fifth Session of the Ministerial Conference, work will focus on the clarification of elements of a possible multilateral framework aimed at enhancing the contribution of competition policy to international trade and development. In this connection, the following elements will be addressed:	24. In the period until the Fifth Session, further work in the Working Group on the Interaction between Trade and Competition Policy will focus on the clarification of:	25. In the period until the Fifth Session, further work in the Working Group on the Interaction between Trade and Competition Policy will focus on the clarification of:

~~removed text~~ as compared to 27 October Draft
added text as compared to 27 October Draft
text moved within a paragraph for purposes of comparing to 27 October Draft

21

Comparison of Draft Ministerial Declarations from WTO Doha Ministerial

Draft Ministerial Declaration 28 September 2001	Draft Ministerial Declaration 27 October 2001	Draft Ministerial Declaration 13 November 2001	Ministerial Declaration 14 November 2001
core principles, including transparency, non-discrimination and procedural fairness, and provisions on hard core cartels; modalities for voluntary cooperation; and, support for progressive reinforcement of competition institutions in developing countries through capacity building. ~~In the course of negotiations,~~ full account shall be taken of the situation of developing and least-developed country participants and appropriate flexibility provided to address them.	core principles, including transparency, non-discrimination and procedural fairness, and provisions on hardcore cartels; modalities for voluntary cooperation; support for progressive reinforcement of competition institutions in developing countries through capacity building; and negotiating modalities, including the question of participation. Full account shall be taken of the needs of developing and least-developed country participants and appropriate flexibility provided to address them. At the Fifth Session, a decision will be taken on modalities of negotiations in this area. We commit ourselves to ensuring that appropriate arrangements are made for the provision of technical assistance and support for capacity building throughout, and as an element of the outcome.	core principles, including transparency, non-discrimination and procedural fairness, and provisions on hardcore cartels; modalities for voluntary cooperation; and support for progressive reinforcement of competition institutions in developing countries through capacity building. Full account shall be taken of the needs of developing and least-developed country participants and appropriate flexibility provided to address them.	core principles, including transparency, non-discrimination and procedural fairness, and provisions on hardcore cartels; modalities for voluntary cooperation; and support for progressive reinforcement of competition institutions in developing countries through capacity building. Full account shall be taken of the needs of developing and least-developed country participants and appropriate flexibility provided to address them.
We commit ourselves to ensure that appropriate arrangements are made for the provision of technical assistance and support for capacity building ~~both during the negotiations~~ and as an element of the ~~agreement to be negotiated~~.			
OR			
21. The Working Group on the Interaction between Trade and Competition Policy shall undertake further focused analytical work, based on proposals by Members. A report on this work shall be presented to the Fifth Session of the Ministerial Conference.			
TRANSPARENCY IN GOVERNMENT PROCUREMENT	TRANSPARENCY IN GOVERNMENT PROCUREMENT	TRANSPARENCY IN GOVERNMENT PROCUREMENT	TRANSPARENCY IN GOVERNMENT PROCUREMENT
22. We agree to negotiations on a multilateral agreement on transpar-	22. We agree to negotiations on a multilateral agreement on transpar-	26. We agree to negotiations on a multilateral agreement on transpar-	26. Recognizing the case for a multilateral agreement on transpar-

~~removed text~~ as compared to 27 October Draft
added text as compared to 27 October Draft
text moved within a paragraph for purposes of comparing to 27 October Draft

Comparison of Draft Ministerial Declarations from WTO Doha Ministerial

Draft Ministerial Declaration 28 September 2001	Draft Ministerial Declaration 27 October 2001	Draft Ministerial Declaration 13 November 2001	Ministerial Declaration 14 November 2001
ency in government procurement,	ency in government procurement,	ency in government procurement,	ency in government procurement and the need for enhanced technical assistance and capacity building in this area, we agree that negotiations will take place after the Fifth Session of the Ministerial Conference on the basis of a decision to be taken, by explicit consensus, at that Session on modalities of negotiations. These
building on the progress that has been made in the Working Group on Transparency in Government Procurement and taking into account participants' development priorities. The negotiations shall be limited to the transparency aspects and will not restrict the scope for countries to give preferences to domestic supplies and suppliers. ~~Issues relating to compliance with any new obligations to be agreed~~ shall be addressed in the negotiations, taking into account the situation of developing and least-developed country participants.	building on the progress that has been made in the Working Group on Transparency in Government Procurement and taking into account participants' development priorities, especially those of least-developed country participants. The negotiations shall be limited to the transparency aspects and therefore will not restrict the scope for countries to give preferences to domestic supplies and suppliers. Matters related to the nature of commitments and their implementation shall be addressed in the negotiations, taking into account the situation of developing and least-developed country participants. In the case of developing and least-developed countries, it is recognized that the implementation of the outcome shall be related to their capacities to implement and the technical assistance provided.	building on the progress that has been made in the Working Group on Transparency in Government Procurement and taking into account participants' development priorities, especially those of least-developed country participants. The negotiations shall be limited to the transparency aspects and therefore will not restrict the scope for countries to give preferences to domestic supplies and suppliers. Matters related to the nature of commitments and their implementation shall be addressed in the negotiations, taking into account the situation of developing and least-developed country participants. In the case of developing and least-developed countries, it is recognized that the implementation of the outcome shall be related to their capacities to implement and the technical assistance provided.	negotiations will build on the progress made in the Working Group on Transparency in Government Procurement by that time and take into account participants' development priorities, especially those of least-developed country participants. Negotiations shall be limited to the transparency aspects and therefore will not restrict the scope for countries to give preferences to domestic supplies and suppliers.
We commit ourselves to ensure that ~~appropriate arrangements are made for the provision~~ of technical assistance and support for capacity building both during the negotiations ~~and as an element of the agree-~~	We commit ourselves to ensuring adequate technical assistance and support for capacity building both during the negotiations and after their conclusion.	We commit ourselves to ensuring adequate technical assistance and support for capacity building both during the negotiations and after their conclusion.	We commit ourselves to ensuring adequate technical assistance and support for capacity building both during the negotiations and after their conclusion.

~~removed text~~ as compared to 27 October Draft
added text as compared to 27 October Draft
text moved within a paragraph for purposes of comparing to 27 October Draft

23

Comparison of Draft Ministerial Declarations from WTO Doha Ministerial

Draft Ministerial Declaration 28 September 2001	Draft Ministerial Declaration 27 October 2001	Draft Ministerial Declaration 13 November 2001	Ministerial Declaration 14 November 2001
~~ment to be negotiated~~.			
TRADE FACILITATION	TRADE FACILITATION	TRADE FACILITATION	TRADE FACILITATION
23. We agree to negotiations which shall build upon	23. With the aim of further expediting the movement, release and clearance of goods including goods in transit, we agree to negotiations which shall build upon	27. With the aim of further expediting the movement, release and clearance of goods including goods in transit, we agree to negotiations which shall build upon	27. Recognizing the case for further expediting the movement, release and clearance of goods, including goods in transit, and the need for enhanced technical assistance and capacity building in this area, we agree that negotiations will take place after the Fifth Session of the Ministerial Conference on the basis of a decision to be taken, by explicit consensus, at that Session on modalities of negotiations. In the period until the Fifth Session, the Council for Trade in Goods shall review and as appropriate, clarify and improve relevant aspects of
Articles V, VIII and X of the GATT 1994, taking into account existing WTO provisions on matters related to customs and other procedures and formalities to expedite movement, release and clearance of goods. ~~Issues relating to compliance with any new obligations to be agreed~~ shall be addressed in the negotiations, taking into account the situation of developing and least-developed country participants.	Articles V, VIII and X of the GATT 1994 by clarifying and improving elements of those Articles, taking into account, as appropriate, existing WTO provisions on matters related to customs and other procedures and formalities for goods trade. Matters related to the nature of any additional commitments and their implementation shall be addressed in the negotiations, taking into account the situation of developing and least-developed country participants. In the case of developing and least-developed countries, it is recognized that the implementation of the outcome shall be related to their capacities to implement and the technical assistance provided.	Articles V, VIII and X of the GATT 1994 by clarifying and improving elements of those Articles, taking into account, as appropriate, existing WTO provisions on matters related to customs and other procedures and formalities for goods trade. Matters related to the nature of any additional commitments and their implementation shall be addressed in the negotiations, taking into account the situation of developing and least-developed country participants. In the case of developing and least-developed countries, it is recognized that the implementation of the outcome shall be related to their capacities to implement and the technical assistance provided.	Articles V, VIII and X of the GATT 1994 and identify the trade facilitation needs and priorities of Members, in particular developing and least-developed countries.
We commit ourselves to ensure that ~~appropriate arrange-~~	We commit ourselves to ensuring adequate	We commit ourselves to ensuring adequate	We commit ourselves to ensuring adequate

~~removed text~~ as compared to 27 October Draft
added text as compared to 27 October Draft
text moved within a paragraph for purposes of comparing to 27 October Draft

24

Comparison of Draft Ministerial Declarations from WTO Doha Ministerial

Draft Ministerial Declaration 28 September 2001	Draft Ministerial Declaration 27 October 2001	Draft Ministerial Declaration 13 November 2001	Ministerial Declaration 14 November 2001
~~ments are made for the provision of~~ technical assistance and support for capacity building both during the negotiations and as ~~an element of the agreement to be negotiated~~.	technical assistance and support for capacity building both during the negotiations and after their conclusion.	technical assistance and support for capacity building both during the negotiations and after their conclusion.	technical assistance and support for capacity building <u>in this area.</u>
WTO RULES	WTO RULES	WTO RULES	WTO RULES
24. We agree to negotiations aimed at clarifying and improving disciplines under the existing Agreements on Implementation of Article VI of the GATT 1994 and on Subsidies and Countervailing Measures [...], taking into account the needs of developing and least-developed ~~country~~ participants.	24. In the light of the increasing application of these instruments by Members, we agree to negotiations aimed at clarifying and improving disciplines under the Agreements on Implementation of Article VI of the GATT 1994 and on Subsidies and Countervailing Measures, while preserving the basic concepts and principles underlying them and taking into account the needs of developing and least-developed participants. In the initial phase of the negotiations, participants will indicate the provisions that they seek to clarify and improve. In the context of these negotiations, participants shall also aim to clarify and improve WTO disciplines on fisheries subsidies, taking into account the importance of this sector to developing countries.	28. In the light of experience and of the increasing application of these instruments by Members, we agree to negotiations aimed at clarifying and improving disciplines under the Agreements on Implementation of Article VI of the GATT 1994 and on Subsidies and Countervailing Measures, while preserving the basic concepts, principles and <u>effectiveness of these agreements, their objectives [and instruments] [and procedures]</u>, and taking into account the needs of developing and least-developed participants. In the initial phase of the negotiations, participants will indicate the provisions that they seek to clarify and improve, <u>including disciplines on trade distorting practices, in the subsequent phase.</u> In the context of these negotiations, participants shall also aim to clarify and improve WTO disciplines on fisheries subsidies, taking into account the importance of this sector to developing countries.	28. In the light of experience and of the increasing application of these instruments by Members, we agree to negotiations aimed at clarifying and improving disciplines under the Agreements on Implementation of Article VI of the GATT 1994 and on Subsidies and Countervailing Measures, while preserving the basic concepts, principles and <u>effectiveness of these Agreements and their instruments and objectives,</u> and taking into account the needs of developing and least-developed participants. In the initial phase of the negotiations, participants will indicate the provisions, <u>including disciplines on trade distorting practices</u>, that they seek to clarify and improve <u>in the subsequent phase</u>. In the context of these negotiations, participants shall also aim to clarify and improve WTO disciplines on fisheries subsidies, taking into account the importance of this sector to developing countries. <u>We note that fisheries subsidies are also referred to in paragraph 31.</u>
25. We also agree to negotiations	25. We also agree to negotiations	29. We also agree to negotiations	29. We also agree to negotiations

~~removed text~~ as compared to 27 October Draft
<u>added text</u> as compared to 27 October Draft
text moved within a paragraph for purposes of comparing to 27 October Draft

25

Comparison of Draft Ministerial Declarations from WTO Doha Ministerial

Draft Ministerial Declaration 28 September 2001	Draft Ministerial Declaration 27 October 2001	Draft Ministerial Declaration 13 November 2001	Ministerial Declaration 14 November 2001
aimed at clarifying and improving disciplines and procedures under the existing WTO provisions applying to regional trade agreements. ~~Issues relating to the application of any new obligations to existing regional trade agreements shall be addressed during the negotiations. Participants~~ shall also take into account the developmental aspects of regional trade agreements.	aimed at clarifying and improving disciplines and procedures under the existing WTO provisions applying to regional trade agreements. The negotiations shall take into account the developmental aspects of regional trade agreements.	aimed at clarifying and improving disciplines and procedures under the existing WTO provisions applying to regional trade agreements. The negotiations shall take into account the developmental aspects of regional trade agreements.	aimed at clarifying and improving disciplines and procedures under the existing WTO provisions applying to regional trade agreements. The negotiations shall take into account the developmental aspects of regional trade agreements.
~~AMENDMENT OF THE~~ DISPUTE SETTLEMENT UNDERSTANDING	DISPUTE SETTLEMENT UNDERSTANDING	DISPUTE SETTLEMENT UNDERSTANDING	DISPUTE SETTLEMENT UNDERSTANDING
26. We agree to negotiations on ~~possible amendments to~~ the Dispute Settlement Understanding ~~on the basis of proposals by Members.~~	26. We agree to negotiations on improvements and clarifications of the Dispute Settlement Understanding.	30. We agree to negotiations on improvements and clarifications of the Dispute Settlement Understanding.	30. We agree to negotiations on improvements and clarifications of the Dispute Settlement Understanding.
The negotiations should be based on the work done thus far and aim ~~to produce a balanced package of amendments~~ no later than May 2003, at which time we will take steps to ensure that the amendments enter into force as soon as possible thereafter.	The negotiations should be based on the work done thus far as well as any additional proposals by Members, and aim to agree on improvements and clarifications not later than May 2003, at which time we will take steps to ensure that the results enter into force as soon as possible thereafter.	The negotiations should be based on the work done thus far as well as any additional proposals by Members, and aim to agree on improvements and clarifications not later than May 2003, at which time we will take steps to ensure that the results enter into force as soon as possible thereafter.	The negotiations should be based on the work done thus far as well as any additional proposals by Members, and aim to agree on improvements and clarifications not later than May 2003, at which time we will take steps to ensure that the results enter into force as soon as possible thereafter.
TRADE AND ENVIRONMENT	TRADE AND ENVIRONMENT	TRADE AND ENVIRONMENT	TRADE AND ENVIRONMENT
		31. [With a view to enhancing the mutual supportiveness of trade and environment, we agree to negotiations on:	31. With a view to enhancing the mutual supportiveness of trade and environment, we agree to negotiations, without prejudging their outcome, on: (i) the relationship between existing WTO rules and specific

~~removed text~~ as compared to 27 October Draft
added text as compared to 27 October Draft
text moved within a paragraph for purposes of comparing to 27 October Draft

26

Comparison of Draft Ministerial Declarations from WTO Doha Ministerial

Draft Ministerial Declaration 28 September 2001	Draft Ministerial Declaration 27 October 2001	Draft Ministerial Declaration 13 November 2001	Ministerial Declaration 14 November 2001
			trade obligations set out in multilateral environmental agreements (MEAs). The negotiations shall be limited in scope to the applicability of such existing WTO rules as among parties to the MEA in question. The negotiations shall not prejudice the WTO rights of any Member that is not a party to the MEA in question;
		(ii) procedures for regular information exchange between multilateral environmental agreements (MEAs) Secretariats and the relevant WTO Committees, and the criteria for the granting of observer status.]	(ii) procedures for regular information exchange between MEA Secretariats and the relevant WTO committees, and the criteria for the granting of observer status;
		(i) the reduction or, as appropriate, elimination of tariff and non-tariff barriers to environmental goods and services, especially in relation to developing countries, in particular the least-developed among them;	(iii) the reduction or, as appropriate, elimination of tariff and non-tariff barriers to environmental goods and services.
		[We note that fisheries subsidies form part of the negotiations provided for in paragraph 28.]	We note that fisheries subsidies form part of the negotiations provided for in paragraph 28.
27. We instruct the Committee on Trade and Environment to pursue work on all items on its agenda within its current terms of reference, and in particular:	27. We instruct the Committee on Trade and Environment, in pursuing work on all items on its agenda within its current terms of reference, to give particular attention to:	32. We instruct the Committee on Trade and Environment, in pursuing work on all items on its agenda within its current terms of reference, to give particular attention to:	32. We instruct the Committee on Trade and Environment, in pursuing work on all items on its agenda within its current terms of reference, to give particular attention to:
* t~~o address, in pursuance of the WTO's objective of sustainable development,~~	(i) the effect of environmental measures on market access	(i) the effect of environmental measures on market access, [especially in relation to developing countries, in particular the least-developed among them.]	(i) the effect of environmental measures on market access, especially in relation to developing countries, in particular the least-developed among them,
those	and those	and those	and those

~~removed text~~ as compared to 27 October Draft
added text as compared to 27 October Draft
text moved within a paragraph for purposes of comparing to 27 October Draft

27

Comparison of Draft Ministerial Declarations from WTO Doha Ministerial

Draft Ministerial Declaration 28 September 2001	Draft Ministerial Declaration 27 October 2001	Draft Ministerial Declaration 13 November 2001	Ministerial Declaration 14 November 2001
situations in which the elimination or reduction of trade restrictions and distortions would benefit trade, the environment and development;	situations in which the elimination or reduction of trade restrictions and distortions would benefit trade, the environment and development;	situations in which the elimination or reduction of trade restrictions and distortions would benefit trade, the environment and development;	situations in which the elimination or reduction of trade restrictions and distortions would benefit trade, the environment and development;
* ~~to deepen the understanding of~~ the relationship between the multilateral trading system and multilateral environment agreements (MEAs).	(ii) the relationship between the multilateral trading system and multilateral environment agreements (MEAs);	(ii) the relationship between the multilateral trading system and multilateral environment agreements (MEAs);	
	(iii) the relevant provisions of the Agreement on Trade-Related Aspects of Intellectual Property Rights; and	(iii) the relevant provisions of the Agreement on Trade-Related Aspects of Intellectual Property Rights; and	(ii) the relevant provisions of the Agreement on Trade-Related Aspects of Intellectual Property Rights; and
	(iv) labelling.	(iv) labelling [requirements for environmental purposes].	(iii) labelling requirements for environmental purposes.
The Committee on Trade and Environment shall report to the Fifth Session of the Ministerial Conference on these issues.	Work on these issues should include the identification of any need to clarify relevant WTO rules. The Committee shall report to the Fifth Session of the Ministerial Conference and make recommendations, where appropriate, with respect to future action, including the desirability of negotiations.	Work on these issues should include the identification of any need to clarify relevant WTO rules. The Committee shall report on [all items on its agenda] to the Fifth Session of the Ministerial Conference, and make recommendations, where appropriate, with respect to [any] future action, including the desirability of negotiations. [The outcome of this work as well as the negotiations carried out under paragraph 31 shall be compatible with the open and non-discriminatory nature of the multilateral trading system, shall not add to or diminish the rights and obligations of Members under existing WTO agreements, nor alter the balance of these rights and	Work on these issues should include the identification of any need to clarify relevant WTO rules. The Committee shall report to the Fifth Session of the Ministerial Conference, and make recommendations, where appropriate, with respect to future action, including the desirability of negotiations. The outcome of this work as well as the negotiations carried out under paragraph 31(i) and (ii) shall be compatible with the open and non-discriminatory nature of the multilateral trading system, shall not add to or diminish the rights and obligations of Members under existing WTO agreements, in particular the Agreement on the Application of Sanitary and Phytosanitary Measures, nor alter the balance of these rights and

~~removed text~~ as compared to 27 October Draft
added text as compared to 27 October Draft
text moved within a paragraph for purposes of comparing to 27 October Draft

28

Comparison of Draft Ministerial Declarations from WTO Doha Ministerial

Draft Ministerial Declaration 28 September 2001	Draft Ministerial Declaration 27 October 2001	Draft Ministerial Declaration 13 November 2001	Ministerial Declaration 14 November 2001
		obligations, and will take into account the needs of developing and least-developed countries.]	obligations, and will take into account the needs of developing and least-developed countries.
		33. [We recognize the importance of technical assistance and capacity building in the field of trade and environment to developing countries, in particular the least-developed among them. We also encourage that expertise and experience be shared with Members wishing to perform environmental reviews at the national level. A report shall be prepared on these activities for the Fifth Session.]	33. We recognize the importance of technical assistance and capacity building in the field of trade and environment to developing countries, in particular the least-developed among them. We also encourage that expertise and experience be shared with Members wishing to perform environmental reviews at the national level. A report shall be prepared on these activities for the Fifth Session.
28. ~~We direct the Committee on Technical Barriers to Trade to expedite its work on labeling, bearing in mind that any measures in this field should not become disguised restrictions on trade, and report to the Fifth Session of the Ministerial Conference.~~			
ELECTRONIC COMMERCE	ELECTRONIC COMMERCE	ELECTRONIC COMMERCE	ELECTRONIC COMMERCE
29. We take note of the work which has been done in the General Council and other relevant bodies since our Declaration of 20 May 1998 and agree to continue the Work Programme on Electronic Commerce.	28. We take note of the work which has been done in the General Council and other relevant bodies since the Ministerial Declaration of 20 May 1998 and agree to continue the Work Programme on Electronic Commerce. The work to date demonstrates that electronic commerce creates new challenges and opportunities for trade for Members at all stages of development, and we recognize the importance of creating and maintaining an environment which is	34. We take note of the work which has been done in the General Council and other relevant bodies since the Ministerial Declaration of 20 May 1998 and agree to continue the Work Programme on Electronic Commerce. The work to date demonstrates that electronic commerce creates new challenges and opportunities for trade for Members at all stages of development, and we recognize the importance of creating and maintaining an environment which is	34. We take note of the work which has been done in the General Council and other relevant bodies since the Ministerial Declaration of 20 May 1998 and agree to continue the Work Programme on Electronic Commerce. The work to date demonstrates that electronic commerce creates new challenges and opportunities for trade for Members at all stages of development, and we recognize the importance of creating and maintaining an environment which is

~~removed text~~ as compared to 27 October Draft
added text as compared to 27 October Draft
text moved within a paragraph for purposes of comparing to 27 October Draft

Comparison of Draft Ministerial Declarations from WTO Doha Ministerial

Draft Ministerial Declaration 28 September 2001	Draft Ministerial Declaration 27 October 2001	Draft Ministerial Declaration 13 November 2001	Ministerial Declaration 14 November 2001
We instruct the General Council to consider the most appropriate institutional arrangements for handling the Work Programme, and to report on further progress to the Fifth Session of the Ministerial Conference. We ~~agree~~ to maintain ~~our~~ current practice of not imposing customs duties on electronic transmissions until the Fifth Session.	favourable to the future development of electronic commerce. We instruct the General Council to consider the most appropriate institutional arrangements for handling the Work Programme, and to report on further progress to the Fifth Session of the Ministerial Conference. We declare that Members will maintain their current practice of not imposing customs duties on electronic transmissions until the Fifth Session.	favourable to the future development of electronic commerce. We instruct the General Council to consider the most appropriate institutional arrangements for handling the Work Programme, and to report on further progress to the Fifth Session of the Ministerial Conference. We declare that Members will maintain their current practice of not imposing customs duties on electronic transmissions until the Fifth Session.	favourable to the future develop-ment of electronic commerce. We instruct the General Council to consider the most appropriate institutional arrangements for handling the Work Programme, and to report on further progress to the Fifth Session of the Ministerial Conference. We declare that Members will maintain their current practice of not imposing customs duties on electronic transmissions until the Fifth Session.
SMALL ECONOMIES	SMALL ECONOMIES	SMALL ECONOMIES	SMALL ECONOMIES
30.We agree to a work programme, under the auspices of the General Council, to examine issues relating to the trade of small economies. The objective of this work is to frame responses to the trade-related issues identified for the fuller integration of small, vulnerable economies into the multilateral trading system, and not to create a sub-category of WTO Members. The General Council shall review the work programme and make recommendations for action to the Fifth Session of the Ministerial Conference.	29.We agree to a work programme, under the auspices of the General Council, to examine issues relating to the trade of small economies. The objective of this work is to frame responses to the trade-related issues identified for the fuller integration of small, vulnerable economies into the multilateral trading system, and not to create a sub-category of WTO Members. The General Council shall review the work programme and make recommendations for action to the Fifth Session of the Ministerial Conference.	35.We agree to a work programme, under the auspices of the General Council, to examine issues relating to the trade of small economies. The objective of this work is to frame responses to the trade-related issues identified for the fuller integration of small, vulnerable economies into the multilateral trading system, and not to create a sub-category of WTO Members. The General Council shall review the work programme and make recommendations for action to the Fifth Session of the Ministerial Conference.	35.We agree to a work programme, under the auspices of the General Council, to examine issues relating to the trade of small economies. The objective of this work is to frame responses to the trade-related issues identified for the fuller integration of small, vulnerable economies into the multilateral trading system, and not to create a sub-category of WTO Members. The General Council shall review the work programme and make recommendations for action to the Fifth Session of the Ministerial Conference.
TRADE, DEBT AND FINANCE	TRADE, DEBT AND FINANCE	TRADE, DEBT AND FINANCE	TRADE, DEBT AND FINANCE
31. We agree to an examination, under the auspices of the General Council, of the relationship between trade, debt and finance, and of any possible recommendations on steps that might be taken within the	30. We agree to an examination, under the auspices of the General Council, of the relationship between trade, debt and finance, and of any possible recommendations on steps that might be taken within the	36. We agree to an examination, in a Working Group under the auspices of the General Council, of the relationship between trade, debt and finance, and of any possible recommendations on steps that might be taken within the	36. We agree to an examination, in a Working Group under the auspices of the General Council, of the relationship between trade, debt and finance, and of any possible recommendations on steps that might be taken within the

~~removed text~~ as compared to 27 October Draft
added text as compared to 27 October Draft
text moved within a paragraph for purposes of comparing to 27 October Draft

Comparison of Draft Ministerial Declarations from WTO Doha Ministerial

Draft Ministerial Declaration 28 September 2001	Draft Ministerial Declaration 27 October 2001	Draft Ministerial Declaration 13 November 2001	Ministerial Declaration 14 November 2001
mandate and competence of the WTO to enhance the capacity of the multilateral trading system to contribute to a durable solution to the problem of external indebtedness of developing and least-developed countries, and to strengthen the coherence of international trade, financial and monetary policies with a view to safeguarding the multilateral trading system from the effects of financial and monetary instability. We instruct the General Council to consider the most appropriate institutional arrangements for handling ~~this examination and to report on progress~~ to the Fifth Session of the Ministerial Conference.	mandate and competence of the WTO to enhance the capacity of the multilateral trading system to contribute to a durable solution to the problem of external indebtedness of developing and least-developed countries, and to strengthen the coherence of international trade, financial and monetary policies, with a view to safeguarding the multilateral trading system from the effects of financial and monetary instability. We instruct the General Council to consider the most appropriate institutional arrangements for handling this work. The General Council shall report to the Fifth Session of the Ministerial Conference on progress in the examination.	mandate and competence of the WTO to enhance the capacity of the multilateral trading system to contribute to a durable solution to the problem of external indebtedness of developing and least-developed countries, and to strengthen the coherence of international trade and financial policies, with a view to safeguarding the multilateral trading system from the effects of financial and monetary instability. The General Council shall report to the Fifth Session of the Ministerial Conference on progress in the examination.	mandate and competence of the WTO to enhance the capacity of the multilateral trading system to contribute to a durable solution to the problem of external indebtedness of developing and least-developed countries, and to strengthen the coherence of international trade and financial policies, with a view to safeguarding the multilateral trading system from the effects of financial and monetary instability. The General Council shall report to the Fifth Session of the Ministerial Conference on progress in the examination.
TRADE AND TRANSFER OF TECHNOLOGY	TRADE AND TRANSFER OF TECHNOLOGY	TRADE AND TRANSFER OF TECHNOLOGY	TRADE AND TRANSFER OF TECHNOLOGY
32. We agree to an examination, under the auspices of the General Council, of the relationship between trade and transfer of technology, and of any possible recommendations on steps that might be taken within the mandate of the WTO to increase flows of technology to developing countries. We instruct the General Council to consider the most appropriate institutional arrangements for handling this examination and to report on progress to the Fifth Session of the Ministerial Conference.	31. We agree to an examination, under the auspices of the General Council, of the relationship between trade and transfer of technology, and of any possible recommendations on steps that might be taken within the mandate of the WTO to increase flows of technology to developing countries. We instruct the General Council to consider the most appropriate institutional arrangements for handling this work. The General Council shall report to the Fifth Session of the Ministerial Conference on progress in the examination.	37. We agree to an examination, in a Working Group under the auspices of the General Council, of the relationship between trade and transfer of technology, and of any possible recommendations on steps that might be taken within the mandate of the WTO to increase flows of technology to developing countries. The General Council shall report to the Fifth Session of the Ministerial Conference on progress in the examination.	37. We agree to an examination, in a Working Group under the auspices of the General Council, of the relationship between trade and transfer of technology, and of any possible recommendations on steps that might be taken within the mandate of the WTO to increase flows of technology to developing countries. The General Council shall report to the Fifth Session of the Ministerial Conference on progress in the examination.

~~removed text~~ as compared to 27 October Draft
added text as compared to 27 October Draft
text moved within a paragraph for purposes of comparing to 27 October Draft

Comparison of Draft Ministerial Declarations from WTO Doha Ministerial

Draft Ministerial Declaration 28 September 2001 TECHNICAL COOPERATION AND CAPACITY BUILDING	Draft Ministerial Declaration 27 October 2001 TECHNICAL COOPERATION AND CAPACITY BUILDING	Draft Ministerial Declaration 13 November 2001 TECHNICAL COOPERATION AND CAPACITY BUILDING	Ministerial Declaration 14 November 2001 TECHNICAL COOPERATION AND CAPACITY BUILDING
33. We instruct the Secretariat ~~to respond to requests from Members for technical assistance in the context of their~~ mainstreaming of trade into national plans for economic development and strategies for poverty reduction. The delivery of WTO technical assistance shall be designed to assist ~~beneficiary countries to understand~~	32. We confirm that technical cooperation and capacity building are core elements of the development dimension of the multilateral trading system, and we welcome and endorse the New Strategy for WTO Technical Cooperation for Capacity Building, Growth and Integration. We instruct the Secretariat, in coordination with other relevant agencies, to support domestic efforts for mainstreaming trade into national plans for economic development and strategies for poverty reduction. The delivery of WTO technical assistance shall be designed to assist developing and least-developed countries	38. We confirm that technical cooperation and capacity building are core elements of the development dimension of the multilateral trading system, and we welcome and endorse the New Strategy for WTO Technical Cooperation for Capacity Building, Growth and Integration. We instruct the Secretariat, in coordination with other relevant agencies, to support domestic efforts for mainstreaming trade into national plans for economic development and strategies for poverty reduction. The delivery of WTO technical assistance shall be designed to assist developing and least-developed countries	38. We confirm that technical cooperation and capacity building are core elements of the development dimension of the multilateral trading system, and we welcome and endorse the New Strategy for WTO Technical Cooperation for Capacity Building, Growth and Integration. We instruct the Secretariat, in coordination with other relevant agencies, to support domestic efforts for mainstreaming trade into national plans for economic development and strategies for poverty reduction. The delivery of WTO technical assistance shall be designed to assist developing and least-developed countries and low-income countries in transition
WTO rules and disciplines, implement obligations and exercise the rights of membership, including drawing on the benefits of an open, rules-based multilateral trading system. Priority shall also be accorded, ~~in the delivery of trade-related technical assistance, to building capacity for multilateral trade negotiations in developing, least developed, small and vulnerable, and transition economies, including those~~ without representation in Geneva.	to adjust to WTO rules and disciplines, implement obligations and exercise the rights of membership, including drawing on the benefits of an open, rules-based multilateral trading system. Priority shall also be accorded to small, vulnerable, and transition economies, as well as to Members and Observers	to adjust to WTO rules and disciplines, implement obligations and exercise the rights of membership, including drawing on the benefits of an open, rules-based multilateral trading system. Priority shall also be accorded to small, vulnerable, and transition economies, as well as to Members and Observers	to adjust to WTO rules and disciplines, implement obligations and exercise the rights of membership, including drawing on the benefits of an open, rules-based multilateral trading system. Priority shall also be accorded to small, vulnerable, and transition economies, as well as to Members and Observers
	without representation in Geneva. We reaffirm our support for the valuable work of the International Trade Centre, which should be enhanced.	without representation in Geneva. We reaffirm our support for the valuable work of the International Trade Centre, which should be enhanced.	without representation in Geneva. We reaffirm our support for the valuable work of the International Trade Centre, which should be enhanced.

~~removed text~~ as compared to 27 October Draft
added text as compared to 27 October Draft
text moved within a paragraph for purposes of comparing to 27 October Draft

Comparison of Draft Ministerial Declarations from WTO Doha Ministerial

Draft Ministerial Declaration 28 September 2001	Draft Ministerial Declaration 27 October 2001	Draft Ministerial Declaration 13 November 2001	Ministerial Declaration 14 November 2001
We underscore the urgent necessity for the coordinated delivery of technical assistance with relevant international and regional intergovernmental institutions within a coherent policy framework and timetable.	33. We underscore the urgent necessity for the effective coordinated delivery of technical assistance with bilateral donors, in the OECD Development Assistance Committee and relevant international and regional intergovernmental institutions, within a coherent policy framework and timetable. In the coordinated delivery of technical assistance, we instruct the Director-General to consult with the relevant agencies, bilateral donors and beneficiaries, to identify ways of enhancing and rationalizing the Integrated Framework for Trade-Related Technical Assistance to Least-Developed Countries and the Joint Integrated Technical Assistance Programme (JITAP).	39. We underscore the urgent necessity for the effective coordinated delivery of technical assistance with bilateral donors, in the OECD Development Assistance Committee and relevant international and regional intergovernmental institutions, within a coherent policy framework and timetable. In the coordinated delivery of technical assistance, we instruct the Director-General to consult with the relevant agencies, bilateral donors and beneficiaries, to identify ways of enhancing and rationalizing the Integrated Framework for Trade-Related Technical Assistance to Least-Developed Countries and the Joint Integrated Technical Assistance Programme (JITAP).	39. We underscore the urgent necessity for the effective coordinated delivery of technical assistance with bilateral donors, in the OECD Development Assistance Committee and relevant international and regional intergovernmental institutions, within a coherent policy framework and timetable. In the coordinated delivery of technical assistance, we instruct the Director-General to consult with the relevant agencies, bilateral donors and beneficiaries, to identify ways of enhancing and rationalizing the Integrated Framework for Trade-Related Technical Assistance to Least-Developed Countries and the Joint Integrated Technical Assistance Programme (JITAP).
We agree that there is a need for this assistance to benefit from secure and predictable funding. We therefore instruct the Committee on Budget, Finance and Administration to develop a plan for adoption by the General Council in December 2001 that will ensure long-term funding for WTO technical assistance at a level no lower than that of the current year.	34. We agree that there is a need for technical assistance to benefit from secure and predictable funding. We therefore instruct the Committee on Budget, Finance and Administration to develop a plan for adoption by the General Council in December 2001 that will ensure long-term funding for WTO technical assistance at an overall level no lower than that of the current year and commensurate with the activities outlined above.	40. We agree that there is a need for technical assistance to benefit from secure and predictable funding. We therefore instruct the Committee on Budget, Finance and Administration to develop a plan for adoption by the General Council in December 2001 that will ensure long-term funding for WTO technical assistance at an overall level no lower than that of the current year and commensurate with the activities outlined above.	40. We agree that there is a need for technical assistance to benefit from secure and predictable funding. We therefore instruct the Committee on Budget, Finance and Administration to develop a plan for adoption by the General Council in December 2001 that will ensure long-term funding for WTO technical assistance at an overall level no lower than that of the current year and commensurate with the activities outlined above.
		41. We have established firm commitments on technical cooperation and capacity building in various paragraphs in this Ministerial Declaration. We reaffirm these	41. We have established firm commitments on technical cooperation and capacity building in various paragraphs in this Ministerial Declaration. We reaffirm these

~~removed text~~ as compared to 27 October Draft
added text as compared to 27 October Draft
text moved within a paragraph for purposes of comparing to 27 October Draft

Comparison of Draft Ministerial Declarations from WTO Doha Ministerial

Draft Ministerial Declaration 28 September 2001	Draft Ministerial Declaration 27 October 2001	Draft Ministerial Declaration 13 November 2001	Ministerial Declaration 14 November 2001
		specific commitments contained in paragraphs 16, 22, 25-27, 33, 38-40, 42 and 43, and also reaffirm the understanding in paragraph 2 on the important role of sustainably financed technical assistance and capacity-building programmes. We instruct the Director-General to report to the Fifth Session of the Ministerial Conference, with an interim report to the General Council in December 2002 on the implementation and adequacy of these commitments in the identified paragraphs.	specific commitments contained in paragraphs 16, 21, 24, 26, 27, 33, 38-40, 42 and 43, and also reaffirm the understanding in paragraph 2 on the important role of sustainably financed technical assistance and capacity-building programmes. We instruct the Director-General to report to the Fifth Session of the Ministerial Conference, with an interim report to the General Council in December 2002 on the implementation and adequacy of these commitments in the identified paragraphs.
LEAST-DEVELOPED COUNTRIES	LEAST-DEVELOPED COUNTRIES	LEAST-DEVELOPED COUNTRIES	LEAST-DEVELOPED COUNTRIES
34. ~~We recognize that the further integration of~~ the least-developed countries (LDCs) into the trading system requires combined and inter-related action at three levels namely, market access, trade-related technical assistance and capacity building, and LDC's domestic policy reforms.	35. We acknowledge the seriousness of the concerns expressed by the least-developed countries (LDCs) in the Zanzibar Declaration adopted by their Ministers in July 2001. We recognize that the integration of the LDCs into the trading system requires combined and inter-related action at three levels, namely: market access, trade-related technical assistance and capacity building, and supporting domestic measures to mainstream trade priority areas of action into plans for economic development and strategies for poverty reduction. We agree that the meaningful integration of LDCs into the trading system and the global economy will involve efforts by all WTO Members. We commit ourselves to the objective	42. We acknowledge the seriousness of the concerns expressed by the least-developed countries (LDCs) in the Zanzibar Declaration adopted by their Ministers in July 2001. We recognize that the integration of the LDCs into the trading system requires combined and inter-related action at three levels, namely: market access, trade-related technical assistance and capacity building, and supporting domestic measures to mainstream trade priority areas of action into plans for economic development and strategies for poverty reduction. We agree that the meaningful integration of LDCs into the trading system and the global economy will involve efforts by all WTO Members. We commit ourselves to the objective	42. We acknowledge the seriousness of the concerns expressed by the least-developed countries (LDCs) in the Zanzibar Declaration adopted by their Ministers in July 2001. We recognize that the integration of the LDCs into the multilateral trading system requires meaningful market access, support for the diversification of their production and export base, and trade-related technical assistance and capacity building. We agree that the meaningful integration of LDCs into the trading system and the global economy will involve efforts by all WTO Members. We commit ourselves to the objective

~~removed text~~ as compared to 27 October Draft
added text as compared to 27 October Draft
text moved within a paragraph for purposes of comparing to 27 October Draft

34

Comparison of Draft Ministerial Declarations from WTO Doha Ministerial

Draft Ministerial Declaration 28 September 2001	Draft Ministerial Declaration 27 October 2001	Draft Ministerial Declaration 13 November 2001	Ministerial Declaration 14 November 2001
	of duty-free, quota-free market access for products originating from LDCs. In this regard, we welcome the significant market access improvements by WTO Members in advance of the Third UN Conference on LDCs (LDC-III), in Brussels, May 2001. We further commit ourselves to consider additional measures for progressive improvements in market access for LDCs. Accession of LDCs remains a priority for the Membership. We agree to work to accelerate negotiations with acceding LDCs. We instruct the Secretariat to reflect the priority we attach to LDCs' accessions in the annual plans for technical assistance.	of duty-free, quota-free market access for products originating from LDCs. In this regard, we welcome the significant market access improvements by WTO Members in advance of the Third UN Conference on LDCs (LDC-III), in Brussels, May 2001. We further commit ourselves to consider additional measures for progressive improvements in market access for LDCs. Accession of LDCs remains a priority for the Membership. We agree to work to facilitate and accelerate negotiations with acceding LDCs. We instruct the Secretariat to reflect the priority we attach to LDCs' accessions in the annual plans for technical assistance. We reaffirm the commitments we undertook at LDC-III, and	of duty-free, quota-free market access for products originating from LDCs. In this regard, we welcome the significant market access improvements by WTO Members in advance of the Third UN Conference on LDCs (LDC-III), in Brussels, May 2001. We further commit ourselves to consider additional measures for progressive improvements in market access for LDCs. Accession of LDCs remains a priority for the Membership. We agree to work to facilitate and accelerate negotiations with acceding LDCs. We instruct the Secretariat to reflect the priority we attach to LDCs' accessions in the annual plans for technical assistance. We reaffirm the commitments we undertook at LDC-III, and
We agree that the WTO should take into account, in designing its work programme for LDCs, the trade-related elements of the Brussels Declaration and Programme of Action consistent with the WTO's mandate adopted at ~~the Third United Nations Conference on the Least Developed Countries in May 2001~~.	We agree that the WTO should take into account, in designing its work programme for LDCs, the trade-related elements of the Brussels Declaration and Programme of Action, consistent with the WTO's mandate, adopted at LDC-III. We instruct the Sub-Committee for Least-Developed Countries to design such a work programme and to report on the agreed work programme to the General Council at its first meeting in 2002.	agree that the WTO should take into account, in designing its work programme for LDCs, the trade-related elements of the Brussels Declaration and Programme of Action, consistent with the WTO's mandate, adopted at LDC-III. We instruct the Sub-Committee for Least-Developed Countries to design such a work programme and to report on the agreed work programme to the General Council at its first meeting in 2002.	agree that the WTO should take into account, in designing its work programme for LDCs, the trade-related elements of the Brussels Declaration and Programme of Action, consistent with the WTO's mandate, adopted at LDC-III. We instruct the Sub-Committee for Least-Developed Countries to design such a work programme and to report on the agreed work programme to the General Council at its first meeting in 2002.
We ~~acknowledge the value of and~~ endorse the Integrated Framework for Trade-Related Technical Assistance to Least-Developed Countries (IF) as a viable model for LDC's trade development. We ~~appeal to~~ development partners to	36. We endorse the Integrated Framework for Trade-Related Technical Assistance to Least-Developed Countries (IF) as a viable model for LDCs' trade development. We urge development partners to significantly	43. We endorse the Integrated Framework for Trade-Related Technical Assistance to Least-Developed Countries (IF) as a viable model for LDCs' trade development. We urge development partners to significantly	43. We endorse the Integrated Framework for Trade-Related Technical Assistance to Least-Developed Countries (IF) as a viable model for LDCs' trade development. We urge development partners to significantly

~~removed text~~ as compared to 27 October Draft
added text as compared to 27 October Draft
text moved within a paragraph for purposes of comparing to 27 October Draft

35

Comparison of Draft Ministerial Declarations from WTO Doha Ministerial

Draft Ministerial Declaration 28 September 2001	Draft Ministerial Declaration 27 October 2001	Draft Ministerial Declaration 13 November 2001	Ministerial Declaration 14 November 2001
increase contributions to the IF Trust Fund. We urge the core agencies, in coordination with development partners, to explore the enhancement of the IF and the	increase contributions to the IF Trust Fund and WTO extra-budgetary trust funds in favour of LDCs. We urge the core agencies, in coordination with development partners, to explore the enhancement of the IF and the	increase contributions to the IF Trust Fund and WTO extra-budgetary trust funds in favour of LDCs. We urge the core agencies, in coordination with development partners, to explore the enhancement of the IF and the	increase contributions to the IF Trust Fund and WTO extra-budgetary trust funds in favour of LDCs. We urge the core agencies, in coordination with development partners, to explore the enhancement of the IF <u>with a view to addressing the supply-side constraints of LDCs and the</u>
extension of the model. We request the Director-General, following coordination with ~~all the core agencies, to~~ report to Ministers at the Fifth Session of the Ministerial Conference.	extension of the model to all LDCs, following the review of the IF and the appraisal of the ongoing Pilot Scheme in selected LDCs. We request the Director-General, following coordination with heads of the other agencies, to provide an interim report to the General Council in December 2002 and a full report to the Fifth Session of the Ministerial Conference on all issues affecting LDCs.	extension of the model to all LDCs, following the review of the IF and the appraisal of the ongoing Pilot Scheme in selected LDCs. We request the Director-General, following coordination with heads of the other agencies, to provide an interim report to the General Council in December 2002 and a full report to the Fifth Session of the Ministerial Conference on all issues affecting LDCs.	extension of the model to all LDCs, following the review of the IF and the appraisal of the ongoing Pilot Scheme in selected LDCs. We request the Director-General, following coordination with heads of the other agencies, to provide an interim report to the General Council in December 2002 and a full report to the Fifth Session of the Ministerial Conference on all issues affecting LDCs.
SPECIAL AND DIFFERENTIAL TREATMENT	SPECIAL AND DIFFERENTIAL TREATMENT	SPECIAL AND DIFFERENTIAL TREATMENT	SPECIAL AND DIFFERENTIAL TREATMENT
35. ~~Text to be considered, taking into account the report to be submitted by the Committee on Trade and Development.~~	37. We reaffirm that provisions for special and differential treatment are an integral part of the WTO Agreements. We note the concerns expressed regarding their operation in addressing specific constraints faced by developing countries, particularly least-developed countries. In that connection, we also note that some Members have proposed a Framework Agreement on Special and Differential Treatment (WT/GC/W/442). We therefore agree that all special and differential treatment provisions shall be reviewed with a view to strengthening them and making	44. We reaffirm that provisions for special and differential treatment are an integral part of the WTO Agreements. We note the concerns expressed regarding their operation in addressing specific constraints faced by developing countries, particularly least-developed countries. In that connection, we also note that some Members have proposed a Framework Agreement on Special and Differential Treatment (WT/GC/W/442). We therefore agree that all special and differential treatment provisions shall be reviewed with a view to strengthening them and making	44. We reaffirm that provisions for special and differential treatment are an integral part of the WTO Agreements. We note the concerns expressed regarding their operation in addressing specific constraints faced by developing countries, particularly least-developed countries. In that connection, we also note that some Members have proposed a Framework Agreement on Special and Differential Treatment (WT/GC/W/442). We therefore agree that all special and differential treatment provisions shall be reviewed with a view to strengthening them and making

~~removed text~~ as compared to 27 October Draft
<u>added text</u> as compared to 27 October Draft
text moved within a paragraph for purposes of comparing to 27 October Draft

Comparison of Draft Ministerial Declarations from WTO Doha Ministerial

Draft Ministerial Declaration 28 September 2001	Draft Ministerial Declaration 27 October 2001	Draft Ministerial Declaration 13 November 2001	Ministerial Declaration 14 November 2001
	them more precise, effective and operational. In this connection, we endorse the work programme on special and differential treatment set out in the Decision on Implementation-Related Issues and Concerns.	them more precise, effective and operational. In this connection, we endorse the work programme on special and differential treatment set out in the Decision on Implementation-Related Issues and Concerns.	them more precise, effective and operational. In this connection, we endorse the work programme on special and differential treatment set out in the Decision on Implementation-Related Issues and Concerns.
ORGANIZATION AND MANAGEMENT OF THE WORK PROGRAMME	ORGANIZATION AND MANAGEMENT OF THE WORK PROGRAMME	ORGANIZATION AND MANAGEMENT OF THE WORK PROGRAMME	ORGANIZATION AND MANAGEMENT OF THE WORK PROGRAMME
36. The negotiations to be pursued under the terms of this Declaration shall be concluded not later than ... . The Fifth Session of the Ministerial Conference will take stock of progress in the negotiations, provide any necessary political guidance, and take ~~any~~ decisions as necessary. When the results of the negotiations in all areas have been established, a Special Session of the Ministerial Conference will be held to take decisions regarding the adoption and implementation of those results.	38. The negotiations to be pursued under the terms of this Declaration shall be concluded not later than ... . The Fifth Session of the Ministerial Conference will take stock of progress in the negotiations, provide any necessary political guidance, and take decisions as necessary. When the results of the negotiations in all areas have been established, a Special Session of the Ministerial Conference will be held to take decisions regarding the adoption and implementation of those results.	45. The negotiations to be pursued under the terms of this Declaration shall be concluded not later than [1 January 2005]. The Fifth Session of the Ministerial Conference will take stock of progress in the negotiations, provide any necessary political guidance, and take decisions as necessary. When the results of the negotiations in all areas have been established, a Special Session of the Ministerial Conference will be held to take decisions regarding the adoption and implementation of those results.	45. The negotiations to be pursued under the terms of this Declaration shall be concluded not later than 1 January 2005. The Fifth Session of the Ministerial Conference will take stock of progress in the negotiations, provide any necessary political guidance, and take decisions as necessary. When the results of the negotiations in all areas have been established, a Special Session of the Ministerial Conference will be held to take decisions regarding the adoption and implementation of those results.
37. The overall conduct of the negotiations shall be supervised by a Trade Negotiations Committee under the authority of the General Council. The Trade Negotiations Committee shall hold its first meeting not later than .... It shall establish appropriate negotiating mechanisms as required and supervise the progress of the negotiations.	39. The overall conduct of the negotiations shall be supervised by a Trade Negotiations Committee under the authority of the General Council. The Trade Negotiations Committee shall hold its first meeting not later than .... It shall establish appropriate negotiating mechanisms as required and supervise the progress of the negotiations.	46. The overall conduct of the negotiations shall be supervised by a Trade Negotiations Committee under the authority of the General Council. The Trade Negotiations Committee shall hold its first meeting not later than [31 January 2002]. It shall establish appropriate negotiating mechanisms as required and supervise the progress of the negotiations.	46. The overall conduct of the negotiations shall be supervised by a Trade Negotiations Committee under the authority of the General Council. The Trade Negotiations Committee shall hold its first meeting not later than 31 January 2002. It shall establish appropriate negotiating mechanisms as required and supervise the progress of the negotiations.

~~removed text~~ as compared to 27 October Draft
added text as compared to 27 October Draft
text moved within a paragraph for purposes of comparing to 27 October Draft

37

Comparison of Draft Ministerial Declarations from WTO Doha Ministerial

Draft Ministerial Declaration 28 September 2001	Draft Ministerial Declaration 27 October 2001	Draft Ministerial Declaration 13 November 2001	Ministerial Declaration 14 November 2001
38. *With the exception of ~~those related to the amendment of~~ the Dispute Settlement Understanding* The conduct, conclusion and entry into force of the outcome of the negotiations shall, be treated as parts of a single undertaking. However, agreements reached at an early stage may be implemented on a provisional or a definitive basis. Early agreements shall be taken into account in assessing the overall balance of the negotiations.	40. With the exception of the improvements and clarifications of the Dispute Settlement Understanding, the conduct, conclusion and entry into force of the outcome of the negotiations shall be treated as parts of a single undertaking. However, agreements reached at an early stage may be implemented on a provisional or a definitive basis. Early agreements shall be taken into account in assessing the overall balance of the negotiations.	47. With the exception of the improvements and clarifications of the Dispute Settlement Understanding, the conduct, conclusion and entry into force of the outcome of the negotiations shall be treated as parts of a single undertaking. However, agreements reached at an early stage may be implemented on a provisional or a definitive basis. Early agreements shall be taken into account in assessing the overall balance of the negotiations.	47. With the exception of the improvements and clarifications of the Dispute Settlement Understanding, the conduct, conclusion and entry into force of the outcome of the negotiations shall be treated as parts of a single undertaking. However, agreements reached at an early stage may be implemented on a provisional or a definitive basis. Early agreements shall be taken into account in assessing the overall balance of the negotiations.
39. Negotiations shall be open to:	41. Negotiations shall be open to:	48. Negotiations shall be open to:	48. Negotiations shall be open to:
(i) all Members of the WTO;	(i) all Members of the WTO; and	(i) all Members of the WTO; and	(i) all Members of the WTO; and
(ii) States and separate customs territories that inform Members, at a regular meeting of the General Council, of their intention to negotiate the terms of their membership and for whom an accession working party is established.	(ii) States and separate customs territories currently in the process of accession and those that inform Members, at a regular meeting of the General Council, of their intentionto negotiate the terms of their membership and for whom an accession working party is established.	(ii) States and separate customs territories currently in the process of accession and those that inform Members, at a regular meeting of the General Council, of their intention to negotiate the terms of their membership and for whom an accession working partyis established.	(ii) States and separate customs territories currently in the process of accession and those that inform Members, at a regular meeting of the General Council, of their intention to negotiate the terms of their membership and for whom an accession working party is established.
Decisions on the outcomes of the negotiations shall be taken only by WTO Members.	Decisions on the outcomes of the negotiations shall be taken only by WTO Members.	Decisions on the outcomes of the negotiations shall be taken only by WTO Members.	Decisions on the outcomes of the negotiations shall be taken only by WTO Members.
40. The negotiations shall be conducted in a transparent manner among participants, in order to facilitate the effective participation of all. They shall be conducted with a view to ensuring benefits to all participants and to achieving an overall balance in the outcome of the negotiations.	42. The negotiations shall be conducted in a transparent manner among participants, in order to facilitate the effective participation of all. They shall be conducted with a view to ensuring benefits to all participants and to achieving an overall balance in the outcome of the negotiations.	49. The negotiations shall be conducted in a transparent manner among participants, in order to facilitate the effective participation of all. They shall be conducted with a view to ensuring benefits to all participants and to achieving an overall balance in the outcome of the negotiations.	49. The negotiations shall be conducted in a transparent manner among participants, in order to facilitate the effective participation of all. They shall be conducted with a view to ensuring benefits to all participants and to achieving an overall balance in the outcome of the negotiations.

~~removed text~~ as compared to 27 October Draft
added text as compared to 27 October Draft
text moved within a paragraph for purposes of comparing to 27 October Draft

38

Comparison of Draft Ministerial Declarations from WTO Doha Ministerial

Draft Ministerial Declaration 28 September 2001	Draft Ministerial Declaration 27 October 2001	Draft Ministerial Declaration 13 November 2001	Ministerial Declaration 14 November 2001
	43. The negotiations and the other aspects of the Work Programme shall take fully into account the principle of special and differential treatment for developing and least-developed countries embodied in: Part IV of the GATT 1994; the Decision of 28 November 1979 on Differential and More Favourable Treatment, Reciprocity and Fuller Participation of Developing Countries; the Uruguay Round Decision on Measures in Favour of Least-Developed Countries; and all other relevant WTO provisions.	50. The negotiations and the other aspects of the Work Programme shall take fully into account the principle of special and differential treatment for developing and least-developed countries embodied in: Part IV of the GATT 1994; the Decision of 28 November 1979 on Differential and More Favourable Treatment, Reciprocity and Fuller Participation of Developing Countries; the Uruguay Round Decision on Measures in Favour of Least-Developed Countries; and all other relevant WTO provisions.	50. The negotiations and the other aspects of the Work Programme shall take fully into account the principle of special and differential treatment for developing and least-developed countries embodied in: Part IV of the GATT 1994; the Decision of 28 November 1979 on Differential and More Favourable Treatment, Reciprocity and Fuller Participation of Developing Countries; the Uruguay Round Decision on Measures in Favour of Least-Developed Countries; and all other relevant WTO provisions.
41. The Committee on Trade and Development and the Committee on Trade and Environment ~~will~~, within their respective mandates, each act as a forum to identify and debate developmental and environmental aspects of the~~se~~ negotiations, in order to help achieve the objective of having sustainable development appropriately reflected ~~in the negotiations~~.	44. The Committee on Trade and Development and the Committee on Trade and Environment shall, within their respective mandates, each act as a forum to identify and debate developmental and environmental aspects of the negotiations, in order to help achieve the objective of having sustainable development appropriately reflected.	51. The Committee on Trade and Development and the Committee on Trade and Environment shall, within their respective mandates, each act as a forum to identify and debate developmental and environmental aspects of the negotiations, in order to help achieve the objective of having sustainable development appropriately reflected.	51. The Committee on Trade and Development and the Committee on Trade and Environment shall, within their respective mandates, each act as a forum to identify and debate developmental and environmental aspects of the negotiations, in order to help achieve the objective of having sustainable development appropriately reflected.
~~42. The Work Programme as a whole must evolve in a balanced and forward-looking manner which responds to the diverse challenges faced by Members~~. Those elements which do not involve negotiations are also accorded a high priority. They ~~will~~ be pursued under the overall supervision of the General Council, which shall report on progress to the Fifth Session of the Ministerial Conference.	45. Those elements of the Work Programme which do not involve negotiations are also accorded a high priority. They shall be pursued under the overall supervision of the General Council, which shall report on progress to the Fifth Session of the Ministerial Conference.	52. Those elements of the Work Programme which do not involve negotiations are also accorded a high priority. They shall be pursued under the overall supervision of the General Council, which shall report on progress to the Fifth Session of the Ministerial Conference.	52. Those elements of the Work Programme which do not involve negotiations are also accorded a high priority. They shall be pursued under the overall supervision of the General Council, which shall report on progress to the Fifth Session of the Ministerial Conference.

~~removed text~~ as compared to 27 October Draft
added text as compared to 27 October Draft
text moved within a paragraph for purposes of comparing to 27 October Draft

39

Comparison of Draft Ministerial Declarations from WTO Doha Ministerial

Draft Ministerial Declaration 28 September 2001	Draft Ministerial Declaration 27 October 2001	Draft Ministerial Declaration 13 November 2001	Ministerial Declaration 14 November 2001
~~Footnote:~~ ~~1 It is proposed that the issue of the relationship between intellectual property and [access to medicines] [public health] be addressed in a separate declaration.~~			

~~removed text~~ as compared to 27 October Draft
added text as compared to 27 October Draft
text moved within a paragraph for purposes of comparing to 27 October Draft

Appendix 2
Comparison of Draft TRIPs Agreement and Public Health Declarations

Comparison of TRIPS and Public Health Draft Declarations from the WTO Doha Ministerial

Harbinson Draft on TRIPS and Health 11 October 2001	Harbinson Text on TRIPS 21 October 2001	Declaration on the TRIPS Agreement and Public Health Revision 13 November 2001	Declaration on the TRIPS Agreement and Public Health 14 November 2001

Methodological Notes

All comparisons have been made to thOctober 21, 2001 Draft TRIPs and Public Health Declarations. In the October 11 Draft text which has been removed from the October 21 draft appears in ~~strikethru~~.

Text in the November 13 draft, which represents an addition to or change from the October 21 draft appears in <u>under-line.</u>

Text in the November 14 draft, which represents an addition to or change from the October 21 draft appears in <u>under-line.</u>

Text in the November 13 or 14 draft which has been moved within a paragraph appears in *italics.*

In all columns the language has been lined up as closely as possible to the October 21 draft, by adding spaces and lines, and breaking up paragraphs where necessary.

~~removed text~~ as compared to 21 October Draft
<u>added text as</u> compared to 21 October Draft

Comparison of TRIPS and Public Health Draft Declarations from the WTO Doha Ministerial

Harbinson Draft on TRIPS and Health 11 October 2001	Harbinson Text on TRIPS 21 October 2001	Declaration on the TRIPS Agreement and Public Health Revision 13 November 2001	Declaration on the TRIPS Agreement and Public Health 14 November 2001
HARBINSON OCT. 11 DRAFT ON TRIPS AND HEALTH **Date: October 26, 2001** Chairman's Proposals on TRIPS and Health (October 11) Reaffirming our commitment to implementation of the TRIPS Agreement and noting that this Declaration cannot amend rights and obligations under the WTO Agreement; Ministers declare that:	**HARBINSON OCT. 21 TEXT ON TRIPS** **Date: October 26, 2001** 21 October 2001 elements for draft declaration on intellectual property and [access to medicines] [public health]	JOB(01)/155/Rev.1 13 November 2001 **DECLARATION ON THE TRIPS AGREEMENT AND PUBLIC HEALTH** **Revision**	**WORLD TRADE ORGANIZATION** **WT/MIN(01)/DEC/2** 20 November 2001 (01-5860) **MINISTERIAL CONFERENCE** **Fourth Session** **Doha, 9 - 14 November 2001** **DECLARATION ON THE TRIPS AGREEMENT AND PUBLIC HEALTH** Adopted on 14 November 2001
~~Element one: The overall relation between the TRIPS Agreement and measures to protect public health/~~	1. We recognize the gravity of the public health crises afflicting many developing and least-developed countries, especially those resulting from the HIV/AIDS and other pandemics.	1. We recognize the gravity of the public health problems afflicting many developing and least-developed countries, especially those resulting from HIV/AIDS, tuberculosis, malaria and other epidemics.	1. We recognize the gravity of the public health problems afflicting many developing and least-developed countries, especially those resulting from HIV/AIDS, tuberculosis, malaria and other epidemics.
	2. We stress the need for the WTO Agreement on Trade-Related Aspects of Intellectual Property Rights (TRIPS Agreement) to be implemented and interpreted so as to be part of the wider national and international action to address these problems.	2. We stress the need for the WTO Agreement on Trade-Related Aspects of Intellectual Property Rights (TRIPS Agreement) to be part of the wider national and international action to address these problems.	2. We stress the need for the WTO Agreement on Trade-Related Aspects of Intellectual Property Rights (TRIPS Agreement) to be part of the wider national and international action to address these problems.
~~ensure access to medicines.~~ ~~[no text offered]~~	3. We recognize that intellectual property protection is important for the development of new medicines but also that it can affect the prices of medicines. We therefore recognize the need for an appropriate balance within intellectual property systems between the public health objectives of promoting new medicines and of maximizing access to existing medicines and,	3. We recognize that intellectual property protection is important for the development of new medicines. We also recognize the concerns about its effects on prices.	3. We recognize that intellectual property protection is important for the development of new medicines. We also recognize the concerns about its effects on prices.

~~removed text~~ as compared to 21 October Draft
added text as compared to 21 October Draft

5

Comparison of TRIPS and Public Health Draft Declarations from the WTO Doha Ministerial

Harbinson Draft on TRIPS and Health 11 October 2001	Harbinson Text on TRIPS 21 October 2001	Declaration on the TRIPS Agreement and Public Health Revision 13 November 2001	Declaration on the TRIPS Agreement and Public Health 14 November 2001
	in this connection, the need for measures under intellectual property systems to facilitate access to existing medicines.		
~~Element two: Considerations relevant for interpreting~~	4. We emphasize that the TRIPS Agreement permits governments to take measures to [protect public health] ~~[to secure access to medicines at affordable prices]~~.	4. We agree that the TRIPS Agreement does not and should not prevent Members from taking measures to protect public health. Accordingly, while reiterating our commitment to the TRIPS Agreement, we affirm that the Agreement can and should be interpreted and implemented in a manner supportive of WTO Members' right to protect public health and, in particular, to promote access to medicines for all.	4. We agree that the TRIPS Agreement does not and should not prevent Members from taking measures to protect public health. Accordingly, while reiterating our commitment to the TRIPS Agreement, we affirm that the Agreement can and should be interpreted and implemented in a manner supportive of WTO Members' right to protect public health and, in particular, to promote access to medicines for all.
	In this connection, we reaffirm the right of WTO Members to use, to the full,	In this connection, we reaffirm the right of WTO Members to use, to the full,	In this connection, we reaffirm the right of WTO Members to use, to the full,
the provisions of the TRIPS agreement ~~that~~ provide flexibility	the provisions in the TRIPS Agreement which provide flexibility for this purpose, as an integral part of our commitment to the TRIPS Agreement as a whole.	the provisions in the TRIPS Agreement, which provide flexibility for this purpose.	the provisions in the TRIPS Agreement, which provide flexibility for this purpose.
	5. With a view to facilitating the use of this flexibility by providing greater legal certainty, we agree on the following clarifications of the provisions of the TRIPS Agreement, while preserving the rights and obligations of Members under that Agreement:	5. Accordingly and in the light of paragraph 4 above, while maintaining our commitments in the TRIPS Agreement, we recognize that these flexibilities include:	5. Accordingly and in the light of paragraph 4 above, while maintaining our commitments in the TRIPS Agreement, we recognize that these flexibilities include:

~~removed text~~ as compared to 21 October Draft
added text as compared to 21 October Draft

Comparison of TRIPS and Public Health Draft Declarations from the WTO Doha Ministerial

Harbinson Draft on TRIPS and Health 11 October 2001	Harbinson Text on TRIPS 21 October 2001	Declaration on the TRIPS Agreement and Public Health Revision 13 November 2001	Declaration on the TRIPS Agreement and Public Health 14 November 2001
		(a) In applying the customary rules of interpretation of public international law,	(a) In applying the customary rules of interpretation of public international law,
Each provision of the TRIPS Agreement should be read in accordance with the customary rules of interpretation of public international law as reflected in the Vienna Convention on the Law of Treaties. ~~In this regard~~, in assessing the "object and purpose" of the TRIPS Agreement~~[, in terms of Article 31 of~~ the Vienna Convention.]	* Each provision of the TRIPS Agreement should be read in accordance with the customary rules of interpretation of public international law as reflected in the Vienna Convention on the Law of Treaties. In assessing the "object and purpose" of the TRIPS Agreement as called for in the Vienna Convention,	each provision of the TRIPS Agreement shall be read in the light of the object and purpose of the Agreement as expressed, in particular, in its objectives and principles.	each provision of the TRIPS Agreement shall be read in the light of the object and purpose of the Agreement as expressed, in particular, in its objectives and principles.
* [full account shall be taken of all relevant provisions of the TRIPS Agreement, in particular Articles 7 and 8] OR * [each provision of the TRIPS Agreement should be read in the light of Articles 7 and 8 ~~of the Agreement]~~ ~~OR~~ ~~*[full consideration should be taken of the goals and limitations expressed in the preamble, Article 7 and Article 8 and other provisions of the TRIPS Agreement]~~	each provision of the TRIPS Agreement shall be read in the light, in particular, of Articles 7and 8.		
~~Element Three: Grounds on which compulsory licenses can be issued and government use permitted~~ Each Member [has the right to] [may] allow other use of the subject-matter of a patent without the authorization of the right holder, including use by the government or third parties authorized by the government, ~~subject to the provisions of Article 31~~. Each Member	* Each Member has the right to allow other use of the subject-matter of a patent without the authorization of the right holder, including use by the government or third parties authorized by the government. Each Member	(b) Each Member has the right to grant compulsory licences and the	Each Member has the right to grant compulsory licences and the

~~removed text~~ as compared to 21 October Draft
added text as compared to 21 October Draft

7

Comparison of TRIPS and Public Health Draft Declarations from the WTO Doha Ministerial

Harbinson Draft on TRIPS and Health 11 October 2001	Harbinson Text on TRIPS 21 October 2001	Declaration on the TRIPS Agreement and Public Health Revision 13 November 2001	Declaration on the TRIPS Agreement and Public Health 14 November 2001
has the freedom to determine the grounds upon which such use is allowed.	has the freedom to determine the grounds upon which such use is allowed.	freedom to determine the grounds upon which such licences are granted.	freedom to determine the grounds upon which such licences are granted.
~~Element Three(2): Circumstances which warrant not seeking a voluntary license prior to seeking a compulsory license or authorizing government use~~ In case of a national emergency or other circumstances of extreme urgency, ~~the TRIPS Agreement recognizes the right of each Member to issue compulsory licenses without efforts having been first made to seek a voluntary license.~~ Without prejudice to what constitutes a national emergency or other circumstances of extreme urgency, ~~Ministers note that~~ public health crises including those relating to HIV/AIDS and other epidemics ~~(pandemics)~~ can represent ~~such situations.~~	* In case of a national emergency, other circumstances of extreme urgency or public non-commercial use, WTO Members may allow, pursuant to Article 31(b), use without the authorization of the right holder without prior efforts on the part of the user to obtain authorization from the right holder. Without prejudice to the right of each Member to determine what constitutes a national emergency or other circumstances of extreme urgency, public health crises, including those relating to HIV/AIDS and other epidemics, can represent a national emergency or other circumstances of extreme urgency.	(c) Each Member has the right to determine what constitutes a national emergency or other circumstances of extreme urgency, it being understood that public health crises, including those relating to HIV/AIDS, tuberculosis, malaria and other epidemics, can represent a national emergency or other circumstances of extreme urgency.	Each Member has the right to determine what constitutes a national emergency or other circumstances of extreme urgency, it being understood that public health crises, including those relating to HIV/AIDS, tuberculosis, malaria and other epidemics, can represent a national emergency or other circumstances of extreme urgency.
~~Element Four: Exhaustion of intellectual property rights and parallel imports~~ *Each Member is free,* ~~*subject to the provisions of Articles 3 and 4 of the TRIPS Agreement*~~*, to establish its own regime for* ~~*the*~~ *exhaustion* ~~*of intellectual property rights, [it being understood that exhaustion relates to situations where goods to which rights apply have been put on the market by, or*~~	* The effect of the various provisions in the TRIPS Agreement that are relevant to exhaustion of intellectual property rights is to leave each Member free to establish its own regime for such exhaustion, subject to the MFN and national treatment provisions of Articles 3 and 4.	(d) The effect of the provisions in the TRIPS Agreement that are relevant to the exhaustion of intellectual property rights is to leave each Member free to establish its own regime for such exhaustion without challenge, subject to the MFN and national treatment provisions of Articles 3 and 4.	The effect of the provisions in the TRIPS Agreement that are relevant to the exhaustion of intellectual property rights is to leave each Member free to establish its own regime for such exhaustion without challenge, subject to the MFN and national treatment provisions of Articles 3 and 4.

~~removed text~~ as compared to 21 October Draft
added text as compared to 21 October Draft

8

Comparison of TRIPS and Public Health Draft Declarations from the WTO Doha Ministerial

Harbinson Draft on TRIPS and Health 11 October 2001	Harbinson Text on TRIPS 21 October 2001	Declaration on the TRIPS Agreement and Public Health Revision 13 November 2001	Declaration on the TRIPS Agreement and Public Health 14 November 2001
~~*with the consent of, the right holder.]*~~ ~~OR~~ ~~Without prejudice to the exhaustion regime a member has chosen, we recognize that Article 28.1 provides an exclusive importation right for patented pharmaceutical products; that the TRIPS Agreement, pursuant to Article 6, does not provide a mechanism to challenge the exhaustion regime a membe regards as in its best interests so long as those practices comply with Articles 3 and 4; and that patent rights are not exhausted in a market unless the goods to which those rights apply have been put on that market with the consent of the right holder.~~ ~~AND~~ ~~*Whatever the exhaustion regime they may have chosen, Members [are encouraged to take][will take][all necessary] measures to prevent pharmaceuticals [provided][imported] under [tiered or]*~~ *discounted pricing* ~~*schemes or supplied under aid schemes from [being diverted from those for whom they were destined, to markets for which they were not intended] [leaving the market to where they are originally destined or (re-) entering markets for which they were not intended]*~~	[6. We welcome steps to make available medicines at discounted prices or under aid schemes to developing and least-developed countries and encourage Members to take measures to prevent the diversion of such medicines from those for whom they are intended into other markets.]		

~~removed text~~ as compared to 21 October Draft
added text as compared to 21 October Draft

Comparison of TRIPS and Public Health Draft Declarations from the WTO Doha Ministerial

Harbinson Draft on TRIPS and Health 11 October 2001	Harbinson Text on TRIPS 21 October 2001	Declaration on the TRIPS Agreement and Public Health Revision 13 November 2001	Declaration on the TRIPS Agreement and Public Health 14 November 2001
~~Element Three(3):~~ Situation of countries with limited domestic manufacturing capacity	Situation of countries with limited domestic manufacturing capacity in making effective use of compulsory licensing.	6. We recognize that WTO Members with	6. We recognize that WTO Members with
~~If a Member economy who has declared a national emergency or circumstance of extreme urgency within the meaning of Article 31(b) possesses insufficient capacity to manufacture a patented product pursuant to a compulsory license, it would be appropriate for any other Member to afford every assistance to the former by making efforts to obtain authrorization from the right holder on reasonable commercial terms and conditions; and if such efforts have not been successful within a reasonable period of time (having due regard to the seriousness of the health emergency involved), for the latter to supply to the former any excess of the patented product not predominantly required for the supply of the domestic market of the latter pursuant to a compulsory license, subject to the application of the procedural safeguards set out in Article 31.~~		insufficient or no manufacturing capacities in the pharmaceutical sector could face difficulties in making effective use of compulsory licensing under the TRIPS Agreement. We instruct the Council for TRIPS to find an expeditious solution to this problem and to report to the General Council before the end of 2002.	insufficient or no manufacturing capacities in the pharmaceutical sector could face difficulties in making effective use of compulsory licensing under the TRIPS Agreement. We instruct the Council for TRIPS to find an expeditious solution to this problem and to report to the General Council before the end of 2002.

~~removed text~~ as compared to 21 October Draft
added text as compared to 21 October Draft

10

Comparison of TRIPS and Public Health Draft Declarations from the WTO Doha Ministerial

Harbinson Draft on TRIPS and Health 11 October 2001	Harbinson Text on TRIPS 21 October 2001	Declaration on the TRIPS Agreement and Public Health Revision 13 November 2001	Declaration on the TRIPS Agreement and Public Health 14 November 2001
~~Element Five:~~ Transition periods [~~no text offered~~]	Transition periods. [Any other matters.]	7. We reaffirm the commitment of developed-country Members to provide incentives to their enterprises and institutions to promote and encourage technology transfer to least-developed country Members pursuant to Article 66.2. We also agree that the least-developed country Members will not be obliged, with respect to pharmaceutical products, to implement or apply Sections 5 and 7 of Part II of the TRIPS Agreement or to enforce rights provided for under these Sections until 1 January 2016, without prejudice to the right of least-developed country Members to seek other extensions of the transition periods as provided for in Article 66.1 of the TRIPS Agreement. We instruct the Council for TRIPS to take the necessary action to give effect to this pursuant to Article 66.1 of the TRIPS Agreement.	7. We reaffirm the commitment of developed-country Members to provide incentives to their enterprises and institutions to promote and encourage technology transfer to least-developed country Members pursuant to Article 66.2. We also agree that the least-developed country Members will not be obliged, with respect to pharmaceutical products, to implement or apply Sections 5 and 7 of Part II of the TRIPS Agreement or to enforce rights provided for under these Sections until 1 January 2016, without prejudice to the right of least-developed country Members to seek other extensions of the transition periods as provided for in Article 66.1 of the TRIPS Agreement. We instruct the Council for TRIPS to take the necessary action to give effect to this pursuant to Article 66.1 of the TRIPS Agreement.

~~removed text~~ as compared to 21 October Draft
added text as compared to 21 October Draft

Appendix 3
Comparison of Implementation-Related Issues and Concerns Draft Decisions

Comparison of Implementation-Related Issues and Concerns Draft Decisions

Implementation-Related Issues and Concerns Draft Decision 26 September 2001	Implementation-Related Issues and Concerns Draft Decision 27 October 2001	Implementation-Related Issues and Concerns Draft Decision 13 November 2001	Implementation-Related Issues and Concerns Decision 14 November 2001

Methodological Notes

All comparisons have been made to thOctober 27, 2001 Implementation-Related Issues and Concerns Draft. In the September 26, Draft text which has been removed from the October 27 draft appears in ~~strikethru~~.

Text in the November 13 draft, which represents an addition to or change from the October 27 draft appears in underline.

Text in the November 14 draft, which represents an addition to or change from the October 27 draft appears in underline.

Text in the November 13 or 14 draft which has been moved within a paragraph appears in *italics.*

In all columns the language has been lined up as closely as possible to the October 27 draft, by adding spaces and lines, and breaking up paragraphs where necessary.

~~removed text~~ as compared to 27 October Draft
added text as compared to 27 October Draft
moved text for purposes of comparing to 27 October Draft

Comparison of Implementation-Related Issues and Concerns Draft Decisions

Implementation-Related Issues and Concerns Draft Decision 26 September 2001	Implementation-Related Issues and Concerns Draft Decision 27 October 2001	Implementation-Related Issues and Concerns Draft Decision 13 November 2001	Implementation-Related Issues and Concerns Decision 14 November 2001
TEXT: MOORE, HARBINSON PROPOSALS ON IMPLEMENTATION	**JOB(01)/139/Rev.1**	JOB(01)/139/Rev.2	**WORLD TRADE ORGANIZATION** **WT/MIN(01)/17**
26 September 2001	27 October 2001	13 November 2001	20 November 2001 (01-5858) **MINISTERIAL CONFERENCE** **Fourth Session** **Doha, 9 - 14 November 2001**
Draft Decision on Implementation-Related Issues and Concerns	**Implementation-Related Issues and Concerns Draft Decision**	Implementation-Related Issues and Concerns Draft Decision	**IMPLEMENTATION-RELATED ISSUES AND CONCERNS**
3 October 2001/Fourth Session of the Ministerial Conference	**Revision**	Revision	Decision of 14 November 2001
The attached draft Decision on implementation-related issues and concerns is submitted for the consideration of delegations by the Chairman of the General Council and the Director-General. ~~It represents their best judgment of the possible basis at this time for reaching agreement~~	The attached revised draft Decision on implementation-related issues and concerns is submitted for the consideration of delegations by the Chairman of the General Council and the Director-General. It takes into account the results of the work of subsidiary bodies on the implementation issues referred to them as well as comments provided by delegations in further consultations.	The attached revised draft Decision on implementation-related issues and concerns is submitted for the consideration of Members by the Chairman of the Ministerial Conference. It takes into account the results of the work of the facilitator on this subject.	
to address ~~the outstanding~~ implementation-~~related~~ issues ~~and concerns in pursuance~~ of the General Council's Decision of 3 May 2000. ~~By taking action on the proposals outlined in this draft Decision, Members would be addressing elements of more than 40 tirets in addition to the dozen or so previously addressed in one way or another.~~	The revised text is the product of a collective effort by all delegations to address implementation issues in accordance with the terms of the 3 May 2000 Decision of the General Council.	as well as comments provided by Members in the Heads of Delegation process. Apart from textiles and clothing, the revised text proposes compromise solutions in an attempt to deal with the difficulties expressed by Members in respect of certain proposals in the earlier draft text. The text represents the Chairman's best judgement as to what is attainable at this stage.	

~~removed text~~ as compared to 27 October Draft
added text as compared to 27 October Draft
moved text for purposes of comparing to 27 October Draft

5

Comparison of Implementation-Related Issues and Concerns Draft Decisions

Implementation-Related Issues and Concerns Draft Decision 26 September 2001	Implementation-Related Issues and Concerns Draft Decision 27 October 2001	Implementation-Related Issues and Concerns Draft Decision 13 November 2001	Implementation-Related Issues and Concerns Decision 14 November 2001
~~The Chairman and the Director-General believe that this draft represents a credible effort to move the implementation debate to a new level of understanding. The elements included in this draft Decision draw upon important and valuable contributions provided by developing countries, the "G-7" countries* and, more recently, by some developed countries. They also take into account the work ongoing in the subsidiary bodies on issues referred to them. The Chairman and the Director-General also wish to acknowledge the value of the contributions by these bodies and their Chairpersons.~~	For ease of reference, this text follows the numbering of the tirets used by the G-7 countries in their paper on implementation.		
~~As reflected in the draft Decision, further action is proposed both now and at the Ministerial Conference in areas such as sanitary and phytosanitary measures, subsidies and countervailing measures, anti-dumping and textiles. In addition,~~ it is proposed ~~that remaining implementation issues be addressed in the context of the future work programme to be decided on by Ministers at the Fourth Ministerial Confrence.~~	It is proposed that this draft Decision be considered by the General Council on 31 October 2001, when it resumes the Special Session opened and adjourned on 3 October 2001.		
~~*Argentina, Morocco, New Zealand, Norway, Switzerland, Thailand and Uruguay~~			
~~Implementation-Related Issues and Concerns Draft Decision~~			

~~removed text~~ as compared to 27 October Draft
<u>added text</u> as compared to 27 October Draft
moved text for purposes of comparing to 27 October Draft

6

Comparison of Implementation-Related Issues and Concerns Draft Decisions

Implementation-Related Issues and Concerns Draft Decision 26 September 2001	Implementation-Related Issues and Concerns Draft Decision 27 October 2001	Implementation-Related Issues and Concerns Draft Decision 13 November 2001	Implementation-Related Issues and Concerns Decision 14 November 2001
The General Council,	The Ministerial Conference,	The Ministerial Conference,	The Ministerial Conference,
Having regard *to* Articles IV.1, IV.2, IV.5, IX.1, and IX.2 of the Marrakesh Agreement Establishing the World Trade Organization (WTO);	Having regard to Articles IV.1, IV.2, IV.5, IX.1 and IX.2 of the Marrakesh Agreement Establishing the World Trade Organization (WTO);	Having regard to Articles IV.1, IV.2, IV.5, IX.1 and IX.2 of the Marrakesh Agreement Establishing the World Trade Organization (WTO);	Having regard to Articles IV.1, IV.5 and IX of the Marrakesh Agreement Establishing the World Trade Organization (WTO);
Mindful of the importance that Members attach to the increased participation of developing countries in the multilateral trading system, and of the need to ensure that the system responds fully to the needs and interests of all participants;	Mindful of the importance that Members attach to the increased participation of developing countries in the multilateral trading system, and of the need to ensure that the system responds fully to the needs and interests of all participants;	Mindful of the importance that Members attach to the increased participation of developing countries in the multilateral trading system, and of the need to ensure that the system responds fully to the needs and interests of all participants;	Mindful of the importance that Members attach to the increased participation of developing countries in the multilateral trading system, and of the need to ensure that the system responds fully to the needs and interests of all participants;
Determined to take concrete action to address issues and concerns that have been raised by many developing-country Members regarding the implementation of some WTO Agreements and Decisions, including the difficulties and resource constraints that have been encountered in the implementation of obligations in various areas;	Determined to take concrete action to address issues and concerns that have been raised by many developing-country Members regarding the implementation of some WTO Agreements and Decisions, including the difficulties and resource constraints that have been encountered in the implementation of obligations in various areas;	Determined to take concrete action to address issues and concerns that have been raised by many developing-country Members regarding the implementation of some WTO Agreements and Decisions, including the difficulties and resource constraints that have been encountered in the implementation of obligations in various areas;	Determined to take concrete action to address issues and concerns that have been raised by many developing-country Members regarding the implementation of some WTO Agreements and Decisions, including the difficulties and resource constraints that have been encountered in the implementation of obligations in various areas;
Recallingits Decision of 3 May 2000 to meet in special sessions to address outstanding implementation issues, and to assess the existing difficulties, identify ways needed to resolve them, and take decisions for appropriate action not later than the Fourth Session of the Ministerial Conference;	Recalling the 3 May 2000 Decision of the General Council to meet in special sessions to address outstanding implementation issues, and to assess the existing difficulties, identify ways needed to resolve them, and take decisions for appropriate action not later than the Fourth Session of the Ministerial Conference;	Recalling the 3 May 2000 Decision of the General Council to meet in special sessions to address outstanding implementation issues, and to assess the existing difficulties, identify ways needed to resolve them, and take decisions for appropriate action not later than the Fourth Session of the Ministerial Conference;	Recalling the 3 May 2000 Decision of the General Council to meet in special sessions to address outstanding implementation issues, and to assess the existing difficulties, identify ways needed to resolve them, and take decisions for appropriate action not later than the Fourth Session of the Ministerial Conference;
Noting the actions taken by the General Council in pursuance of this mandate at its Special	Noting the actions taken by the General Council in pursuance of this mandate at its Special	Noting the actions taken by the General Council in pursuance of this mandate at its Special	Noting the actions taken by the General Council in pursuance of this mandate at its Special

~~removed text~~ as compared to 27 October Draft
<u>added text</u> as compared to 27 October Draft
moved text for purposes of comparing to 27 October Draft

7

Comparison of Implementation-Related Issues and Concerns Draft Decisions

Implementation-Related Issues and Concerns Draft Decision 26 September 2001	Implementation-Related Issues and Concerns Draft Decision 27 October 2001	Implementation-Related Issues and Concerns Draft Decision 13 November 2001	Implementation-Related Issues and Concerns Decision 14 November 2001
Sessions in October and December 2000 (WT/L/384), as well as the review and further discussion undertaken at the Special Sessions held in April and July 2001, including the referral of additional issues to relevant WTO bodies or their chairpersons for further work;	Sessions in October and December 2000 (WT/L/384), as well as the review and further discussion undertaken at the Special Sessions held in April, July and October 2001, including the referral of additional issues to relevant WTO bodies or their chairpersons for further work;	Sessions in October and December 2000 (WT/L/384), as well as the review and further discussion undertaken at the Special Sessions held in April, July and October 2001, including the referral of additional issues to relevant WTO bodies or their chairpersons for further work;	Sessions in October and December 2000 (WT/L/384), as well as the review and further discussion undertaken at the Special Sessions held in April, July and October 2001, including the referral of additional issues to relevant WTO bodies or their chairpersons for further work;
Noting also the reports on the issues referred to ~~them from subsidiary bodies and their chairpersons and from the Director-General~~, and the discussions as well as the clarifications provided and understandings reached on implementation issues in the intensive informal and formal meetings held under this process since May 2000;	*Noting also* the reports on the issues referred to the General Council from subsidiary bodies and their chairpersons and from the Director-General, and the discussions as well as the clarifications provided and understandings reached on implementation issues in the intensive informal and formal meetings held under this process since May 2000;	*Noting also* the reports on the issues referred to the General Council from subsidiary bodies and their chairpersons and from the Director-General, and the discussions as well as the clarifications provided and understandings reached on implementation issues in the intensive informal and formal meetings held under this process since May 2000;	*Noting also* the reports on the issues referred to the General Council from subsidiary bodies and their chairpersons and from the Director-General, and the discussions as well as the clarifications provided and understandings reached on implementation issues in the intensive informal and formal meetings held under this process since May 2000;
Decides as follows:	*Decides* as follows:	*Decides* as follows:	*Decides* as follows:
~~(i) to take immediate action, as set out in Annex I, to address the implementation difficulties encountered by developing countries in a number of areas;~~			
~~(ii) to develop recommendations for Ministers, based on the proposals set out in Annex II, for decision at the Fourth Session of the Ministerial Conference;~~			
~~(iii) to recommend to Ministers, meeting on the occasion of the Fourth Session of the Ministerial Conference to address other implementation issues in the course of the future work~~			

~~removed text~~ as compared to 27 October Draft
added text as compared to 27 October Draft
moved text for purposes of comparing to 27 October Draft

Comparison of Implementation-Related Issues and Concerns Draft Decisions

Implementation-Related Issues and Concerns Draft Decision 26 September 2001	Implementation-Related Issues and Concerns Draft Decision 27 October 2001	Implementation-Related Issues and Concerns Draft Decision 13 November 2001	Implementation-Related Issues and Concerns Decision 14 November 2001
~~programme of the WTO as provided for in the draft Ministerial Declaration; and~~			
~~(iv) to request the Director-General, consistent with the relevant provisions of the draft Ministerial Declaration, to ensure that WTO technical assistance focuses, on a priority basis, on assisting developing countries to implement existing WTO obligations as well as on increasing their capacity to participate more effectively in future multilateral trade negotiations. In carrying out this mandate, we stress the need for the WTO Secretariat to cooperate more closely with international and regional intergovernmental organizations to as to increase efficiency and synergies and avoid duplication of programmes.~~			
~~Annex I~~			
1. General Agreement on Tariffs and Trade 1994	1. General Agreement on Tariffs and Trade 1994 (GATT 1994)	1. General Agreement on Tariffs and Trade 1994 (GATT 1994)	1. General Agreement on Tariffs and Trade 1994 (GATT 1994)
- Tiret 2 "The General Council reaffirms that Article XVIII of the GATT 1994 is a special and differential treatment provision for developing countries and that recourse to it should be less overous than to Article XII of the GATT 1994."	- Tiret 2 "Reaffirms that Article XVIII of the GATT 1994 is a special and differential treatment provision for developing countries and that recourse to it should be less onerous than to Article XII of the GATT 1994."	- Tiret 2 "Reaffirms that Article XVIII of the GATT 1994 is a special and differential treatment provision for developing countries and that recourse to it should be less onerous than to Article XII of the GATT 1994."	1.1 Reaffirms that Article XVIII of the GATT 1994 is a special and differential treatment provision for developing countries and that recourse to it should be less onerous than to Article XII of the GATT 1994.
- Tiret 4 "Noting the issues raised in the report of the Committee on Market Access	- Tiret 4 "Noting the issues raised in the report of the Chairperson of the Committee on Market Access	- Tiret 4 "Noting the issues raised in the report of the Chairperson of the Committee on Market Access	1.2 Noting the issues raised in the report of the Chairperson of the Committee on Market Access

~~removed text~~ as compared to 27 October Draft
<u>added text</u> as compared to 27 October Draft
moved text for purposes of comparing to 27 October Draft

Comparison of Implementation-Related Issues and Concerns Draft Decisions

Implementation-Related Issues and Concerns Draft Decision 26 September 2001	Implementation-Related Issues and Concerns Draft Decision 27 October 2001	Implementation-Related Issues and Concerns Draft Decision 13 November 2001	Implementation-Related Issues and Concerns Decision 14 November 2001
concerning the meaning to be given to the phrase "substantial ~~supplier~~" in Article XIII of the GATT 1994, the Committee is directed to give further consideration to the issue and make recommendations to the General Council as expeditiously as possible but in any event no later than the ~~Fifth Ministerial Conference~~."	(WT/GC/50) concerning the meaning to be given to the phrase "substantial interest" in paragraph 2(d) of Article XIII of the GATT 1994, the Market Access Committee is directed to give further consideration to the issue and make recommendations to the General Council as expeditiously as possible but in any event not later than the end of 2002."	(WT/GC/50) concerning the meaning to be given to the phrase "substantial interest" in paragraph 2(d) of Article XIII of the GATT 1994, the Market Access Committee is directed to give further consideration to the issue and make recommendations to the General Council as expeditiously as possible but in any event not later than the end of 2002."	(WT/GC/50) concerning the meaning to be given to the phrase "substantial interest" in paragraph 2(d) of Article XIII of the GATT 1994, the Market Access Committee is directed to give further consideration to the issue and make recommendations to the General Council as expeditiously as possible but in any event not later than the end of 2002.
2. Agreement on Agriculture	2. Agreement on Agriculture	2. Agreement on Agriculture	2. Agreement on Agriculture
- Tiret 5 "~~The General Council~~ urges Members to exercise restraint in challenging measures notified under the green box by developing countries to promote rural development and adequately address food security concerns."	- Tiret 5 "Urges Members to exercise restraint in challenging measures notified under the green box by developing countries to promote rural development and adequately address food security concerns."	- Tiret 5 "Urges Members to exercise restraint in challenging measures notified under the green box by developing countries to promote rural development and adequately address food security concerns."	2.1 Urges Members to exercise restraint in challenging measures notified under the green box by developing countries to promote rural development and adequately address food security concerns.
Annex II *1. Agreement on Agriculture* *- Tiret 7* *[Action to be taken on implementation of the Decision on Measures Concerning the Possible Negative Effects of the Reform Programme on Least-Developed and Net Food-Importing Developing Countries in ~~the light of the report of the Committee on Agriculture expected on 28 September 2001.]~~*	- Tiret 7 "Takes note of the report of the Committee on Agriculture (G/AG/11) regarding the implementation of the Decision on Measures Concerning the Possible Negative Effects of the Reform Programme on Least-Developed and Net Food-Importing Developing Countries, and approves the recommendations contained therein regarding (i) food aid; (ii) technical and financial assistance in the context of aid programmes to improve agricultural productivity and infrastructure; (iii) financing normal levels of commer-	- Tiret 7 "Takes note of the report of the Committee on Agriculture (G/AG/11) regarding the implementation of the Decision on Measures Concerning the Possible Negative Effects of the Reform Programme on Least-Developed and Net Food-Importing Developing Countries, and approves the recommendations contained therein regarding (i) food aid; (ii) technical and financial assistance in the context of aid programmes to improve agricultural productivity and infrastructure; (iii) financing normal levels of commer-	2.2 Takes note of the report of the Committee on Agriculture (G/AG/11) regarding the implementation of the Decision on Measures Concerning the Possible Negative Effects of the Reform Programme on Least-Developed and Net Food-Importing Developing Countries, and approves the recommendations contained therein regarding (i) food aid; (ii) technical and financial assistance in the context of aid programmes to improve agricultural productivity and infrastructure; (iii) financing normal levels of commer-

~~removed text~~ as compared to 27 October Draft
added text as compared to 27 October Draft
moved text for purposes of comparing to 27 October Draft

Comparison of Implementation-Related Issues and Concerns Draft Decisions

Implementation-Related Issues and Concerns Draft Decision 26 September 2001	Implementation-Related Issues and Concerns Draft Decision 27 October 2001	Implementation-Related Issues and Concerns Draft Decision 13 November 2001	Implementation-Related Issues and Concerns Decision 14 November 2001
	cial imports of basic foodstuffs; and (iv) review of follow-up."	cial imports of basic foodstuffs; and (iv) review of follow-up."	cial imports of basic foodstuffs; and (iv) review of follow-up.
- Tiret 8 *[~~Action on~~* *the implementation of Article 10.2 of the Agreement on Agriculture ~~to be taken in the light of the report of the Committee on Agriculture expected on 28 September 2001.~~]*	- Tiret 8 "Takes note of the report of the Committee on Agriculture (G/AG/11) regarding the implementation of Article 10.2 of the Agreement on Agriculture, and approves the recommendations and reporting requirements contained therein."	- Tiret 8 "Takes note of the report of the Committee on Agriculture (G/AG/11) regarding the implementation of Article 10.2 of the Agreement on Agriculture, and approves the recommendations and reporting requirements contained therein."	2.3 Takes note of the report of the Committee on Agriculture (G/AG/11) regarding the implementation of Article 10.2 of the Agreement on Agriculture, and approves the recommendations and reporting requirements contained therein.
- Tariff Rate Quotas *"The General Council takes note of the Committee on Agriculture's report on the administration of tariff rate quotas and the submission by Members of addenda to their notifications and endorses the decision by the Committee to keep this matter under review."*	- Tariff Rate Quotas "Takes note of the report of the Committee on Agriculture (G/AG/11) regarding the administration of tariff rate quotas and the submission by Members of addenda to their notifications, and endorses the decision by the Committee to keep this matter under review."	- Tariff Rate Quotas "Takes note of the report of the Committee on Agriculture (G/AG/11) regarding the administration of tariff rate quotas and the submission by Members of addenda to their notifications, and endorses the decision by the Committee to keep this matter under review."	2.4 Takes note of the report of the Committee on Agriculture (G/AG/11) regarding the administration of tariff rate quotas and the submission by Members of addenda to their notifications, and endorses the decision by the Committee to keep this matter under review.
3. Agreement on Sanitary and Phytosanitary Measures	3. Agreement on the Application of Sanitary and Phytosanitary Measures	3. Agreement on the Application of Sanitary and Phytosanitary Measures	3. Agreement on the Application of Sanitary and Phytosanitary Measures
- Tirets 9 and 10 "Where the appropriate level of sanitary and phytosanitary protection allows scope for the phased introduction of new sanitary and phytosanitary measures, the phrase "longer time-frame for compliance" referred to in Article 10.2 of the Agreement on the Application of Sanitary and Phytosanitary Measures, shall be understood to mean normally a period of not less than 6 months. Where the appropriate level of	- Tirets 9 and 10 "Where the appropriate level of sanitary and phytosanitary protection allows scope for the phased introduction of new sanitary and phytosanitary measures, the phrase "longer time-frame for compliance" referred to in Article 10.2 of the Agreement on the Application of Sanitary and Phytosanitary Measures, shall be understood to mean normally a period of not less than 6 months. Where the appropriate level of	- Tirets 9 and 10 "Where the appropriate level of sanitary and phytosanitary protection allows scope for the phased introduction of new sanitary and phytosanitary measures, the phrase "longer time-frame for compliance" referred to in Article 10.2 of the Agreement on the Application of Sanitary and Phytosanitary Measures, shall be understood to mean normally a period of not less than 6 months. Where the appropriate level of	3.1 Where the appropriate level of sanitary and phytosanitary protection allows scope for the phased introduction of new sanitary and phytosanitary measures, the phrase "longer time-frame for compliance" referred to in Article 10.2 of the Agreement on the Application of Sanitary and Phytosanitary Measures, shall be understood to mean normally a period of not less than 6 months. Where the appropriate level of

~~removed text~~ as compared to 27 October Draft
added text as compared to 27 October Draft
moved text for purposes of comparing to 27 October Draft

Comparison of Implementation-Related Issues and Concerns Draft Decisions

Implementation-Related Issues and Concerns Draft Decision 26 September 2001	Implementation-Related Issues and Concerns Draft Decision 27 October 2001	Implementation-Related Issues and Concerns Draft Decision 13 November 2001	Implementation-Related Issues and Concerns Decision 14 November 2001
sanitary and phytosanitary protection does not allow scope for the phased introduction of a new measure, but specific problems are identified by a Member, the Member applying the measure shall upon request enter into consultations with the country with a view to finding a mutually satisfactory solution to the problem while continuing to achieve the importing Member's appropriate level of protection."	sanitary and phytosanitary protection does not allow scope for the phased introduction of a new measure, but specific problems are identified by a Member, the Member applying the measure shall upon request enter into consultations with the country with a view to finding a mutually satisfactory solution to the problem while continuing to achieve the importing Member's appropriate level of protection."	sanitary and phytosanitary protection does not allow scope for the phased introduction of a new measure, but specific problems are identified by a Member, the Member applying the measure shall upon request enter into consultations with the country with a view to finding a mutually satisfactory solution to the problem while continuing to achieve the importing Member's appropriate level of protection."	sanitary and phytosanitary protection does not allow scope for the phased introduction of a new measure, but specific problems are identified by a Member, the Member applying the measure shall upon request enter into consultations with the country with a view to finding a mutually satisfactory solution to the problem while continuing to achieve the importing Member's appropriate level of protection.
- Tiret 11 "Subject to the conditions specified in paragraph 2 of Annex ~~B~~ to the Agreement on the Application of Sanitary and Phytosanitary Measures the phrase "reasonable interval" shall be understood to mean normally a period of not less than 6 months. It is understood that timeframes for specific measures have to be considered in the context of the particular circumstances of the measure, actions necessary to implement the measure, ~~and the fact that SPS~~ measures can contribute to trade liberalization."	- Tiret 11 "Subject to the conditions specified in paragraph 2 of Annex B to the Agreement on the Application of Sanitary and Phytosanitary Measures, the phrase "reasonable interval" shall be understood to mean normally a period of not less than 6 months. It is understood that timeframes for specific measures have to be considered in the context of the particular circumstances of the measure and actions necessary to implement it. The entry into force of measures which contribute to the liberalization of trade should not be unnecessarily delayed."	- Tiret 11 "Subject to the conditions specified in paragraph 2 of Annex B to the Agreement on the Application of Sanitary and Phytosanitary Measures, the phrase "reasonable interval" shall be understood to mean normally a period of not less than 6 months. It is understood that timeframes for specific measures have to be considered in the context of the particular circumstances of the measure and actions necessary to implement it. The entry into force of measures which contribute to the liberalization of trade should not be unnecessarily delayed."	3.2 Subject to the conditions specified in paragraph 2 of Annex B to the Agreement on the Application of Sanitary and Phytosanitary Measures, the phrase "reasonable interval" shall be understood to mean normally a period of not less than 6 months. It is understood that timeframes for specific measures have to be considered in the context of the particular circumstances of the measure and actions necessary to implement it. The entry into force of measures which contribute to the liberalization of trade should not be unnecessarily delayed.
- Tiret 12 [~~Action to be taken in the light of the work~~ of the Committee on Sanitary and Phytosanitary Measures.]	- Tiret 12 "Takes note of the Decision of the Committee on Sanitary and Phytosanitary Measures (G/SPS/19) regarding equivalence, and instructs the Committee to develop expeditiously the specific programme to further the implementation of Article 4 of the Agree-	- Tiret 12 "Takes note of the Decision of the Committee on Sanitary and Phytosanitary Measures (G/SPS/19) regarding equivalence, and instructs the Committee to develop expeditiously the specific programme to further the implementation of Article 4 of the Agree-	3.3 Takes note of the Decision of the Committee on Sanitary and Phytosanitary Measures (G/SPS/19) regarding equivalence, and instructs the Committee to develop expeditiously the specific programme to further the implementation of Article 4 of the Agree-

~~removed text~~ as compared to 27 October Draft
<u>added text</u> as compared to 27 October Draft
moved text for purposes of comparing to 27 October Draft

12

Comparison of Implementation-Related Issues and Concerns Draft Decisions

Implementation-Related Issues and Concerns Draft Decision 26 September 2001	Implementation-Related Issues and Concerns Draft Decision 27 October 2001	Implementation-Related Issues and Concerns Draft Decision 13 November 2001	Implementation-Related Issues and Concerns Decision 14 November 2001
	ment on the Application of Sanitary and Phytosanitary Measures."	ment on the Application of Sanitary and Phytosanitary Measures."	ment on the Application of Sanitary and Phytosanitary Measures.
- Tiret 15 "Pursuant to the provision of Article 12.7 of the Agreement on the Application of Sanitary and Phytosanitary Measures, the Committee on Sanitary and Phytosanitary Measures is instructed to review the operation and implementation of the Agreement on Sanitary and Phytosanitary Measures at least once every four years."	- Tiret 15 "Pursuant to the provisions of Article 12.7 of the Agreement on the Application of Sanitary and Phytosanitary Measures, the Committee on Sanitary and Phytosanitary Measures is instructed to review the operation and implementation of the Agreement on Sanitary and Phytosanitary Measures at least once every four years."	- Tiret 15 "Pursuant to the provisions of Article 12.7 of the Agreement on the Application of Sanitary and Phytosanitary Measures, the Committee on Sanitary and Phytosanitary Measures is instructed to review the operation and implementation of the Agreement on Sanitary and Phytosanitary Measures at least once every four years."	3.4 Pursuant to the provisions of Article 12.7 of the Agreement on the Application of Sanitary and Phytosanitary Measures, the Committee on Sanitary and Phytosanitary Measures is instructed to review the operation and implementation of the Agreement on Sanitary and Phytosanitary Measures at least once every four years.
- International standard setting organizations	- International standard setting organizations	- International standard setting organizations	3.5
"~~The General Council notes with satisfaction the~~ actions taken to date by the Director-General to facilitate the increased participation of Members at different levels of development in the work of the relevant international standard setting organizations, as well as to coordinate efforts with these organizations and financial institutions to identify SPS-related technical assistance needs and how best to address them.	"(i) Takes note of the actions taken to date by the Director-General to facilitate the increased participation of Members at different levels of development in the work of the relevant international standard setting organizations as well as his efforts to coordinate with these organizations and financial institutions in identifying SPS-related technical assistance needs and how best to address them; and	"(i) Takes note of the actions taken to date by the Director-General to facilitate the increased participation of Members at different levels of development in the work of the relevant international standard setting organizations as well as his efforts to coordinate with these organizations and financial institutions in identifying SPS-related technical assistance needs and how best to address them; and	(i) Takes note of the actions taken to date by the Director-General to facilitate the increased participation of Members at different levels of development in the work of the relevant international standard setting organizations as well as his efforts to coordinate with these organizations and financial institutions in identifying SPS-related technical assistance needs and how best to address them; and
The General Council urges the Director-General to continue his cooperative efforts with these organizations and institutions in that regard."	(ii) urges the Director-General to continue his cooperative efforts with these organizations and institutions in this regard, including with a view to according priority to the effective participation of least-developed countries and facilitating the provision of technical and financial	(ii) urges the Director-General to continue his cooperative efforts with these organizations and institutions in this regard, including with a view to according priority to the effective participation of least-developed countries and facilitating the provision of technical and financial	(ii) urges the Director-General to continue his cooperative efforts with these organizations and institutions in this regard, including with a view to according priority to the effective participation of least-developed countries and facilitating the provision of technical and financial

~~removed text~~ as compared to 27 October Draft
added text as compared to 27 October Draft
moved text for purposes of comparing to 27 October Draft

13

Comparison of Implementation-Related Issues and Concerns Draft Decisions

Implementation-Related Issues and Concerns Draft Decision 26 September 2001	Implementation-Related Issues and Concerns Draft Decision 27 October 2001	Implementation-Related Issues and Concerns Draft Decision 13 November 2001	Implementation-Related Issues and Concerns Decision 14 November 2001
	assistance for this purpose."	assistance for this purpose."	assistance for this purpose.
	- Proposals by Least-Developed Countries "(i) Urges Members to provide, to the extent possible, the financial and technical assistance necessary to enable least-developed countries to respond adequately to the introduction of any new SPS measures which may have significant negative effects on their trade; and	- Proposals by Least-Developed Countries "(i) Urges Members to provide, to the extent possible, the financial and technical assistance necessary to enable least-developed countries to respond adequately to the introduction of any new SPS measures which may have significant negative effects on their trade; and	3.6 (i) Urges Members to provide, to the extent possible, the financial and technical assistance necessary to enable least-developed countries to respond adequately to the introduction of any new SPS measures which may have significant negative effects on their trade; and
	(ii) urges Members to ensure that technical assistance is provided to least-developed countries with a view to responding to the special problems faced by them in implementing the Agreement on the Application of Sanitary and Phytosanitary Measures."	(ii) urges Members to ensure that technical assistance is provided to least-developed countries with a view to responding to the special problems faced by them in implementing the Agreement on the Application of Sanitary and Phytosanitary Measures."	(ii) urges Members to ensure that technical assistance is provided to least-developed countries with a view to responding to the special problems faced by them in implementing the Agreement on the Application of Sanitary and Phytosanitary Measures.
2. Agreement on Textiles and Clothing	4. Agreement on Textiles and Clothing	4. Agreement on Textiles and Clothing	4. Agreement on Textiles and Clothing
"Recalling the Ministerial Declarations of Singapore and Geneva under which Members reaffirmed their commitment to full and faithful implementation of the Agreement on Textiles and Clothing, the Ministerial Conference agrees."	"Recalling the Ministerial Declarations of Singapore and Geneva under which Members reaffirmed their commitment to full and faithful implementation of the Agreement on Textiles and Clothing, the Ministerial Conference agrees:"	"Recalling the Ministerial Declarations of Singapore and Geneva under which Members reaffirmed their commitment to full and faithful implementation of the Agreement on Textiles and Clothing, the Ministerial Conference agrees:"	Reaffirms the commitment to full and faithful implementation of the Agreement on Textiles and Clothing, and agrees:
- Tirets 16 & 24 *"that the provisions of the Agreement relating to the early integration of products and the elimination of quota restrictions should be effectively utilised."*	- Tirets 16 & 24 "that the provisions of the Agreement relating to the early integration of products and the elimination of quota restrictions should be effectively utilised."	- Tirets 16 & 24 "that the provisions of the Agreement relating to the early integration of products and the elimination of quota restrictions should be effectively utilised."	4.1 that the provisions of the Agreement relating to the early integration of products and the elimination of quota restrictions should be effectively utilised.

~~removed text~~ as compared to 27 October Draft
added text as compared to 27 October Draft
moved text for purposes of comparing to 27 October Draft

14

Comparison of Implementation-Related Issues and Concerns Draft Decisions

Implementation-Related Issues and Concerns Draft Decision 26 September 2001	Implementation-Related Issues and Concerns Draft Decision 27 October 2001	Implementation-Related Issues and Concerns Draft Decision 13 November 2001	Implementation-Related Issues and Concerns Decision 14 November 2001
- Tirets 20, 21 & 25 *"to calculate the quota levels for small suppliers for the remaining years of the Agreement by applying the most favourable methodology available in respect of those Members under the growth-on-growth provisions from the beginning of the implementation period; to extend the same treatment to least developed countries; and, where possible, to eliminate quota restrictions on imports of such Members."*	- Tirets 20, 21 & 25 "that when calculating the quota levels for small suppliers for the remaining years of the Agreement, Members will apply the most favourable methodology available in respect of those Members under the growth-on-growth provisions from the beginning of the implementation period; to extend the same treatment to least-developed countries; and, where possible, to eliminate quota restrictions on imports of such Members."	- Tirets 20, 21 & 25 "that when calculating the quota levels for small suppliers for the remaining years of the Agreement, Members will apply the most favourable methodology available in respect of those Members under the growth-on-growth provisions from the beginning of the implementation period; to extend the same treatment to least-developed countries; and, where possible, to eliminate quota restrictions on imports of such Members."	
- Tirets 17 & 22 *"to calculate the quota levels for the remaining years of the Agreement with respect to other restrained Members as if implementation of the growth-on-growth provision for stage 3 had been advanced to 1 January 2000."*	- Tirets 17 & 22 "that Members will calculate the quota levels for the remaining years of the Agreement with respect to other restrained Members as if implementation of the growth-on-growth provision for stage 3 had been advanced to 1 January 2000."	- Tirets 17 & 22 "that Members will calculate the quota levels for the remaining years of the Agreement with respect to other restrained Members as if implementation of the growth-on-growth provision for stage 3 had been advanced to 1 January 2000."	
- Tirets 18, 23, 26 & 27 *"to exercise particular consideration and restraint before initiating investigations in the context of contingent trade remedies on textile and clothing exports from developing countries."*	- Tirets 18, 23, 26 & 27 "that Members will exercise particular consideration and restraint before initiating investigations in the context of contingent trade remedies on textile and clothing exports from developing countries."	- Tirets 18, 23, 26 & 27 "that Members will exercise particular consideration and restraint before initiating investigations in the context of contingent trade remedies on textile and clothing exports from developing countries."	4.2 that Members will exercise particular consideration before initiating investigations in the context of antidumping remedies on textile and clothing exports from developing countries previously subject to quantitative restrictions under the Agreement for a period of two years following full integration of this Agreement into the WTO.
- Tirets 19 & 29 *"that ~~Members~~, without prejudice to their rights and obligations, shall notify any changes in their rules of origin concerning products falling under the coverage*	- Tirets 19 & 29 "that without prejudice to their rights and obligations, Members shall notify any changes in their rules of origin concerning products falling under the coverage	- Tirets 19 & 29 "that without prejudice to their rights and obligations, Members shall notify any changes in their rules of origin concerning products falling under the coverage	4.3 that without prejudice to their rights and obligations, Members shall notify any changes in their rules of origin concerning products falling under the coverage

~~removed text~~ as compared to 27 October Draft
added text as compared to 27 October Draft
moved text for purposes of comparing to 27 October Draft

15

Comparison of Implementation-Related Issues and Concerns Draft Decisions

Implementation-Related Issues and Concerns Draft Decision 26 September 2001	Implementation-Related Issues and Concerns Draft Decision 27 October 2001	Implementation-Related Issues and Concerns Draft Decision 13 November 2001	Implementation-Related Issues and Concerns Decision 14 November 2001
of the Agreement to the Committee on Rules of Origin which may examine them<s>before they are applied."</s>	of the Agreement to the Committee on Rules of Origin which may decide to examine them."	of the Agreement to the Committee on Rules of Origin which may decide to examine them."	of the Agreement to the Committee on Rules of Origin which may decide to examine them. <u>Requests the Council for Trade in Goods to examine the following proposals:</u> <u>4.4 that when calculating the quota levels for small suppliers for the remaining years of the Agreement, Members will apply the most favourable methodology available in respect of those Members under the growth-on-growth provisions from the beginning of the implementation period; extend the same treatment to least-developed countries; and, where possible, eliminate quota restrictions on imports of such Members;</u> <u>4.5 that Members will calculate the quota levels for the remaining years of the Agreement with respect to other restrained Members as if implementation of the growth-on-growth provision for stage 3 had been advanced to 1 January 2000; and make recommendations to the General Council by 31 July 2002 for appropriate action.</u>
4. Agreement of Technical Barriers to Trade	5. Agreement on Technical Barriers to Trade	5. Agreement on Technical Barriers to Trade	5. Agreement on Technical Barriers to Trade
- Tirets 31 & 32	- Tirets 31&32	- Tirets 31&32	5.1
"<s>The General Council</s> confirms the approach to technical assistance being developed by the Committee on Technical Barriers to Trade, reflecting the results of the	"Confirms the approach to technical assistance being developed by the Committee on Technical Barriers to Trade, reflecting the results of the	"Confirms the approach to technical assistance being developed by the Committee on Technical Barriers to Trade, reflecting the results of the	Confirms the approach to technical assistance being developed by the Committee on Technical Barriers to Trade, reflecting the results of the

<s>removed text</s> as compared to 27 October Draft
<u>added text</u> as compared to 27 October Draft
moved text for purposes of comparing to 27 October Draft

16

Comparison of Implementation-Related Issues and Concerns Draft Decisions

Implementation-Related Issues and Concerns Draft Decision 26 September 2001	Implementation-Related Issues and Concerns Draft Decision 27 October 2001	Implementation-Related Issues and Concerns Draft Decision 13 November 2001	Implementation-Related Issues and Concerns Decision 14 November 2001
trienneial review work in this area, and mandate this work to continue."	triennial review work in this area, and mandates this work to continue."	triennial review work in this area, and mandates this work to continue."	triennial review work in this area, and mandates this work to continue.
- Tiret 35 "Subject to the conditions specified in paragraph 12 of Article 2 of the Agreement on Technical Barriers to Trade, the phrase "reasonable interval" shall be understood to mean normally a period of not less than 6 months, except when this would be ineffective in fulfilling the legitimate objectives pursed."	- Tiret 35 "Subject to the conditions specified in paragraph 12 of Article 2 of the Agreement on Technical Barriers to Trade, the phrase "reasonable interval" shall be understood to mean normally a period of not less than 6 months, except when this would be ineffective in fulfilling the legitimate objectives pursued."	- Tiret 35 "Subject to the conditions specified in paragraph 12 of Article 2 of the Agreement on Technical Barriers to Trade, the phrase "reasonable interval" shall be understood to mean normally a period of not less than 6 months, except when this would be ineffective in fulfilling the legitimate objectives pursued."	5.2 Subject to the conditions specified in paragraph 12 of Article 2 of the Agreement on Technical Barriers to Trade, the phrase "reasonable interval" shall be understood to mean normally a period of not less than 6 months, except when this would be ineffective in fulfilling the legitimate objectives pursued.
- International standard setting organizations "~~The General Council notes with satisfaction the notions~~	- International standard setting organizations "(i) Takes note of the actions	- International standard setting organizations "(i) Takes note of the actions	5.3 (i) Takes note of the actions
taken to date by the Director-General in facilitating the increased participation of Members at different levels of development in the work of the relevant international standard setting organizations, as well as to coordinate efforts with these organizations and financial institutions to identify TBT-related technical assistance needs and how best to address them.	taken to date by the Director-General to facilitate the increased participation of Members at different levels of development in the work of the relevant international standard setting organizations as well as his efforts to coordinate with these organizations and financial institutions in identifyingTBT-related technical assistance needs and how best to address them; and	taken to date by the Director-General to facilitate the increased participation of Members at different levels of development in the work of the relevant international standard setting organizations as well as his efforts to coordinate with these organizations and financial institutions in identifying TBT-related technical assistance needs and how best to address them; and	taken to date by the Director-General to facilitate the increased participation of Members at different levels of development in the work of the relevant international standard setting organizations as well as his efforts to coordinate with these organizations and financial institutions in identifying TBT-related technical assistance needs and how best to address them; and
~~The General Council~~ urges the Director-General to continue his cooperative efforts with these organizations and institutions ~~in that regard."~~	(ii) urges the Director-General to continue his cooperative efforts with these organizations and institutions, including with a view to according priority to the effective participation of least-developed countries and facilitating the provision of technical and financial assistance for this purpose.".	(ii) urges the Director-General to continue his cooperative efforts with these organizations and institutions, including with a view to according priority to the effective participation of least-developed countries and facilitating the provision of technical and financial assistance for this purpose."	(ii) urges the Director-General to continue his cooperative efforts with these organizations and institutions, including with a view to according priority to the effective participation of least-developed countries and facilitating the provision of technical and financial assistance for this purpose.

~~removed text~~ as compared to 27 October Draft
<u>added text</u> as compared to 27 October Draft
moved text for purposes of comparing to 27 October Draft

Comparison of Implementation-Related Issues and Concerns Draft Decisions

Implementation-Related Issues and Concerns Draft Decision 26 September 2001	Implementation-Related Issues and Concerns Draft Decision 27 October 2001	Implementation-Related Issues and Concerns Draft Decision 13 November 2001	Implementation-Related Issues and Concerns Decision 14 November 2001
	- Proposals by Least-Developed Countries	- Proposals by Least-Developed Countries	5.4
	"(i) Urges Members to provide, to the extent possible, the financial and technical assistance necessary to enable least-developed countries to respond adequately to the introduction of any new TBT measures which may have significant negative effects on their trade; and	"(i) Urges Members to provide, to the extent possible, the financial and technical assistance necessary to enable least-developed countries to respond adequately to the introduction of any new TBT measures which may have significant negative effects on their trade; and	(i) Urges Members to provide, to the extent possible, the financial and technical assistance necessary to enable least-developed countries to respond adequately to the introduction of any new TBT measures which may have significant negative effects on their trade; and
	(ii) urges Members to ensure that technical assistance is provided to least-developed countries with a view to responding to the special problems faced by them in implementing the Agreement on Technical Barriers to Trade."	(ii) urges Members to ensure that technical assistance is provided to least-developed countries with a view to responding to the special problems faced by them in implementing the Agreement on Technical Barriers to Trade."	(ii) urges Members to ensure that technical assistance is provided to least-developed countries with a view to responding to the special problems faced by them in implementing the Agreement on Technical Barriers to Trade.
5. Agreement on Trade-Related Investment Measures	6. Agreement on Trade-Related Investment Measures	6. Agreement on Trade-Related Investment Measures	6. Agreement on Trade-Related Investment Measures
- Tiret 36 "~~The General Council notes with satisfaction~~ the actions taken by the Council for Trade in Goods in regard to requests from some developing-country Members for the extension of the five-year transitional period provided for in Article 5.2 of Agreement on Trade-Related Investment Measures."	- Tiret 36 "Takes note of the actions taken by the Council for Trade in Goods in regard to requests from some developing-country Members for the extension of the five-year transitional period provided for in Article 5.2 of Agreement on Trade-Related Investment Measures."	- Tiret 36 "Takes note of the actions taken by the Council for Trade in Goods in regard to requests from some developing-country Members for the extension of the five-year transitional period provided for in Article 5.2 of Agreement on Trade-Related Investment Measures."	6.1 Takes note of the actions taken by the Council for Trade in Goods in regard to requests from some developing-country Members for the extension of the five-year transitional period provided for in Article 5.2 of Agreement on Trade-Related Investment Measures.
	- Proposal by Least-Developed Countries	- Proposal by Least-Developed Countries	
	"Urges the Council for Trade in Goods to consider positively requests that may be made by least-developed countries under	"Urges the Council for Trade in Goods to consider positively requests that may be made by least-developed countries under	6.2 Urges the Council for Trade in Goods to consider positively requests that may be made by least-developed countries under

~~removed text~~ as compared to 27 October Draft
<u>added text</u> as compared to 27 October Draft
moved text for purposes of comparing to 27 October Draft

18

Comparison of Implementation-Related Issues and Concerns Draft Decisions

Implementation-Related Issues and Concerns Draft Decision 26 September 2001	Implementation-Related Issues and Concerns Draft Decision 27 October 2001	Implementation-Related Issues and Concerns Draft Decision 13 November 2001	Implementation-Related Issues and Concerns Decision 14 November 2001
	Article 5.3 of the TRIMs Agreement or Article IX.3 of the WTO Agreement, as well as to take into consideration the particular circumstances of least-developed countries when setting the terms and conditions including time-frames."	Article 5.3 of the TRIMs Agreement or Article IX.3 of the WTO Agreement, as well as to take into consideration the particular circumstances of least-developed countries when setting the terms and conditions including time-frames."	Article 5.3 of the TRIMs Agreement or Article IX.3 of the WTO Agreement, as well as to take into consideration the particular circumstances of least-developed countries when setting the terms and conditions including time-frames.
3. Agreement on the Implementation of Article VI of the General Agreement on Tariffs and Trade 1994	7. Agreement on the Implementation of Article VI of the General Agreement on Tariffs and Trade 1994	7. Agreement on the Implementation of Article VI of the General Agreement on Tariffs and Trade 1994	7. Agreement on the Implementation of Article VI of the General Agreement on Tariffs and Trade 1994
- Tiret 41 ~~The Ministerial Conference~~ *agrees that investigating authorities shall examine with special care any application for the initiation of an anti-dumping investigation where an investigation of the same product from the same Member resulted in a negative finding within the 365 days prior to the filing of the application. Unless this pre-initiation examination indicates that circumstances have changed, the investigation shall not proceed.*	- Tiret 41 "Agrees that investigating authorities shall examine with special care any application for the initiation of an anti-dumping investigation where an investigation of the same product from the same Member resulted in a negative finding within the 365 days prior to the filing of the application and that, unless this pre-initiation examination indicates that circumstances have changed, the investigation shall not proceed."	- Tiret 41 "Agrees that investigating authorities shall examine with special care any application for the initiation of an anti-dumping investigation where an investigation of the same product from the same Member resulted in a negative finding within the 365 days prior to the filing of the application and that, unless this pre-initiation examination indicates that circumstances have changed, the investigation shall not proceed."	7.1 Agrees that investigating authorities shall examine with special care any application for the initiation of an anti-dumping investigation where an investigation of the same product from the same Member resulted in a negative finding within the 365 days prior to the filing of the application and that, unless this pre-initiation examination indicates that circumstances have changed, the investigation shall not proceed.
- Tiret 45 ~~The Ministerial Conference~~ *recognizes that, while Article 15 of the Agreement on the Implementation of Article VI of the General Agreement on Tariffs and Trade 1994 is a mandatory provision, the modalities for its application would benefit from clarification. Accordingly, the Committee on Anti-Dumping Practices is instructed, through its working group on Implementation, to examine this issue and to draw up appropriate*	- Tiret 45 "Recognizes that, while Article 15 of the Agreement on the Implementation of Article VI of the General Agreement on Tariffs and Trade 1994 is a mandatory provision, the modalities for its application would benefit from clarification. Accordingly, the Committee on Anti-Dumping Practices is instructed, through its working group on Implementation, to examine this issue and to draw up appropriate	- Tiret 45 "Recognizes that, while Article 15 of the Agreement on the Implementation of Article VI of the General Agreement on Tariffs and Trade 1994 is a mandatory provision, the modalities for its application would benefit from clarification. Accordingly, the Committee on Anti-Dumping Practices is instructed, through its working group on Implementation, to examine this issue and to draw up appropriate	7.2 Recognizes that, while Article 15 of the Agreement on the Implementation of Article VI of the General Agreement on Tariffs and Trade 1994 is a mandatory provision, the modalities for its application would benefit from clarification. Accordingly, the Committee on Anti-Dumping Practices is instructed, through its working group on Implementation, to examine this issue and to draw up appropriate

~~removed text~~ as compared to 27 October Draft
<u>added text</u> as compared to 27 October Draft
moved text for purposes of comparing to 27 October Draft

Comparison of Implementation-Related Issues and Concerns Draft Decisions

Implementation-Related Issues and Concerns Draft Decision 26 September 2001	Implementation-Related Issues and Concerns Draft Decision 27 October 2001	Implementation-Related Issues and Concerns Draft Decision 13 November 2001	Implementation-Related Issues and Concerns Decision 14 November 2001
recommendations within twelve months on how to operationalize this provision.	recommendations within twelve months on how to operationalize this provision."	recommendations within twelve months on how to operationalize this provision."	recommendations within twelve months on how to operationalize this provision.
- Tiret 49 ~~The Ministerial Conference~~ *notes that Article 5.8 of the Agreement on the Implementation of Article VI of the General Agreement on Tariffs and Trade 1994 does not specify the time-frame to be used in determining the volume of dumped imports, and that this lack of specificity creates uncertainties in the implementation of the provision. The Committee on Anti-Dumping Practices is instructed, through its working group on Implementation, to study this issue and draw up recommendations within 12 months, with a view to ensuring the maximum possible predictability and objectivity in the application of time frames.*	- Tiret 49 "Takes note that Article 5.8 of the Agreement on the Implementation of Article VI of the General Agreement on Tariffs and Trade 1994 does not specify the time-frame to be used in determining the volume of dumped imports, and that this lack of specificity creates uncertainties in the implementation of the provision. The Committee on Anti-Dumping Practices is instructed, through its working group on Implementation, to study this issue and draw up recommendations within 12 months, with a view to ensuring the maximum possible predictability and objectivity in the application of time frames."	- Tiret 49 "Takes note that Article 5.8 of the Agreement on the Implementation of Article VI of the General Agreement on Tariffs and Trade 1994 does not specify the time-frame to be used in determining the volume of dumped imports, and that this lack of specificity creates uncertainties in the implementation of the provision. The Committee on Anti-Dumping Practices is instructed, through its working group on Implementation, to study this issue and draw up recommendations within 12 months, with a view to ensuring the maximum possible predictability and objectivity in the application of time frames."	7.3 Takes note that Article 5.8 of the Agreement on the Implementation of Article VI of the General Agreement on Tariffs and Trade 1994 does not specify the time-frame to be used in determining the volume of dumped imports, and that this lack of specificity creates uncertainties in the implementation of the provision. The Committee on Anti-Dumping Practices is instructed, through its working group on Implementation, to study this issue and draw up recommendations within 12 months, with a view to ensuring the maximum possible predictability and objectivity in the application of time frames.
- Tiret 55 ~~The Ministerial Conference~~ *notes that Article 18.6 of the Agreement on the Implementation of Article VI of the General Agreement on Tariffs and Trade 1994 requires the Committee on Anti-Dumping Practices to review annually the implementation and operation of the Agreement taking into account the objectives thereof. The Committee on Anti-Dumping Practices is requested to draw up guidelines for the improvement of annual reviews, and to report its views and recommendations to the General Council for subsequent*	- Tiret 55 "Takes note that Article 18.6 of the Agreement on the Implementation of Article VI of the General Agreement on Tariffs and Trade 1994 requires the Committee on Anti-Dumping Practices to review annually the implementation and operation of the Agreement taking into account the objectives thereof. The Committee on Anti-dumping Practices is instructed to draw up guidelines for the improvement of annual reviews and to report its views and recommendations to the General Council for subsequent	- Tiret 55 "Takes note that Article 18.6 of the Agreement on the Implementation of Article VI of the General Agreement on Tariffs and Trade 1994 requires the Committee on Anti-Dumping Practices to review annually the implementation and operation of the Agreement taking into account the objectives thereof. The Committee on Anti-dumping Practices is instructed to draw up guidelines for the improvement of annual reviews and to report its views and recommendations to the General Council for subsequent	7.4 Takes note that Article 18.6 of the Agreement on the Implementation of Article VI of the General Agreement on Tariffs and Trade 1994 requires the Committee on Anti-Dumping Practices to review annually the implementation and operation of the Agreement taking into account the objectives thereof. The Committee on Anti-dumping Practices is instructed to draw up guidelines for the improvement of annual reviews and to report its views and recommendations to the General Council for subsequent

~~removed text~~ as compared to 27 October Draft
added text as compared to 27 October Draft
moved text for purposes of comparing to 27 October Draft

Comparison of Implementation-Related Issues and Concerns Draft Decisions

Implementation-Related Issues and Concerns Draft Decision 26 September 2001	Implementation-Related Issues and Concerns Draft Decision 27 October 2001	Implementation-Related Issues and Concerns Draft Decision 13 November 2001	Implementation-Related Issues and Concerns Decision 14 November 2001
decision within 12 months.	decision within 12 months."	decision within 12 months."	decision within 12 months.
6. Agreement on the Implementation of Article VII of the General Agreement on Tariffs and Trade 1994	8. Agreement on the Implementation of Article VII of the General Agreement on Tariffs and Trade 1994	8. Agreement on the Implementation of Article VII of the General Agreement on Tariffs and Trade 1994	8. Agreement on the Implementation of Article VII of the General Agreement on Tariffs and Trade 1994
- Article 20.1 "The General Council notes ~~with satisfaction~~ the actions taken by the Committee on Customs Valuation in regard to the requests from a number of developing-country Members for the extension of the five-year transitional period provided for in Article 20.1 of Agreement on the Implementation of Article VII of the General Agreement on Tariffs and Trade 1994."	- Article 20.1 "Takes note of the actions taken by the Committee on Customs Valuation in regard to the requests from a number of developing-country Members for the extension of the five-year transitional period provided for in Article 20.1 of Agreement on the Implementation of Article VII of the General Agreement on Tariffs and Trade 1994."	- Article 20.1 "Takes note of the actions taken by the Committee on Customs Valuation in regard to the requests from a number of developing-country Members for the extension of the five-year transitional period provided for in Article 20.1 of Agreement on the Implementation of Article VII of the General Agreement on Tariffs and Trade 1994."	8.1 Takes note of the actions taken by the Committee on Customs Valuation in regard to the requests from a number of developing-country Members for the extension of the five-year transitional period provided for in Article 20.1 of Agreement on the Implementation of Article VII of the General Agreement on Tariffs and Trade 1994.
- Article 20.3	- Proposal by Least-Developed Countries	- Proposal by Least-Developed Countries	
~~"The General Council endorses the comprehensive approach to technical assistance developed by the Committee on Customs Valuation and mandates the Committee to continue this work."~~	"Urges the Council for Trade in Goods to give positive consideration to requests that may be made by least-developed country Members under paragraphs 1 and 2 of Annex III of the Customs Valuation Agreement or under Article IX.3 of the WTO Agreement, as well as to take into consideration the particular circumstances of least-developed countries when setting the terms and conditions including time-frames."	"Urges the Council for Trade in Goods to give positive consideration to requests that may be made by least-developed country Members under paragraphs 1 and 2 of Annex III of the Customs Valuation Agreement or under Article IX.3 of the WTO Agreement, as well as to take into consideration the particular circumstances of least-	8.2 Urges the Council for Trade in Goods to give positive consideration to requests that may be made by least-developed country Members under paragraphs 1 and 2 of Annex III of the Customs Valuation Agreement or under Article IX.3 of the WTO Agreement, as well as to take into consideration the particular circumstances of least-developed countries when setting the terms and conditions including time-frames.

~~removed text~~ as compared to 27 October Draft
added text as compared to 27 October Draft
moved text for purposes of comparing to 27 October Draft

Comparison of Implementation-Related Issues and Concerns Draft Decisions

Implementation-Related Issues and Concerns Draft Decision 26 September 2001	Implementation-Related Issues and Concerns Draft Decision 27 October 2001	Implementation-Related Issues and Concerns Draft Decision 13 November 2001	Implementation-Related Issues and Concerns Decision 14 November 2001
4. Agreement on the Implementation of Article VII of the General Agreement on Tariffs and Trade 1994			
- Tiret 56 *"~~The General Council agrees that~~* *when the Customs Administration of an importing Member has reasonable grounds to doubt the accuracy of the value declared, it may seek assistance from the Customs Administration of an exporting Member on the value of the good imported. In that case the exporting Member ~~should~~ offer cooperation and assistance,*	- Tiret 56 "Underlines the importance of strengthening cooperation between the customs administrations of Members in the prevention of customs fraud. In this regard, it is agreed that, further to the 1994 Ministerial Decision Regarding Cases Where Customs Administrations Have Reasons to Doubt the Truth or Accuracy of the Declared Value, when the customs administration of an importing Member has reasonable grounds to doubt the truth or accuracy of the declared value, it may seek assistance from the customs administration of an exporting Member on the value of the good concerned. In such cases, the exporting Member shall offer cooperation and assistance,	assistance, <u>consistent with its domestic laws and procedures,</u>	8.3 Underlines the importance of strengthening cooperation between the customs administrations of Members in the prevention of customs fraud. In this regard, it is agreed that, further to the 1994 Ministerial Decision Regarding Cases Where Customs Administrations Have Reasons to Doubt the Truth or Accuracy of the Declared Value, when the customs administration of an importing Member has reasonable grounds to doubt the truth or accuracy of the declared value, it may seek assistance from the customs administration of an exporting Member on the value of the good concerned. In such cases, the exporting Member shall offer cooperation and assistance, <u>consistent with its domestic laws and procedures,</u>
including information on the ~~export~~ value of the goods imported if available. Any information provided in this context shall be treated in accordance with the provisions of Article 10 of the Agreement on the Implementation of Article VII of the GATT 1994."	including furnishing, where possible, information on the value of the good concerned. Any information provided in this context shall be treated in accordance with Article 10 of the Customs Valuation Agreement. Furthermore, recognizing the legitimate concerns expressed by the customs administrations of several importing Members on the accuracy of the declared value, the Committee on Customs Valuation is directed to identify and assess practical means	including furnishing information on the <u>export</u> value of the good concerned. Any information provided in this context shall be treated in accordance with Article 10 of the Customs Valuation Agreement. Furthermore, recognizing the legitimate concerns expressed by the customs administrations of several importing Members on the accuracy of the declared value, the Committee on Customs Valuation is directed to identify and assess practical means	including furnishing information on the <u>export</u> value of the good concerned. Any information provided in this context shall be treated in accordance with Article 10 of the Customs Valuation Agreement. Furthermore, recognizing the legitimate concerns expressed by the customs administrations of several importing Members on the accuracy of the declared value, the Committee on Customs Valuation is directed to identify and assess practical means

~~removed text~~ as compared to 27 October Draft
<u>added text</u> as compared to 27 October Draft
moved text for purposes of comparing to 27 October Draft

22

Comparison of Implementation-Related Issues and Concerns Draft Decisions

Implementation-Related Issues and Concerns Draft Decision 26 September 2001	Implementation-Related Issues and Concerns Draft Decision 27 October 2001	Implementation-Related Issues and Concerns Draft Decision 13 November 2001	Implementation-Related Issues and Concerns Decision 14 November 2001
	to address such concerns, including the exchange of information on export values and to report to the General Council by the end of 2002 at the latest."	to address such concerns, including the exchange of information on export values and to report to the General Council by the end of 2002 at the latest."	to address such concerns, including the exchange of information on export values and to report to the General Council by the end of 2002 at the latest.
5. Agreement on Rules of Origin	9. Agreement on Rules of Origin	9. Agreement on Rules of Origin	9. Agreement on Rules of Origin
	- Tiret 62 "Takes note of the report of the Committee on Rules of Origin (G/RO/48) regarding progress on the harmonization work programme, and urges the Committee to complete its work by the end of 2001."	- Tiret 62 "Takes note of the report of the Committee on Rules of Origin (G/RO/48) regarding progress on the harmonization work programme, and urges the Committee to complete its work by the end of 2001."	9.1 Takes note of the report of the Committee on Rules of Origin (G/RO/48) regarding progress on the harmonization work programme, and urges the Committee to complete its work by the end of 2001.
- Tiret 63 *"The Ministerial Conference agrees that any interim arrangements on rules of origin implemented by Members in the transitional period before the entry into force of the results of the harmonisation work programme shall be consistent with the Agreement on Rules of Origin, particularly Articles 2 and 5 thereof. Without prejudice to Members' rights and obligations, such arrangements may be examined by the Committee on Rules of Origin."*	- Tiret 63 "Agrees that any interim arrangements on rules of origin implemented by Members in the transitional period before the entry into force of the results of the harmonisation work programme shall be consistent with the Agreement on Rules of Origin, particularly Articles 2 and 5 thereof. Without prejudice to Members' rights and obligations, such arrangements may be examined by the Committee on Rules of Origin."	- Tiret 63 "Agrees that any interim arrangements on rules of origin implemented by Members in the transitional period before the entry into force of the results of the harmonisation work programme shall be consistent with the Agreement on Rules of Origin, particularly Articles 2 and 5 thereof. Without prejudice to Members' rights and obligations, such arrangements may be examined by the Committee on Rules of Origin."	9.2 Agrees that any interim arrangements on rules of origin implemented by Members in the transitional period before the entry into force of the results of the harmonisation work programme shall be consistent with the Agreement on Rules of Origin, particularly Articles 2 and 5 thereof. Without prejudice to Members' rights and obligations, such arrangements may be examined by the Committee on Rules of Origin.
7. Agreement on Subsidies and Countervailing Measures	10. Agreement on Subsidies and Countervailing Measures	10. Agreement on Subsidies and Countervailing Measures	10. Agreement on Subsidies and Countervailing Measures
-Tirets 67, 82, and 83 "The General Council agrees that Annex VII(b) to the Agreement on Subsidies and Countervailing Measures includes the Members that are listed therein	- Tiret 67 "Agrees that Annex VII(b) to the Agreement on Subsidies and Countervailing Measures includes the Members that are listed therein	- Tiret 67 "Agrees that Annex VII(b) to the Agreement on Subsidies and Countervailing Measures includes the Members that are listed therein	10.1 Agrees that Annex VII(b) to the Agreement on Subsidies and Countervailing Measures includes the Members that are listed therein

~~removed text~~ as compared to 27 October Draft
added text as compared to 27 October Draft
moved text for purposes of comparing to 27 October Draft

23

Comparison of Implementation-Related Issues and Concerns Draft Decisions

Implementation-Related Issues and Concerns Draft Decision 26 September 2001	Implementation-Related Issues and Concerns Draft Decision 27 October 2001	Implementation-Related Issues and Concerns Draft Decision 13 November 2001	Implementation-Related Issues and Concerns Decision 14 November 2001
until their GNP per capita reaches US $1,000 in constant 1990 dollars ~~for three consecutive years."~~	until their GNP per capita reaches US $1,000 in constant 1990 dollars.	until their GNP per capita reaches US $1,000 in constant 1990 dollars for three consecutive years.	until their GNP per capita reaches US $1,000 in constant 1990 dollars for three consecutive years.
[~~Action to be taken in the light of the report of the Committee on Subsidies and Countervailing Measures on the implementation of Article 27 as it relates to particular issues concerning developing-country Members with a small percentage share of exports in import markets and in global trade~~.]	This decision will enter into effect upon the adoption by the Committee on Subsidies and Countervailing Measures of an appropriate methodology for calculating constant 1990 dollars,	This decision will enter into effect upon the adoption by the Committee on Subsidies and Countervailing Measures of an appropriate methodology for calculating constant 1990 dollars. If, however, the Committee on Subsidies and Countervailing Measures does not reach a consensus agreement on an appropriate methodology by	This decision will enter into effect upon the adoption by the Committee on Subsidies and Countervailing Measures of an appropriate methodology for calculating constant 1990 dollars. If, however, the Committee on Subsidies and Countervailing Measures does not reach a consensus agreement on an appropriate methodology by
	but in any case not later than 1 January 2003.	1 January 2003, the methodology proposed by the Chairman of the Committee set forth in G/SCM/38, Annex 2 shall be applied.	1 January 2003, the methodology proposed by the Chairman of the Committee set forth in G/SCM/38, Appendix 2 shall be applied.
"The General Council agrees that if a Member has been excluded from Annex VII to the Agreement on Subsidies and Countervailing Measures, it nevertheless shall be re-included in it if its GNP per capita falls back below US$1,000."	In this process, the Committee shall take into account that a Member shall not leave Annex VII(b) so long as	A Member shall not leave Annex VII(b) so long as	A Member shall not leave Annex VII(b) so long as
	its GNP per capita in current dollars has not reached US $1000 based upon the most recent data from the World Bank."	its GNP per capita in current dollars has not reached US $1000 based upon the most recent data from the World Bank."	its GNP per capita in current dollars has not reached US $1000 based upon the most recent data from the World Bank.
- Tiret 68 [Decision to be taken in the light of the work of the Committee on Subsidies and Countervailing Measures.]			
	- Tiret 69 "Takes note of the proposal to treat measures implemented by developing countries with a view to achieving legitimate development goals, such as regional growth, technology research and development funding, production diversification and development and implementa-	- Tiret 69 "Takes note of the proposal to treat measures implemented by developing countries with a view to achieving legitimate development goals, such as regional growth, technology research and development funding, production diversification and development and implementa-	10.2 Takes note of the proposal to treat measures implemented by developing countries with a view to achieving legitimate development goals, such as regional growth, technology research and development funding, production diversification and development and implementa-

~~removed text~~ as compared to 27 October Draft
added text as compared to 27 October Draft
moved text for purposes of comparing to 27 October Draft

Comparison of Implementation-Related Issues and Concerns Draft Decisions

Implementation-Related Issues and Concerns Draft Decision 26 September 2001	Implementation-Related Issues and Concerns Draft Decision 27 October 2001	Implementation-Related Issues and Concerns Draft Decision 13 November 2001	Implementation-Related Issues and Concerns Decision 14 November 2001
	tion of environmentally sound methods of production as non-actionable subsidies, and agrees that this issue be addressed in accordance with paragraph 13 below. During the course of the negotiations, Members shall exercise due restraint with respect to challenging such measures."	tion of environmentally sound methods of production as non-actionable subsidies, and agrees that this issue be addressed in accordance with paragraph 13 below. During the course of the negotiations, Members are urged to exercise due restraint with respect to challenging such measures."	tion of environmentally sound methods of production as non-actionable subsidies, and agrees that this issue be addressed in accordance with paragraph 13 below. During the course of the negotiations, Members are urged to exercise due restraint with respect to challenging such measures.
~~- Tirets 74 & 75~~ ~~"The Ministerial Conference urges Members to apply, where possible, a higher de minimis level in countervailing duty investigations of products originating in developing country Members, than the levels set forth in Articles 27.10 and 27.11 of the Agreement on Subsidies and Countervailing Measures."~~			
- Tiret 80 "~~The General Council instructs the~~ Committee on Subsidies and Countervailing Measures ~~to~~ review the provisions of the Agreement on Subsidies and Countervailing Measures regarding countervailing duty investigations, and to report ~~it by the Fourth Ministerial Conference.~~"	- Tiret 80 "Agrees that the Committee on Subsidies and Countervailing Measures shall continue its review of the provisions of the Agreement on Subsidies and Countervailing Measures regarding countervailing duty investigations and report to the General Council by 31 July 2002."	- Tiret 80 "Agrees that the Committee on Subsidies and Countervailing Measures shall continue its review of the provisions of the Agreement on Subsidies and Countervailing Measures regarding countervailing duty investigations and report to the General Council by 31 July 2002."	10.3 Agrees that the Committee on Subsidies and Countervailing Measures shall continue its review of the provisions of the Agreement on Subsidies and Countervailing Measures regarding countervailing duty investigations and report to the General Council by 31 July 2002.
	- Tiret 82 "Agrees that if a Member has been excluded from the list in paragraph (b) of Annex VII to the Agreement on Subsidies and Countervailing Measures, it shall be re-included in it when its GNP per capita falls back below US$ 1,000."	- Tiret 82 "Agrees that if a Member has been excluded from the list in paragraph (b) of Annex VII to the Agreement on Subsidies and Countervailing Measures, it shall be re-included in it when its GNP per capita falls back below US$ 1,000."	10.4 Agrees that if a Member has been excluded from the list in paragraph (b) of Annex VII to the Agreement on Subsidies and Countervailing Measures, it shall be re-included in it when its GNP per capita falls back below US$ 1,000.

~~removed text~~ as compared to 27 October Draft
added text as compared to 27 October Draft
moved text for purposes of comparing to 27 October Draft

25

Comparison of Implementation-Related Issues and Concerns Draft Decisions

Implementation-Related Issues and Concerns Draft Decision 26 September 2001	Implementation-Related Issues and Concerns Draft Decision 27 October 2001	Implementation-Related Issues and Concerns Draft Decision 13 November 2001	Implementation-Related Issues and Concerns Decision 14 November 2001
8. General Agreement on Trade in Services (GATS) ~~- Tiret 85~~ ~~"Recalling and reaffirming the provisions of the General Agreement on Trade in Services, the General Council notes that Members agree that administrative practices should not impede full and faithful implementation of their commitments under the General Agreement on Trade in Services, particularly as regards the supply of services under Mode 4."~~			
	- Proposal by Least-Developed Countries	- Proposal by Least-Developed Countries	10.5
	"Subject to the provisions of Articles 27.5 and 27.6, it is reaffirmed that least-developed country Members are exempt from the prohibition on export subsidies set forth in Article 3.1(a) of the Agreement on Subsidies and Countervailing Measures, and thus have flexibility to finance their exporters, consistent with their development needs. It is understood that the eight-year period in Article 27.5 within which a least-developed country Member must phase out its export subsidies in respect of a product in which it is export-competitive begins from the date export competitiveness exists within the meaning of Article 27.6."	"Subject to the provisions of Articles 27.5 and 27.6, it is reaffirmed that least-developed country Members are exempt from the prohibition on export subsidies set forth in Article 3.1(a) of the Agreement on Subsidies and Countervailing Measures, and thus have flexibility to finance their exporters, consistent with their development needs. It is understood that the eight-year period in Article 27.5 within which a least-developed country Member must phase out its export subsidies in respect of a product in which it is export-competitive begins from the date export competitiveness exists within the meaning of Article 27.6."	Subject to the provisions of Articles 27.5 and 27.6, it is reaffirmed that least-developed country Members are exempt from the prohibition on export subsidies set forth in Article 3.1(a) of the Agreement on Subsidies and Countervailing Measures, and thus have flexibility to finance their exporters, consistent with their development needs. It is understood that the eight-year period in Article 27.5 within which a least-developed country Member must phase out its export subsidies in respect of a product in which it is export-competitive begins from the date export competitiveness exists within the meaning of Article 27.6.
- Article 27.4	- Article 27.4 "Having regard to the particular situation of certain developing-country Members, directs the Committee on Subsidies and	- Article 27.4 "Having regard to the particular situation of certain developing-country Members, directs the Committee on Subsidies and	10.6 Having regard to the particular situation of certain developing-country Members, directs the Committee on Subsidies and

~~removed text~~ as compared to 27 October Draft
<u>added text</u> as compared to 27 October Draft
moved text for purposes of comparing to 27 October Draft

Comparison of Implementation-Related Issues and Concerns Draft Decisions

Implementation-Related Issues and Concerns Draft Decision 26 September 2001	Implementation-Related Issues and Concerns Draft Decision 27 October 2001	Implementation-Related Issues and Concerns Draft Decision 13 November 2001	Implementation-Related Issues and Concerns Decision 14 November 2001
~~[Finalization of the Annex I decision on Article 27.4 in the light of the work of the Committee on Subsidies and Countervailing Measures.]~~	Countervailing Measures to extend the transition period, under the rubric of Article 27.4 of the Agreement on Subsidies and Countervailing Measures, for certain export subsidies provided by such Members, pursuant to the procedures set forth in document G/SCM/W/471."	Countervailing Measures to extend the transition period, under the rubric of Article 27.4 of the Agreement on Subsidies and Countervailing Measures, for certain export subsidies provided by such Members, pursuant to the procedures set forth in document G/SCM/W/471/Rev.1. Furthermore, when considering a request for an extension of the transition period under the rubric of Article 27.4 of the Agreement on Subsidies and Countervailing Measures, and in order to avoid that Member at similar stages of development and having a similar order of magnitude of share in world trade are treated differently in terms of receiving such extensions for the same eligible programmes and the length of such extensions, directs the Committee to extend the transition period for those developing countries, after taking into account the relative competitiveness in relation to other developing country Members who have requested extension of the transition period following the procedures set forth in document G/SCM/W/471/Rev.1."	Countervailing Measures to extend the transition period, under the rubric of Article 27.4 of the Agreement on Subsidies and Countervailing Measures, for certain export subsidies provided by such Members, pursuant to the procedures set forth in document G/SCM/39. Furthermore, when considering a request for an extension of the transition period under the rubric of Article 27.4 of the Agreement on Subsidies and Countervailing Measures, and in order to avoid that Members at similar stages of development and having a similar order of magnitude of share in world trade are treated differently in terms of receiving such extensions for the same eligible programmes and the length of such extensions, directs the Committee to extend the transition period for those developing countries, after taking into account the relative competitiveness in relation to other developing country Members who have requested extension of the transition period following the procedures set forth in document G/SCM/39.
9. TRIPS Agreement *7. TRIPS Agreement*	11. Agreement on Trade-Related Aspects of Intellectual Property Rights (TRIPS)	11. Agreement on Trade-Related Aspects of Intellectual Property Rights (TRIPS)	11. Agreement on Trade-Related Aspects of Intellectual Property Rights (TRIPS)
- Tiret 89 "~~The Ministerial Conference~~ *directs the TRIPS Council to continue its examination of the scope and modalities for complaints of the types provided for under subparagraphs 1(b) and 1(c)*	- Tiret 89 "The TRIPS Council is directed to continue its examination of the scope and modalities for complaints of the types provided for under subparagraphs 1(b) and 1(c)	- Tiret 89 "The TRIPS Council is directed to continue its examination of the scope and modalities for complaints of the types provided for under subparagraphs 1(b) and 1(c)	11.1 The TRIPS Council is directed to continue its examination of the scope and modalities for complaints of the types provided for under subparagraphs 1(b) and 1(c)

~~removed text~~ as compared to 27 October Draft
added text as compared to 27 October Draft
moved text for purposes of comparing to 27 October Draft

Comparison of Implementation-Related Issues and Concerns Draft Decisions

Implementation-Related Issues and Concerns Draft Decision 26 September 2001	Implementation-Related Issues and Concerns Draft Decision 27 October 2001	Implementation-Related Issues and Concerns Draft Decision 13 November 2001	Implementation-Related Issues and Concerns Decision 14 November 2001
of Article XXIII of GATT 1994 and make recommendations to the Fifth Session of the Ministerial Conference. ~~The Ministerial Conference~~ *agrees that Members, in the meantime, will not initiate such complaints."*	of Article XXIII of GATT 1994 and make recommendations to the Fifth Session of the Ministerial Conference. It is agreed that, in the meantime, Members will not initiate such complaints under the TRIPS Agreement."	of Article XXIII of GATT 1994 and make recommendations to the Fifth Session of the Ministerial Conference. It is agreed that, in the meantime, Members will not initiate such complaints under the TRIPS Agreement."	of Article XXIII of GATT 1994 and make recommendations to the Fifth Session of the Ministerial Conference. It is agreed that, in the meantime, Members will not initiate such complaints under the TRIPS Agreement.
- Tiret 90 ~~"With a view to facilitating the implementation of the TRIPS Agreement the General Council requests Members to submit to the TRIPS Council information regarding measures implementing~~ Article 66.2. These submissions shall be subject to a review in the TRIPS Council, ~~and serve as reference in drawing up an illustrative list of incentives~~. This information shall be updated by Members annually thereafter."	- Tiret 90 "Reaffirming that the provisions of Article 66.2 of the TRIPS Agreement are mandatory, it is agreed that the TRIPS Council shall put in place a mechanism for ensuring the monitoring and full implementation of the obligations in question. To this end, developed-country Members shall submit prior to the end of 2002 detailed reports on the functioning in practice of the incentives provided to their enterprises for the transfer of technology in pursuance of their commitments under Article 66.2. These submissions shall be subject to a review in the TRIPS Council and information shall be updated by Members annually."	- Tiret 90 "Reaffirming that the provisions of Article 66.2 of the TRIPS Agreement are mandatory, it is agreed that the TRIPS Council shall put in place a mechanism for ensuring the monitoring and full implementation of the obligations in question. To this end, developed-country Members shall submit prior to the end of 2002 detailed reports on the functioning in practice of the incentives provided to their enterprises for the transfer of technology in pursuance of their commitments under Article 66.2. These submissions shall be subject to a review in the TRIPS Council and information shall be updated by Members annually."	11.2 Reaffirming that the provisions of Article 66.2 of the TRIPS Agreement are mandatory, it is agreed that the TRIPS Council shall put in place a mechanism for ensuring the monitoring and full implementation of the obligations in question. To this end, developed-country Members shall submit prior to the end of 2002 detailed reports on the functioning in practice of the incentives provided to their enterprises for the transfer of technology in pursuance of their commitments under Article 66.2. These submissions shall be subject to a review in the TRIPS Council and information shall be updated by Members annually.
10. Cross-cutting Issues *8. Cross-cutting Issues*	12. Cross-cutting Issues	12. Cross-cutting Issues	12. Cross-cutting Issues
- Tiret 96 *[~~Action to be taken in light of the report of the Committee on Trade and Development due on 28 September. This issue is also referred to in the Draft Ministerial Declaration~~.]*	- Tiret 96 "The Committee on Trade and Development is instructed: (i) to identify those special and differential treatment provisions that are already mandatory in nature	- Tiret 96 "The Committee on Trade and Development is instructed: (i) to identify those special and differential treatment provisions that are already mandatory in nature	12.1 The Committee on Trade and Development is instructed: (i) to identify those special and differential treatment provisions that are already mandatory in nature and

~~removed text~~ as compared to 27 October Draft
added text as compared to 27 October Draft
moved text for purposes of comparing to 27 October Draft

Comparison of Implementation-Related Issues and Concerns Draft Decisions

Implementation-Related Issues and Concerns Draft Decision 26 September 2001	Implementation-Related Issues and Concerns Draft Decision 27 October 2001	Implementation-Related Issues and Concerns Draft Decision 13 November 2001	Implementation-Related Issues and Concerns Decision 14 November 2001
	and those that are non-binding in character, to consider the legal and practical implications for developed and developing Members of converting special and differential treatment measures into mandatory provisions, to identify those that Members consider should be made mandatory, and to report to the General Council with clear recommendations for a decision by July 2002;	and those that are non-binding in character, to consider the legal and practical implications for developed and developing Members of converting special and differential treatment measures into mandatory provisions, to identify those that Members consider should be made mandatory, and to report to the General Council with clear recommendations for a decision by July 2002;	those that are non-binding in character, to consider the legal and practical implications for developed and developing Members of converting special and differential treatment measures into mandatory provisions, to identify those that Members consider should be made mandatory, and to report to the General Council with clear recommendations for a decision by July 2002;
	(ii) to examine additional ways in which special and differential treatment provisions can be made more effective, to consider ways, including improved information flows, in which developing countries, in particular the least-developed countries, may be assisted to make best use of special and differential treatment provisions, and to report to the General Council with clear recommendations for a decision by July 2002; and	(ii) to examine additional ways in which special and differential treatment provisions can be made more effective, to consider ways, including improved information flows, in which developing countries, in particular the least-developed countries, may be assisted to make best use of special and differential treatment provisions, and to report to the General Council with clear recommendations for a decision by July 2002; and	(ii) to examine additional ways in which special and differential treatment provisions can be made more effective, to consider ways, including improved information flows, in which developing countries, in particular the least-developed countries, may be assisted to make best use of special and differential treatment provisions, and to report to the General Council with clear recommendations for a decision by July 2002; and
	(iii) to consider, in the context of the work programme adopted at the Fourth Session of the Ministerial Conference, how special and differential treatment may be incorporated into the architecture of WTO rules.	(iii) to consider, in the context of the work programme adopted at the Fourth Session of the Ministerial Conference, how special and differential treatment may be incorporated into the architecture of WTO rules.	(iii) to consider, in the context of the work programme adopted at the Fourth Session of the Ministerial Conference, how special and differential treatment may be incorporated into the architecture of WTO rules.
	The work of the Committee on Trade and Development in this regard shall take fully into consideration previous work undertaken as noted in WT/COMTD/W/77/Rev.1. It will also be without prejudice to	The work of the Committee on Trade and Development in this regard shall take fully into consideration previous work undertaken as noted in WT/COMTD/W/77/Rev.1. It will also be without prejudice to	The work of the Committee on Trade and Development in this regard shall take fully into consideration previous work undertaken as noted in WT/COMTD/W/77/Rev.1. It will also be without prejudice to

~~removed text~~ as compared to 27 October Draft
added text as compared to 27 October Draft
moved text for purposes of comparing to 27 October Draft

29

Comparison of Implementation-Related Issues and Concerns Draft Decisions

Implementation-Related Issues and Concerns Draft Decision 26 September 2001	Implementation-Related Issues and Concerns Draft Decision 27 October 2001	Implementation-Related Issues and Concerns Draft Decision 13 November 2001	Implementation-Related Issues and Concerns Decision 14 November 2001
	work in respect of implementation of WTO Agreements in the General Council and in other Councils and Committees."	work in respect of implementation of WTO Agreements in the General Council and in other Councils and Committees."	work in respect of implementation of WTO Agreements in the General Council and in other Councils and Committees.
- Tiret 97 "~~The General Council~~ reaffirms that preferences granted to developing countries pursuant to the "Enabling Clause" should be generalised, non-reciprocal and non-discriminatory."	- Tiret 97 " Reaffirms that preferences granted to developing countries pursuant to the Decision of the Contracting Parties of 28 November 1979 ("Enabling Clause") should be generalised, non-reciprocal and non-discriminatory."	- Tiret 97 " Reaffirms that preferences granted to developing countries pursuant to the Decision of the Contracting Parties of 28 November 1979 ("Enabling Clause") should be generalised, non-reciprocal and non-discriminatory."	12.2 Reaffirms that preferences granted to developing countries pursuant to the Decision of the Contracting Parties of 28 November 1979 ("Enabling Clause") should be generalised, non-reciprocal and non-discriminatory.
	13. Outstanding Implementation Issues	13. Outstanding Implementation Issues	13. Outstanding Implementation Issues
	Agrees that outstanding implementation issues be addressed in accordance with paragraph 12 of the Ministerial Declaration (WT/MIN(01)/DEC/-).	Agrees that outstanding implementation issues be addressed in accordance with paragraph 12 of the Ministerial Declaration (WT/MIN(01)/DEC/-).	Agrees that outstanding implementation issues be addressed in accordance with paragraph 12 of the Ministerial Declaration (WT/MIN(01)/DEC/1).

~~removed text~~ as compared to 27 October Draft
<u>added text</u> as compared to 27 October Draft
moved text for purposes of comparing to 27 October Draft

Comparison of Implementation-Related Issues and Concerns Draft Decisions

Implementation-Related Issues and Concerns Draft Decision 26 September 2001	Implementation-Related Issues and Concerns Draft Decision 27 October 2001	Implementation-Related Issues and Concerns Draft Decision 13 November 2001	Implementation-Related Issues and Concerns Decision 14 November 2001
	14. Final Provisions	14. Final Provisions	14. Final Provisions
	Requests the Director-General, consistent with paragraphs 32 to 36 of the Ministerial Declaration (WT/MIN(01)/DEC/-), to ensure that WTO technical assistance focuses, on a priority basis, on assisting developing countries to implement existing WTO obligations as well as on increasing their capacity to participate more effectively in future multilateral trade negotiations. In carrying out this mandate, the WTO Secretariat should cooperate more closely with international and regional intergovernmental organisations so as to increase efficiency and synergies and avoid duplication of programmes.	Requests the Director-General, consistent with paragraphs 38 to 43 of the Ministerial Declaration (WT/MIN(01)/DEC/-), to ensure that WTO technical assistance focuses, on a priority basis, on assisting developing countries to implement existing WTO obligations as well as on increasing their capacity to participate more effectively in future multilateral trade negotiations. In carrying out this mandate, the WTO Secretariat should cooperate more closely with international and regional intergovernmental organisations so as to increase efficiency and synergies and avoid duplication of programmes.	Requests the Director-General, consistent with paragraphs 38 to 43 of the Ministerial Declaration (WT/MIN(01)/DEC/1), to ensure that WTO technical assistance focuses, on a priority basis, on assisting developing countries to implement existing WTO obligations as well as on increasing their capacity to participate more effectively in future multilateral trade negotiations. In carrying out this mandate, the WTO Secretariat should cooperate more closely with international and regional intergovernmental organisations so as to increase efficiency and synergies and avoid duplication of programmes.

~~removed text~~ as compared to 27 October Draft
added text as compared to 27 October Draft
moved text for purposes of comparing to 27 October Draft

Appendix 4
Ministerial Declaration
WT/MIN(01)/DEC/1
(20 November 2001)

WORLD TRADE ORGANIZATION

WT/MIN(01)/DEC/1
20 November 2001

(01-5859)

MINISTERIAL CONFERENCE
Fourth Session
Doha, 9 - 14 November 2001

MINISTERIAL DECLARATION

Adopted on 14 November 2001

1. The multilateral trading system embodied in the World Trade Organization has contributed significantly to economic growth, development and employment throughout the past fifty years. We are determined, particularly in the light of the global economic slowdown, to maintain the process of reform and liberalization of trade policies, thus ensuring that the system plays its full part in promoting recovery, growth and development. We therefore strongly reaffirm the principles and objectives set out in the Marrakesh Agreement Establishing the World Trade Organization, and pledge to reject the use of protectionism.

2. International trade can play a major role in the promotion of economic development and the alleviation of poverty. We recognize the need for all our peoples to benefit from the increased opportunities and welfare gains that the multilateral trading system generates. The majority of WTO Members are developing countries. We seek to place their needs and interests at the heart of the Work Programme adopted in this Declaration. Recalling the Preamble to the Marrakesh Agreement, we shall continue to make positive efforts designed to ensure that developing countries, and especially the least-developed among them, secure a share in the growth of world trade commensurate with the needs of their economic development. In this context, enhanced market access, balanced rules, and well targeted, sustainably financed technical assistance and capacity-building programmes have important roles to play.

3. We recognize the particular vulnerability of the least-developed countries and the special structural difficulties they face in the global economy. We are committed to addressing the marginalization of least-developed countries in international trade and to improving their effective participation in the multilateral trading system. We recall the commitments made by Ministers at our meetings in Marrakesh, Singapore and Geneva, and by the international community at the Third UN Conference on Least-Developed Countries in Brussels, to help least-developed countries secure beneficial and meaningful integration into the multilateral trading system and the global economy. We are determined that the WTO will play its part in building effectively on these commitments under the Work Programme we are establishing.

4. We stress our commitment to the WTO as the unique forum for global trade rule-making and liberalization, while also recognizing that regional trade agreements can play an important role in promoting the liberalization and expansion of trade and in fostering development.

5. We are aware that the challenges Members face in a rapidly changing international environment cannot be addressed through measures taken in the trade field alone. We shall continue to work with the Bretton Woods institutions for greater coherence in global economic policy-making.

6. We strongly reaffirm our commitment to the objective of sustainable development, as stated in the Preamble to the Marrakesh Agreement. We are convinced that the aims of upholding and

safeguarding an open and non-discriminatory multilateral trading system, and acting for the protection of the environment and the promotion of sustainable development can and must be mutually supportive. We take note of the efforts by Members to conduct national environmental assessments of trade policies on a voluntary basis. We recognize that under WTO rules no country should be prevented from taking measures for the protection of human, animal or plant life or health, or of the environment at the levels it considers appropriate, subject to the requirement that they are not applied in a manner which would constitute a means of arbitrary or unjustifiable discrimination between countries where the same conditions prevail, or a disguised restriction on international trade, and are otherwise in accordance with the provisions of the WTO Agreements. We welcome the WTO's continued cooperation with UNEP and other inter-governmental environmental organizations. We encourage efforts to promote cooperation between the WTO and relevant international environmental and developmental organizations, especially in the lead-up to the World Summit on Sustainable Development to be held in Johannesburg, South Africa, in September 2002.

7. We reaffirm the right of Members under the General Agreement on Trade in Services to regulate, and to introduce new regulations on, the supply of services.

8. We reaffirm our declaration made at the Singapore Ministerial Conference regarding internationally recognized core labour standards. We take note of work under way in the International Labour Organization (ILO) on the social dimension of globalization.

9. We note with particular satisfaction that this Conference has completed the WTO accession procedures for China and Chinese Taipei. We also welcome the accession as new Members, since our last Session, of Albania, Croatia, Georgia, Jordan, Lithuania, Moldova and Oman, and note the extensive market-access commitments already made by these countries on accession. These accessions will greatly strengthen the multilateral trading system, as will those of the 28 countries now negotiating their accession. We therefore attach great importance to concluding accession proceedings as quickly as possible. In particular, we are committed to accelerating the accession of least-developed countries.

10. Recognizing the challenges posed by an expanding WTO membership, we confirm our collective responsibility to ensure internal transparency and the effective participation of all Members. While emphasizing the intergovernmental character of the organization, we are committed to making the WTO's operations more transparent, including through more effective and prompt dissemination of information, and to improve dialogue with the public. We shall therefore at the national and multilateral levels continue to promote a better public understanding of the WTO and to communicate the benefits of a liberal, rules-based multilateral trading system.

11. In view of these considerations, we hereby agree to undertake the broad and balanced Work Programme set out below. This incorporates both an expanded negotiating agenda and other important decisions and activities necessary to address the challenges facing the multilateral trading system.

WORK PROGRAMME

IMPLEMENTATION-RELATED ISSUES AND CONCERNS

12. We attach the utmost importance to the implementation-related issues and concerns raised by Members and are determined to find appropriate solutions to them. In this connection, and having regard to the General Council Decisions of 3 May and 15 December 2000, we further adopt the Decision on Implementation-Related Issues and Concerns in document WT/MIN(01)/17 to address a number of implementation problems faced by Members. We agree that negotiations on outstanding implementation issues shall be an integral part of the Work Programme we are establishing, and that

agreements reached at an early stage in these negotiations shall be treated in accordance with the provisions of paragraph 47 below. In this regard, we shall proceed as follows: (a) where we provide a specific negotiating mandate in this Declaration, the relevant implementation issues shall be addressed under that mandate; (b) the other outstanding implementation issues shall be addressed as a matter of priority by the relevant WTO bodies, which shall report to the Trade Negotiations Committee, established under paragraph 46 below, by the end of 2002 for appropriate action.

AGRICULTURE

13. We recognize the work already undertaken in the negotiations initiated in early 2000 under Article 20 of the Agreement on Agriculture, including the large number of negotiating proposals submitted on behalf of a total of 121 Members. We recall the long-term objective referred to in the Agreement to establish a fair and market-oriented trading system through a programme of fundamental reform encompassing strengthened rules and specific commitments on support and protection in order to correct and prevent restrictions and distortions in world agricultural markets. We reconfirm our commitment to this programme. Building on the work carried out to date and without prejudging the outcome of the negotiations we commit ourselves to comprehensive negotiations aimed at: substantial improvements in market access; reductions of, with a view to phasing out, all forms of export subsidies; and substantial reductions in trade-distorting domestic support. We agree that special and differential treatment for developing countries shall be an integral part of all elements of the negotiations and shall be embodied in the Schedules of concessions and commitments and as appropriate in the rules and disciplines to be negotiated, so as to be operationally effective and to enable developing countries to effectively take account of their development needs, including food security and rural development. We take note of the non-trade concerns reflected in the negotiating proposals submitted by Members and confirm that non-trade concerns will be taken into account in the negotiations as provided for in the Agreement on Agriculture.

14. Modalities for the further commitments, including provisions for special and differential treatment, shall be established no later than 31 March 2003. Participants shall submit their comprehensive draft Schedules based on these modalities no later than the date of the Fifth Session of the Ministerial Conference. The negotiations, including with respect to rules and disciplines and related legal texts, shall be concluded as part and at the date of conclusion of the negotiating agenda as a whole.

SERVICES

15. The negotiations on trade in services shall be conducted with a view to promoting the economic growth of all trading partners and the development of developing and least-developed countries. We recognize the work already undertaken in the negotiations, initiated in January 2000 under Article XIX of the General Agreement on Trade in Services, and the large number of proposals submitted by Members on a wide range of sectors and several horizontal issues, as well as on movement of natural persons. We reaffirm the Guidelines and Procedures for the Negotiations adopted by the Council for Trade in Services on 28 March 2001 as the basis for continuing the negotiations, with a view to achieving the objectives of the General Agreement on Trade in Services, as stipulated in the Preamble, Article IV and Article XIX of that Agreement. Participants shall submit initial requests for specific commitments by 30 June 2002 and initial offers by 31 March 2003.

MARKET ACCESS FOR NON-AGRICULTURAL PRODUCTS

16. We agree to negotiations which shall aim, by modalities to be agreed, to reduce or as appropriate eliminate tariffs, including the reduction or elimination of tariff peaks, high tariffs, and

tariff escalation, as well as non-tariff barriers, in particular on products of export interest to developing countries. Product coverage shall be comprehensive and without *a priori* exclusions. The negotiations shall take fully into account the special needs and interests of developing and least-developed country participants, including through less than full reciprocity in reduction commitments, in accordance with the relevant provisions of Article XXVIII *bis* of GATT 1994 and the provisions cited in paragraph 50 below. To this end, the modalities to be agreed will include appropriate studies and capacity-building measures to assist least-developed countries to participate effectively in the negotiations.

TRADE-RELATED ASPECTS OF INTELLECTUAL PROPERTY RIGHTS

17. We stress the importance we attach to implementation and interpretation of the Agreement on Trade-Related Aspects of Intellectual Property Rights (TRIPS Agreement) in a manner supportive of public health, by promoting both access to existing medicines and research and development into new medicines and, in this connection, are adopting a separate Declaration.

18. With a view to completing the work started in the Council for Trade-Related Aspects of Intellectual Property Rights (Council for TRIPS) on the implementation of Article 23.4, we agree to negotiate the establishment of a multilateral system of notification and registration of geographical indications for wines and spirits by the Fifth Session of the Ministerial Conference. We note that issues related to the extension of the protection of geographical indications provided for in Article 23 to products other than wines and spirits will be addressed in the Council for TRIPS pursuant to paragraph 12 of this Declaration.

19. We instruct the Council for TRIPS, in pursuing its work programme including under the review of Article 27.3(b), the review of the implementation of the TRIPS Agreement under Article 71.1 and the work foreseen pursuant to paragraph 12 of this Declaration, to examine, *inter alia*, the relationship between the TRIPS Agreement and the Convention on Biological Diversity, the protection of traditional knowledge and folklore, and other relevant new developments raised by Members pursuant to Article 71.1. In undertaking this work, the TRIPS Council shall be guided by the objectives and principles set out in Articles 7 and 8 of the TRIPS Agreement and shall take fully into account the development dimension.

RELATIONSHIP BETWEEN TRADE AND INVESTMENT

20. Recognizing the case for a multilateral framework to secure transparent, stable and predictable conditions for long-term cross-border investment, particularly foreign direct investment, that will contribute to the expansion of trade, and the need for enhanced technical assistance and capacity-building in this area as referred to in paragraph 21, we agree that negotiations will take place after the Fifth Session of the Ministerial Conference on the basis of a decision to be taken, by explicit consensus, at that Session on modalities of negotiations.

21. We recognize the needs of developing and least-developed countries for enhanced support for technical assistance and capacity building in this area, including policy analysis and development so that they may better evaluate the implications of closer multilateral cooperation for their development policies and objectives, and human and institutional development. To this end, we shall work in cooperation with other relevant intergovernmental organisations, including UNCTAD, and through appropriate regional and bilateral channels, to provide strengthened and adequately resourced assistance to respond to these needs.

22. In the period until the Fifth Session, further work in the Working Group on the Relationship Between Trade and Investment will focus on the clarification of: scope and definition; transparency;

non-discrimination; modalities for pre-establishment commitments based on a GATS-type, positive list approach; development provisions; exceptions and balance-of-payments safeguards; consultation and the settlement of disputes between Members. Any framework should reflect in a balanced manner the interests of home and host countries, and take due account of the development policies and objectives of host governments as well as their right to regulate in the public interest. The special development, trade and financial needs of developing and least-developed countries should be taken into account as an integral part of any framework, which should enable Members to undertake obligations and commitments commensurate with their individual needs and circumstances. Due regard should be paid to other relevant WTO provisions. Account should be taken, as appropriate, of existing bilateral and regional arrangements on investment.

INTERACTION BETWEEN TRADE AND COMPETITION POLICY

23. Recognizing the case for a multilateral framework to enhance the contribution of competition policy to international trade and development, and the need for enhanced technical assistance and capacity-building in this area as referred to in paragraph 24, we agree that negotiations will take place after the Fifth Session of the Ministerial Conference on the basis of a decision to be taken, by explicit consensus, at that Session on modalities of negotiations.

24. We recognize the needs of developing and least-developed countries for enhanced support for technical assistance and capacity building in this area, including policy analysis and development so that they may better evaluate the implications of closer multilateral cooperation for their development policies and objectives, and human and institutional development. To this end, we shall work in cooperation with other relevant intergovernmental organisations, including UNCTAD, and through appropriate regional and bilateral channels, to provide strengthened and adequately resourced assistance to respond to these needs.

25. In the period until the Fifth Session, further work in the Working Group on the Interaction between Trade and Competition Policy will focus on the clarification of: core principles, including transparency, non-discrimination and procedural fairness, and provisions on hardcore cartels; modalities for voluntary cooperation; and support for progressive reinforcement of competition institutions in developing countries through capacity building. Full account shall be taken of the needs of developing and least-developed country participants and appropriate flexibility provided to address them.

TRANSPARENCY IN GOVERNMENT PROCUREMENT

26. Recognizing the case for a multilateral agreement on transparency in government procurement and the need for enhanced technical assistance and capacity building in this area, we agree that negotiations will take place after the Fifth Session of the Ministerial Conference on the basis of a decision to be taken, by explicit consensus, at that Session on modalities of negotiations. These negotiations will build on the progress made in the Working Group on Transparency in Government Procurement by that time and take into account participants' development priorities, especially those of least-developed country participants. Negotiations shall be limited to the transparency aspects and therefore will not restrict the scope for countries to give preferences to domestic supplies and suppliers. We commit ourselves to ensuring adequate technical assistance and support for capacity building both during the negotiations and after their conclusion.

WT/MIN(01)/DEC/1
Page 6

TRADE FACILITATION

27. Recognizing the case for further expediting the movement, release and clearance of goods, including goods in transit, and the need for enhanced technical assistance and capacity building in this area, we agree that negotiations will take place after the Fifth Session of the Ministerial Conference on the basis of a decision to be taken, by explicit consensus, at that Session on modalities of negotiations. In the period until the Fifth Session, the Council for Trade in Goods shall review and as appropriate, clarify and improve relevant aspects of Articles V, VIII and X of the GATT 1994 and identify the trade facilitation needs and priorities of Members, in particular developing and least-developed countries. We commit ourselves to ensuring adequate technical assistance and support for capacity building in this area.

WTO RULES

28. In the light of experience and of the increasing application of these instruments by Members, we agree to negotiations aimed at clarifying and improving disciplines under the Agreements on Implementation of Article VI of the GATT 1994 and on Subsidies and Countervailing Measures, while preserving the basic concepts, principles and effectiveness of these Agreements and their instruments and objectives, and taking into account the needs of developing and least-developed participants. In the initial phase of the negotiations, participants will indicate the provisions, including disciplines on trade distorting practices, that they seek to clarify and improve in the subsequent phase. In the context of these negotiations, participants shall also aim to clarify and improve WTO disciplines on fisheries subsidies, taking into account the importance of this sector to developing countries. We note that fisheries subsidies are also referred to in paragraph 31.

29. We also agree to negotiations aimed at clarifying and improving disciplines and procedures under the existing WTO provisions applying to regional trade agreements. The negotiations shall take into account the developmental aspects of regional trade agreements.

DISPUTE SETTLEMENT UNDERSTANDING

30. We agree to negotiations on improvements and clarifications of the Dispute Settlement Understanding. The negotiations should be based on the work done thus far as well as any additional proposals by Members, and aim to agree on improvements and clarifications not later than May 2003, at which time we will take steps to ensure that the results enter into force as soon as possible thereafter.

TRADE AND ENVIRONMENT

31. With a view to enhancing the mutual supportiveness of trade and environment, we agree to negotiations, without prejudging their outcome, on:

(i) the relationship between existing WTO rules and specific trade obligations set out in multilateral environmental agreements (MEAs). The negotiations shall be limited in scope to the applicability of such existing WTO rules as among parties to the MEA in question. The negotiations shall not prejudice the WTO rights of any Member that is not a party to the MEA in question;

(ii) procedures for regular information exchange between MEA Secretariats and the relevant WTO committees, and the criteria for the granting of observer status;

(iii) the reduction or, as appropriate, elimination of tariff and non-tariff barriers to environmental goods and services.

We note that fisheries subsidies form part of the negotiations provided for in paragraph 28.

32. We instruct the Committee on Trade and Environment, in pursuing work on all items on its agenda within its current terms of reference, to give particular attention to:

(i) the effect of environmental measures on market access, especially in relation to developing countries, in particular the least-developed among them, and those situations in which the elimination or reduction of trade restrictions and distortions would benefit trade, the environment and development;

(ii) the relevant provisions of the Agreement on Trade-Related Aspects of Intellectual Property Rights; and

(iii) labelling requirements for environmental purposes.

Work on these issues should include the identification of any need to clarify relevant WTO rules. The Committee shall report to the Fifth Session of the Ministerial Conference, and make recommendations, where appropriate, with respect to future action, including the desirability of negotiations. The outcome of this work as well as the negotiations carried out under paragraph 31(i) and (ii) shall be compatible with the open and non-discriminatory nature of the multilateral trading system, shall not add to or diminish the rights and obligations of Members under existing WTO agreements, in particular the Agreement on the Application of Sanitary and Phytosanitary Measures, nor alter the balance of these rights and obligations, and will take into account the needs of developing and least-developed countries.

33. We recognize the importance of technical assistance and capacity building in the field of trade and environment to developing countries, in particular the least-developed among them. We also encourage that expertise and experience be shared with Members wishing to perform environmental reviews at the national level. A report shall be prepared on these activities for the Fifth Session.

ELECTRONIC COMMERCE

34. We take note of the work which has been done in the General Council and other relevant bodies since the Ministerial Declaration of 20 May 1998 and agree to continue the Work Programme on Electronic Commerce. The work to date demonstrates that electronic commerce creates new challenges and opportunities for trade for Members at all stages of development, and we recognize the importance of creating and maintaining an environment which is favourable to the future development of electronic commerce. We instruct the General Council to consider the most appropriate institutional arrangements for handling the Work Programme, and to report on further progress to the Fifth Session of the Ministerial Conference. We declare that Members will maintain their current practice of not imposing customs duties on electronic transmissions until the Fifth Session.

SMALL ECONOMIES

35. We agree to a work programme, under the auspices of the General Council, to examine issues relating to the trade of small economies. The objective of this work is to frame responses to the trade-

related issues identified for the fuller integration of small, vulnerable economies into the multilateral trading system, and not to create a sub-category of WTO Members. The General Council shall review the work programme and make recommendations for action to the Fifth Session of the Ministerial Conference.

TRADE, DEBT AND FINANCE

36. We agree to an examination, in a Working Group under the auspices of the General Council, of the relationship between trade, debt and finance, and of any possible recommendations on steps that might be taken within the mandate and competence of the WTO to enhance the capacity of the multilateral trading system to contribute to a durable solution to the problem of external indebtedness of developing and least-developed countries, and to strengthen the coherence of international trade and financial policies, with a view to safeguarding the multilateral trading system from the effects of financial and monetary instability. The General Council shall report to the Fifth Session of the Ministerial Conference on progress in the examination.

TRADE AND TRANSFER OF TECHNOLOGY

37. We agree to an examination, in a Working Group under the auspices of the General Council, of the relationship between trade and transfer of technology, and of any possible recommendations on steps that might be taken within the mandate of the WTO to increase flows of technology to developing countries. The General Council shall report to the Fifth Session of the Ministerial Conference on progress in the examination.

TECHNICAL COOPERATION AND CAPACITY BUILDING

38. We confirm that technical cooperation and capacity building are core elements of the development dimension of the multilateral trading system, and we welcome and endorse the New Strategy for WTO Technical Cooperation for Capacity Building, Growth and Integration. We instruct the Secretariat, in coordination with other relevant agencies, to support domestic efforts for mainstreaming trade into national plans for economic development and strategies for poverty reduction. The delivery of WTO technical assistance shall be designed to assist developing and least-developed countries and low-income countries in transition to adjust to WTO rules and disciplines, implement obligations and exercise the rights of membership, including drawing on the benefits of an open, rules-based multilateral trading system. Priority shall also be accorded to small, vulnerable, and transition economies, as well as to Members and Observers without representation in Geneva. We reaffirm our support for the valuable work of the International Trade Centre, which should be enhanced.

39. We underscore the urgent necessity for the effective coordinated delivery of technical assistance with bilateral donors, in the OECD Development Assistance Committee and relevant international and regional intergovernmental institutions, within a coherent policy framework and timetable. In the coordinated delivery of technical assistance, we instruct the Director-General to consult with the relevant agencies, bilateral donors and beneficiaries, to identify ways of enhancing and rationalizing the Integrated Framework for Trade-Related Technical Assistance to Least-Developed Countries and the Joint Integrated Technical Assistance Programme (JITAP).

40. We agree that there is a need for technical assistance to benefit from secure and predictable funding. We therefore instruct the Committee on Budget, Finance and Administration to develop a plan for adoption by the General Council in December 2001 that will ensure long-term funding for

WTO technical assistance at an overall level no lower than that of the current year and commensurate with the activities outlined above.

41. We have established firm commitments on technical cooperation and capacity building in various paragraphs in this Ministerial Declaration. We reaffirm these specific commitments contained in paragraphs 16, 21, 24, 26, 27, 33, 38-40, 42 and 43, and also reaffirm the understanding in paragraph 2 on the important role of sustainably financed technical assistance and capacity-building programmes. We instruct the Director-General to report to the Fifth Session of the Ministerial Conference, with an interim report to the General Council in December 2002 on the implementation and adequacy of these commitments in the identified paragraphs.

LEAST-DEVELOPED COUNTRIES

42. We acknowledge the seriousness of the concerns expressed by the least-developed countries (LDCs) in the Zanzibar Declaration adopted by their Ministers in July 2001. We recognize that the integration of the LDCs into the multilateral trading system requires meaningful market access, support for the diversification of their production and export base, and trade-related technical assistance and capacity building. We agree that the meaningful integration of LDCs into the trading system and the global economy will involve efforts by all WTO Members. We commit ourselves to the objective of duty-free, quota-free market access for products originating from LDCs. In this regard, we welcome the significant market access improvements by WTO Members in advance of the Third UN Conference on LDCs (LDC-III), in Brussels, May 2001. We further commit ourselves to consider additional measures for progressive improvements in market access for LDCs. Accession of LDCs remains a priority for the Membership. We agree to work to facilitate and accelerate negotiations with acceding LDCs. We instruct the Secretariat to reflect the priority we attach to LDCs' accessions in the annual plans for technical assistance. We reaffirm the commitments we undertook at LDC-III, and agree that the WTO should take into account, in designing its work programme for LDCs, the trade-related elements of the Brussels Declaration and Programme of Action, consistent with the WTO's mandate, adopted at LDC-III. We instruct the Sub-Committee for Least-Developed Countries to design such a work programme and to report on the agreed work programme to the General Council at its first meeting in 2002.

43. We endorse the Integrated Framework for Trade-Related Technical Assistance to Least-Developed Countries (IF) as a viable model for LDCs' trade development. We urge development partners to significantly increase contributions to the IF Trust Fund and WTO extra-budgetary trust funds in favour of LDCs. We urge the core agencies, in coordination with development partners, to explore the enhancement of the IF with a view to addressing the supply-side constraints of LDCs and the extension of the model to all LDCs, following the review of the IF and the appraisal of the ongoing Pilot Scheme in selected LDCs. We request the Director-General, following coordination with heads of the other agencies, to provide an interim report to the General Council in December 2002 and a full report to the Fifth Session of the Ministerial Conference on all issues affecting LDCs.

SPECIAL AND DIFFERENTIAL TREATMENT

44. We reaffirm that provisions for special and differential treatment are an integral part of the WTO Agreements. We note the concerns expressed regarding their operation in addressing specific constraints faced by developing countries, particularly least-developed countries. In that connection, we also note that some Members have proposed a Framework Agreement on Special and Differential Treatment (WT/GC/W/442). We therefore agree that all special and differential treatment provisions shall be reviewed with a view to strengthening them and making them more precise, effective and operational. In this connection, we endorse the work programme on special and differential treatment set out in the Decision on Implementation-Related Issues and Concerns.

ORGANIZATION AND MANAGEMENT OF THE WORK PROGRAMME

45. The negotiations to be pursued under the terms of this Declaration shall be concluded not later than 1 January 2005. The Fifth Session of the Ministerial Conference will take stock of progress in the negotiations, provide any necessary political guidance, and take decisions as necessary. When the results of the negotiations in all areas have been established, a Special Session of the Ministerial Conference will be held to take decisions regarding the adoption and implementation of those results.

46. The overall conduct of the negotiations shall be supervised by a Trade Negotiations Committee under the authority of the General Council. The Trade Negotiations Committee shall hold its first meeting not later than 31 January 2002. It shall establish appropriate negotiating mechanisms as required and supervise the progress of the negotiations.

47. With the exception of the improvements and clarifications of the Dispute Settlement Understanding, the conduct, conclusion and entry into force of the outcome of the negotiations shall be treated as parts of a single undertaking. However, agreements reached at an early stage may be implemented on a provisional or a definitive basis. Early agreements shall be taken into account in assessing the overall balance of the negotiations.

48. Negotiations shall be open to:

(i) all Members of the WTO; and

(ii) States and separate customs territories currently in the process of accession and those that inform Members, at a regular meeting of the General Council, of their intention to negotiate the terms of their membership and for whom an accession working party is established.

Decisions on the outcomes of the negotiations shall be taken only by WTO Members.

49. The negotiations shall be conducted in a transparent manner among participants, in order to facilitate the effective participation of all. They shall be conducted with a view to ensuring benefits to all participants and to achieving an overall balance in the outcome of the negotiations.

50. The negotiations and the other aspects of the Work Programme shall take fully into account the principle of special and differential treatment for developing and least-developed countries embodied in: Part IV of the GATT 1994; the Decision of 28 November 1979 on Differential and More Favourable Treatment, Reciprocity and Fuller Participation of Developing Countries; the Uruguay Round Decision on Measures in Favour of Least-Developed Countries; and all other relevant WTO provisions.

51. The Committee on Trade and Development and the Committee on Trade and Environment shall, within their respective mandates, each act as a forum to identify and debate developmental and environmental aspects of the negotiations, in order to help achieve the objective of having sustainable development appropriately reflected.

52. Those elements of the Work Programme which do not involve negotiations are also accorded a high priority. They shall be pursued under the overall supervision of the General Council, which shall report on progress to the Fifth Session of the Ministerial Conference.

____

Appendix 5
Declaration on TRIPs Agreement and Public Health
WT/MIN(01)/DEC/2
(20 November 2001)

WORLD TRADE ORGANIZATION

WT/MIN(01)/DEC/2
20 November 2001

(01-5860)

MINISTERIAL CONFERENCE
Fourth Session
Doha, 9 - 14 November 2001

DECLARATION ON THE TRIPS AGREEMENT AND PUBLIC HEALTH

Adopted on 14 November 2001

1. We recognize the gravity of the public health problems afflicting many developing and least-developed countries, especially those resulting from HIV/AIDS, tuberculosis, malaria and other epidemics.

2. We stress the need for the WTO Agreement on Trade-Related Aspects of Intellectual Property Rights (TRIPS Agreement) to be part of the wider national and international action to address these problems.

3. We recognize that intellectual property protection is important for the development of new medicines. We also recognize the concerns about its effects on prices.

4. We agree that the TRIPS Agreement does not and should not prevent Members from taking measures to protect public health. Accordingly, while reiterating our commitment to the TRIPS Agreement, we affirm that the Agreement can and should be interpreted and implemented in a manner supportive of WTO Members' right to protect public health and, in particular, to promote access to medicines for all.

In this connection, we reaffirm the right of WTO Members to use, to the full, the provisions in the TRIPS Agreement, which provide flexibility for this purpose.

5. Accordingly and in the light of paragraph 4 above, while maintaining our commitments in the TRIPS Agreement, we recognize that these flexibilities include:

(a) In applying the customary rules of interpretation of public international law, each provision of the TRIPS Agreement shall be read in the light of the object and purpose of the Agreement as expressed, in particular, in its objectives and principles.

(b) Each Member has the right to grant compulsory licences and the freedom to determine the grounds upon which such licences are granted.

(c) Each Member has the right to determine what constitutes a national emergency or other circumstances of extreme urgency, it being understood that public health crises, including those relating to HIV/AIDS, tuberculosis, malaria and other epidemics, can represent a national emergency or other circumstances of extreme urgency.

(d) The effect of the provisions in the TRIPS Agreement that are relevant to the exhaustion of intellectual property rights is to leave each Member free to establish its own regime for such exhaustion without challenge, subject to the MFN and national treatment provisions of Articles 3 and 4.

./.

WT/MIN(01)/DEC/2
Page 2

6. We recognize that WTO Members with insufficient or no manufacturing capacities in the pharmaceutical sector could face difficulties in making effective use of compulsory licensing under the TRIPS Agreement. We instruct the Council for TRIPS to find an expeditious solution to this problem and to report to the General Council before the end of 2002.

7. We reaffirm the commitment of developed-country Members to provide incentives to their enterprises and institutions to promote and encourage technology transfer to least-developed country Members pursuant to Article 66.2. We also agree that the least-developed country Members will not be obliged, with respect to pharmaceutical products, to implement or apply Sections 5 and 7 of Part II of the TRIPS Agreement or to enforce rights provided for under these Sections until 1 January 2016, without prejudice to the right of least-developed country Members to seek other extensions of the transition periods as provided for in Article 66.1 of the TRIPS Agreement. We instruct the Council for TRIPS to take the necessary action to give effect to this pursuant to Article 66.1 of the TRIPS Agreement.

Appendix 6
Implementation-Related Issues and Concerns Decision
WT/MIN(01)/17
(20 November 2001)

WORLD TRADE ORGANIZATION

WT/MIN(01)/17
20 November 2001

(01-5858)

MINISTERIAL CONFERENCE
Fourth Session
Doha, 9 - 14 November 2001

IMPLEMENTATION-RELATED ISSUES AND CONCERNS

Decision of 14 November 2001

The Ministerial Conference,

Having regard to Articles IV.1, IV.5 and IX of the Marrakesh Agreement Establishing the World Trade Organization (WTO);

Mindful of the importance that Members attach to the increased participation of developing countries in the multilateral trading system, and of the need to ensure that the system responds fully to the needs and interests of all participants;

Determined to take concrete action to address issues and concerns that have been raised by many developing-country Members regarding the implementation of some WTO Agreements and Decisions, including the difficulties and resource constraints that have been encountered in the implementation of obligations in various areas;

Recalling the 3 May 2000 Decision of the General Council to meet in special sessions to address outstanding implementation issues, and to assess the existing difficulties, identify ways needed to resolve them, and take decisions for appropriate action not later than the Fourth Session of the Ministerial Conference;

Noting the actions taken by the General Council in pursuance of this mandate at its Special Sessions in October and December 2000 (WT/L/384), as well as the review and further discussion undertaken at the Special Sessions held in April, July and October 2001, including the referral of additional issues to relevant WTO bodies or their chairpersons for further work;

Noting also the reports on the issues referred to the General Council from subsidiary bodies and their chairpersons and from the Director-General, and the discussions as well as the clarifications provided and understandings reached on implementation issues in the intensive informal and formal meetings held under this process since May 2000;

Decides as follows:

1. General Agreement on Tariffs and Trade 1994 (GATT 1994)

   1.1 Reaffirms that Article XVIII of the GATT 1994 is a special and differential treatment provision for developing countries and that recourse to it should be less onerous than to Article XII of the GATT 1994.

1.2 Noting the issues raised in the report of the Chairperson of the Committee on Market Access (WT/GC/50) concerning the meaning to be given to the phrase "substantial interest" in paragraph 2(d) of Article XIII of the GATT 1994, the Market Access Committee is directed to give further consideration to the issue and make recommendations to the General Council as expeditiously as possible but in any event not later than the end of 2002.

2. Agreement on Agriculture

2.1 Urges Members to exercise restraint in challenging measures notified under the green box by developing countries to promote rural development and adequately address food security concerns.

2.2 Takes note of the report of the Committee on Agriculture (G/AG/11) regarding the implementation of the Decision on Measures Concerning the Possible Negative Effects of the Reform Programme on Least-Developed and Net Food-Importing Developing Countries, and approves the recommendations contained therein regarding (i) food aid; (ii) technical and financial assistance in the context of aid programmes to improve agricultural productivity and infrastructure; (iii) financing normal levels of commercial imports of basic foodstuffs; and (iv) review of follow-up.

2.3 Takes note of the report of the Committee on Agriculture (G/AG/11) regarding the implementation of Article 10.2 of the Agreement on Agriculture, and approves the recommendations and reporting requirements contained therein.

2.4 Takes note of the report of the Committee on Agriculture (G/AG/11) regarding the administration of tariff rate quotas and the submission by Members of addenda to their notifications, and endorses the decision by the Committee to keep this matter under review.

3. Agreement on the Application of Sanitary and Phytosanitary Measures

3.1 Where the appropriate level of sanitary and phytosanitary protection allows scope for the phased introduction of new sanitary and phytosanitary measures, the phrase "longer time-frame for compliance" referred to in Article 10.2 of the Agreement on the Application of Sanitary and Phytosanitary Measures, shall be understood to mean normally a period of not less than 6 months. Where the appropriate level of sanitary and phytosanitary protection does not allow scope for the phased introduction of a new measure, but specific problems are identified by a Member, the Member applying the measure shall upon request enter into consultations with the country with a view to finding a mutually satisfactory solution to the problem while continuing to achieve the importing Member's appropriate level of protection.

3.2 Subject to the conditions specified in paragraph 2 of Annex B to the Agreement on the Application of Sanitary and Phytosanitary Measures, the phrase "reasonable interval" shall be understood to mean normally a period of not less than 6 months. It is understood that timeframes for specific measures have to be considered in the context of the particular circumstances of the measure and actions necessary to implement it. The entry into force of measures which contribute to the liberalization of trade should not be unnecessarily delayed.

3.3 Takes note of the Decision of the Committee on Sanitary and Phytosanitary Measures (G/SPS/19) regarding equivalence, and instructs the Committee to develop expeditiously the specific programme to further the implementation of Article 4 of the Agreement on the Application of Sanitary and Phytosanitary Measures.

3.4 Pursuant to the provisions of Article 12.7 of the Agreement on the Application of Sanitary and Phytosanitary Measures, the Committee on Sanitary and Phytosanitary Measures is instructed to review the operation and implementation of the Agreement on Sanitary and Phytosanitary Measures at least once every four years.

3.5 (i) Takes note of the actions taken to date by the Director-General to facilitate the increased participation of Members at different levels of development in the work of the relevant international standard setting organizations as well as his efforts to coordinate with these organizations and financial institutions in identifying SPS-related technical assistance needs and how best to address them; and

(ii) urges the Director-General to continue his cooperative efforts with these organizations and institutions in this regard, including with a view to according priority to the effective participation of least-developed countries and facilitating the provision of technical and financial assistance for this purpose.

3.6 (i) Urges Members to provide, to the extent possible, the financial and technical assistance necessary to enable least-developed countries to respond adequately to the introduction of any new SPS measures which may have significant negative effects on their trade; and

(ii) urges Members to ensure that technical assistance is provided to least-developed countries with a view to responding to the special problems faced by them in implementing the Agreement on the Application of Sanitary and Phytosanitary Measures.

4. Agreement on Textiles and Clothing

Reaffirms the commitment to full and faithful implementation of the Agreement on Textiles and Clothing, and agrees:

4.1 that the provisions of the Agreement relating to the early integration of products and the elimination of quota restrictions should be effectively utilised.

4.2 that Members will exercise particular consideration before initiating investigations in the context of antidumping remedies on textile and clothing exports from developing countries previously subject to quantitative restrictions under the Agreement for a period of two years following full integration of this Agreement into the WTO.

4.3 that without prejudice to their rights and obligations, Members shall notify any changes in their rules of origin concerning products falling under the coverage of the Agreement to the Committee on Rules of Origin which may decide to examine them.

Requests the Council for Trade in Goods to examine the following proposals:

4.4 that when calculating the quota levels for small suppliers for the remaining years of the Agreement, Members will apply the most favourable methodology available in respect of those Members under the growth-on-growth provisions from the beginning of the implementation period; extend the same treatment to least-developed countries; and, where possible, eliminate quota restrictions on imports of such Members;

4.5 that Members will calculate the quota levels for the remaining years of the Agreement with respect to other restrained Members as if implementation of the growth-on-growth provision for stage 3 had been advanced to 1 January 2000;

and make recommendations to the General Council by 31 July 2002 for appropriate action.

5. Agreement on Technical Barriers to Trade

5.1 Confirms the approach to technical assistance being developed by the Committee on Technical Barriers to Trade, reflecting the results of the triennial review work in this area, and mandates this work to continue.

5.2 Subject to the conditions specified in paragraph 12 of Article 2 of the Agreement on Technical Barriers to Trade, the phrase "reasonable interval" shall be understood to mean normally a period of not less than 6 months, except when this would be ineffective in fulfilling the legitimate objectives pursued.

5.3 (i) Takes note of the actions taken to date by the Director-General to facilitate the increased participation of Members at different levels of development in the work of the relevant international standard setting organizations as well as his efforts to coordinate with these organizations and financial institutions in identifying TBT-related technical assistance needs and how best to address them; and

(ii) urges the Director-General to continue his cooperative efforts with these organizations and institutions, including with a view to according priority to the effective participation of least-developed countries and facilitating the provision of technical and financial assistance for this purpose.

5.4 (i) Urges Members to provide, to the extent possible, the financial and technical assistance necessary to enable least-developed countries to respond adequately to the introduction of any new TBT measures which may have significant negative effects on their trade; and

(ii) urges Members to ensure that technical assistance is provided to least-developed countries with a view to responding to the special problems faced by them in implementing the Agreement on Technical Barriers to Trade.

6. Agreement on Trade-Related Investment Measures

6.1 Takes note of the actions taken by the Council for Trade in Goods in regard to requests from some developing-country Members for the extension of the five-year transitional period provided for in Article 5.2 of Agreement on Trade-Related Investment Measures.

6.2 Urges the Council for Trade in Goods to consider positively requests that may be made by least-developed countries under Article 5.3 of the TRIMs Agreement or Article IX.3 of the WTO Agreement, as well as to take into consideration the particular circumstances of least-developed countries when setting the terms and conditions including time-frames.

7. Agreement on the Implementation of Article VI of the General Agreement on Tariffs and Trade 1994

7.1 Agrees that investigating authorities shall examine with special care any application for the initiation of an anti-dumping investigation where an investigation of the same product from the same Member resulted in a negative finding within the 365 days prior to the filing of the application and that, unless this pre-initiation examination indicates that circumstances have changed, the investigation shall not proceed.

7.2 Recognizes that, while Article 15 of the Agreement on the Implementation of Article VI of the General Agreement on Tariffs and Trade 1994 is a mandatory provision, the modalities for its application would benefit from clarification. Accordingly, the Committee on Anti-Dumping Practices is instructed, through its working group on Implementation, to examine this issue and to draw up appropriate recommendations within twelve months on how to operationalize this provision.

7.3 Takes note that Article 5.8 of the Agreement on the Implementation of Article VI of the General Agreement on Tariffs and Trade 1994 does not specify the time-frame to be used in determining the volume of dumped imports, and that this lack of specificity creates uncertainties in the implementation of the provision. The Committee on Anti-Dumping Practices is instructed, through its working group on Implementation, to study this issue and draw up recommendations within 12 months, with a view to ensuring the maximum possible predictability and objectivity in the application of time frames.

7.4 Takes note that Article 18.6 of the Agreement on the Implementation of Article VI of the General Agreement on Tariffs and Trade 1994 requires the Committee on Anti-Dumping Practices to review annually the implementation and operation of the Agreement taking into account the objectives thereof. The Committee on Anti-dumping Practices is instructed to draw up guidelines for the improvement of annual reviews and to report its views and recommendations to the General Council for subsequent decision within 12 months.

8. Agreement on the Implementation of Article VII of the General Agreement on Tariffs and Trade 1994

8.1 Takes note of the actions taken by the Committee on Customs Valuation in regard to the requests from a number of developing-country Members for the extension of the five-year transitional period provided for in Article 20.1 of Agreement on the Implementation of Article VII of the General Agreement on Tariffs and Trade 1994.

8.2 Urges the Council for Trade in Goods to give positive consideration to requests that may be made by least-developed country Members under paragraphs 1 and 2 of Annex III of the Customs Valuation Agreement or under Article IX.3 of the WTO Agreement, as well as to take into consideration the particular circumstances of least-developed countries when setting the terms and conditions including time-frames.

8.3 Underlines the importance of strengthening cooperation between the customs administrations of Members in the prevention of customs fraud. In this regard, it is agreed that, further to the 1994 Ministerial Decision Regarding Cases Where Customs Administrations Have Reasons to Doubt the Truth or Accuracy of the

WT/MIN(01)/17
Page 6

Declared Value, when the customs administration of an importing Member has reasonable grounds to doubt the truth or accuracy of the declared value, it may seek assistance from the customs administration of an exporting Member on the value of the good concerned. In such cases, the exporting Member shall offer cooperation and assistance, consistent with its domestic laws and procedures, including furnishing information on the export value of the good concerned. Any information provided in this context shall be treated in accordance with Article 10 of the Customs Valuation Agreement. Furthermore, recognizing the legitimate concerns expressed by the customs administrations of several importing Members on the accuracy of the declared value, the Committee on Customs Valuation is directed to identify and assess practical means to address such concerns, including the exchange of information on export values and to report to the General Council by the end of 2002 at the latest.

9. Agreement on Rules of Origin

9.1 Takes note of the report of the Committee on Rules of Origin (G/RO/48) regarding progress on the harmonization work programme, and urges the Committee to complete its work by the end of 2001.

9.2 Agrees that any interim arrangements on rules of origin implemented by Members in the transitional period before the entry into force of the results of the harmonisation work programme shall be consistent with the Agreement on Rules of Origin, particularly Articles 2 and 5 thereof. Without prejudice to Members' rights and obligations, such arrangements may be examined by the Committee on Rules of Origin.

10. Agreement on Subsidies and Countervailing Measures

10.1 Agrees that Annex VII(b) to the Agreement on Subsidies and Countervailing Measures includes the Members that are listed therein until their GNP per capita reaches US $1,000 in constant 1990 dollars for three consecutive years. This decision will enter into effect upon the adoption by the Committee on Subsidies and Countervailing Measures of an appropriate methodology for calculating constant 1990 dollars. If, however, the Committee on Subsidies and Countervailing Measures does not reach a consensus agreement on an appropriate methodology by 1 January 2003, the methodology proposed by the Chairman of the Committee set forth in G/SCM/38, Appendix 2 shall be applied. A Member shall not leave Annex VII(b) so long as its GNP per capita in current dollars has not reached US $1000 based upon the most recent data from the World Bank.

10.2 Takes note of the proposal to treat measures implemented by developing countries with a view to achieving legitimate development goals, such as regional growth, technology research and development funding, production diversification and development and implementation of environmentally sound methods of production as non-actionable subsidies, and agrees that this issue be addressed in accordance with paragraph 13 below. During the course of the negotiations, Members are urged to exercise due restraint with respect to challenging such measures.

10.3 Agrees that the Committee on Subsidies and Countervailing Measures shall continue its review of the provisions of the Agreement on Subsidies and Countervailing

Measures regarding countervailing duty investigations and report to the General Council by 31 July 2002.

10.4 Agrees that if a Member has been excluded from the list in paragraph (b) of Annex VII to the Agreement on Subsidies and Countervailing Measures, it shall be re-included in it when its GNP per capita falls back below US$ 1,000.

10.5 Subject to the provisions of Articles 27.5 and 27.6, it is reaffirmed that least-developed country Members are exempt from the prohibition on export subsidies set forth in Article 3.1(a) of the Agreement on Subsidies and Countervailing Measures, and thus have flexibility to finance their exporters, consistent with their development needs. It is understood that the eight-year period in Article 27.5 within which a least-developed country Member must phase out its export subsidies in respect of a product in which it is export-competitive begins from the date export competitiveness exists within the meaning of Article 27.6.

10.6 Having regard to the particular situation of certain developing-country Members, directs the Committee on Subsidies and Countervailing Measures to extend the transition period, under the rubric of Article 27.4 of the Agreement on Subsidies and Countervailing Measures, for certain export subsidies provided by such Members, pursuant to the procedures set forth in document G/SCM/39. Furthermore, when considering a request for an extension of the transition period under the rubric of Article 27.4 of the Agreement on Subsidies and Countervailing Measures, and in order to avoid that Members at similar stages of development and having a similar order of magnitude of share in world trade are treated differently in terms of receiving such extensions for the same eligible programmes and the length of such extensions, directs the Committee to extend the transition period for those developing countries, after taking into account the relative competitiveness in relation to other developing-country Members who have requested extension of the transition period following the procedures set forth in document G/SCM/39.

11. Agreement on Trade-Related Aspects of Intellectual Property Rights (TRIPS)

11.1 The TRIPS Council is directed to continue its examination of the scope and modalities for complaints of the types provided for under subparagraphs 1(b) and 1(c) of Article XXIII of GATT 1994 and make recommendations to the Fifth Session of the Ministerial Conference. It is agreed that, in the meantime, Members will not initiate such complaints under the TRIPS Agreement.

11.2 Reaffirming that the provisions of Article 66.2 of the TRIPS Agreement are mandatory, it is agreed that the TRIPS Council shall put in place a mechanism for ensuring the monitoring and full implementation of the obligations in question. To this end, developed-country Members shall submit prior to the end of 2002 detailed reports on the functioning in practice of the incentives provided to their enterprises for the transfer of technology in pursuance of their commitments under Article 66.2. These submissions shall be subject to a review in the TRIPS Council and information shall be updated by Members annually.

WT/MIN(01)/17
Page 8

12. Cross-cutting Issues

12.1 The Committee on Trade and Development is instructed:

(i) to identify those special and differential treatment provisions that are already mandatory in nature and those that are non-binding in character, to consider the legal and practical implications for developed and developing Members of converting special and differential treatment measures into mandatory provisions, to identify those that Members consider should be made mandatory, and to report to the General Council with clear recommendations for a decision by July 2002;

(ii) to examine additional ways in which special and differential treatment provisions can be made more effective, to consider ways, including improved information flows, in which developing countries, in particular the least-developed countries, may be assisted to make best use of special and differential treatment provisions, and to report to the General Council with clear recommendations for a decision by July 2002; and

(iii) to consider, in the context of the work programme adopted at the Fourth Session of the Ministerial Conference, how special and differential treatment may be incorporated into the architecture of WTO rules.

The work of the Committee on Trade and Development in this regard shall take fully into consideration previous work undertaken as noted in WT/COMTD/W/77/Rev.1. It will also be without prejudice to work in respect of implementation of WTO Agreements in the General Council and in other Councils and Committees.

12.2 Reaffirms that preferences granted to developing countries pursuant to the Decision of the Contracting Parties of 28 November 1979 ("Enabling Clause")[1] should be generalised, non-reciprocal and non-discriminatory.

13. Outstanding Implementation Issues[2]

Agrees that outstanding implementation issues be addressed in accordance with paragraph 12 of the Ministerial Declaration (WT/MIN(01)/DEC/1).

14. Final Provisions

Requests the Director-General, consistent with paragraphs 38 to 43 of the Ministerial Declaration (WT/MIN(01)/DEC/1), to ensure that WTO technical assistance focuses, on a priority basis, on assisting developing countries to implement existing WTO obligations as well as on increasing their capacity to participate more effectively in future multilateral trade negotiations. In carrying out this mandate, the WTO Secretariat should cooperate more closely with international and regional intergovernmental organisations so as to increase efficiency and synergies and avoid duplication of programmes.

---

[1] BISD 26S/203.

[2] A list of these issues is compiled in document Job(01)/152/Rev.1.

Appendix 7
Compiliation of Outstanding Implementation Issues Raised by Members
JOB(01)/152/Rev.1, (27 October 2001)

JOB(01)/152/Rev.1 27 October 2001

Compilation of Outstanding Implementation Issues Raised by Members

Revision

This compilation is being circulated by the Secretariat with a view to assisting delegations in their consideration of the outstanding implementation issues. It should be read together with the draft Decision on Implementation-Related Issues and Concerns (Job(01)/139/Rev.1). It lists outstanding implementation issues raised in the draft Ministerial Text of 19 October 1999 (Job(99)/5868/Rev.1) and those subsequently raised by Members during consultations. For ease of reference, the text retains the numbering of the tirets used by the G-7 countries in their paper on implementation.

---

1. <u>General Agreement on Tariffs and Trade 1994</u>

- Tiret 1
  Only the Committee on Balance-of-Payments shall have the authority to examine the overall justification of BOP measures.

- Tiret 3
  A complete review of Article XVIII shall be undertaken with a view to ensure that it subserves the original objective of facilitating the progressive development of economies in developing countries and to allow them to implement programmes and policies of economic development designed to raise the general standard of living of their people.

2. <u>Agreement on Agriculture</u>

- Tiret 6
  If in the calculation of the AMS, domestic support prices are lower than the external reference price (so as to ensure access of poor households to basic foodstuffs), thereby resulting in negative product specific support, then Members shall be allowed to increase their non-product specific support by an equivalent amount.

3. <u>Agreement on the Application of Sanitary and Phytosanitary Measures</u>

   Proposal by Brazil, 17 October 2001

- Where the introduction of SPS measures may have significant effect on trade opportunities for products of interest to developing countries, Members shall notify the WTO and inform the concerned Member prior to the application of such measures and, in addition, to the relevant provisions of paragraph 5 of Annex B and Article 7, shall notify final rules or subsequent decisions derived from a previously notified measure.

4. <u>Agreement on Technical Barriers to Trade</u>

- Tiret 33
  Article 11 shall be made obligatory so that technical assistance and cooperation is provided to developing countries.

JOB(01)/152/Rev.1
Page 2

- Tiret 34
  Acceptance by developed-country importers of self-declaration regarding adherence to standards by developing-country exporters. This provision should be introduced in Article 12.

5. Agreement on Trade-Related Investment Measures

- Tiret 37
  Developing countries shall have another opportunity to notify existing TRIMs measures which they would be then allowed to maintain till the end of the new transition period.

- Tiret 38
  The provisions of Article 5.3 must be suitably amended and made mandatory.

- Tiret 39
  Developing countries shall be exempted from the disciplines on the application of domestic content requirement by providing for an enabling provision in Articles 2 and 4 to this effect.

- Tiret 40
  Specific provisions shall be included in the Agreement to provide developing countries the necessary flexibility to implement development policies (intended to address, among others, social, regional, economic, and technological concerns) that may help reduce the disparities they face *vis-à-vis* developed countries.

6. Agreement on Implementation of Article VI of the GATT 1994

- Tiret 42
  Under Article 9.1 the lesser duty rule shall be made mandatory.

- Tiret 43
  Article 2.2 shall be clarified in order to make appropriate comparison with respect to the margin of dumping.

- Tiret 44
  Provisions of the Agreement shall be improved with a view to prevent the imposition of arbitrary or primarily protectionist measures. The provisions to be revisited should include, *inter alia*, (i) the criteria, methodology, and procedures of the reviews specified in the Agreement (expeditious review for new exporters, final review, reviews upon request), (ii) the definition of the product motivating the investigation, (iii) the determination of the margin of dumping, (iv) the imposition and collection of duties, (v) the "cumulation" clauses.

- Tiret 46
  The existing de minimis dumping margin of 2 per cent of export price below which no anti-dumping duty can be imposed (Article 5.8), needs to be raised to 5 per cent for developing countries.

- Tiret 47
  The proposed de minimis dumping margin of 5 per cent is applied not only in new cases but also in refund and review cases.

- Tiret 48
  The threshold volume of dumped imports which shall normally be regarded as negligible (Article 5.8) should be increased from the existing 3 per cent to [5 per cent] [7 per cent] for imports from developing countries.

- Tiret 50
  The substantial quantities test should be increased from the present threshold of 20 per cent to at least 40 per cent.

- Tiret 51
  Article 2.4.1 shall include details of dealing with foreign exchange rate fluctuations during the process of dumping.

- Tiret 52
  Article 3 shall contain a detailed provision dealing with the determination of the material retardation of the establishment of a domestic industry as stipulated in footnote 9.

- Tiret 53
  There should be a provision in the Agreement, which provides a presumption of dumping of imports from developed countries into developing countries, provided certain conditions are met.

- Tiret 54
  Article 17 should be suitably modified so that the general standard of review laid down in the WTO dispute settlement mechanism applies equally and totally to disputes in the anti-dumping area.

Proposals by Least-Developed Countries, 22 October 2001

- The General Council agrees that simplified procedures for taking anti-dumping action shall be devised for the use of LDCs.

- The General Council agrees that the threshold for volume of imports referred to in Article 5.8 of the Agreement shall be increased from 3 percent to 7 percent in the case of LDCs. LDCs shall be exempted from cumulation.

7. <u>Agreement on Implementation of Article VII of GATT 1994</u>

- Tiret 57
  The addition of cost of services such as engineering, development, and design work, which are supplied directly or indirectly by the buyer free of charge or at reduced cost for the production of goods under import, shall be included in Article 8:1(b)(iv).

- Tiret 58
  The residual method of determining customs value under Article 7 shall be inclusive of all residual eventualities, thus allowing valuation based on domestic market price or export price in a third country with appropriate adjustments.

- Tiret 59
  The Agreement should be amended to provide for the highest value when more than one transaction value of identical or similar goods is found.

- Tiret 60
  Buying commissions should be taken into account in the determination of customs value of imported goods as it forms a legitimate component of the landed cost of imported goods.

- Tiret 61
  Persons associated with each other as sole agents, sole distributors, and sole concessionaires, howsoever described, should automatically be deemed "related".

8. Agreement on Subsidies and Countervailing Measures

- Tiret 64
  Article 8:1 of the Subsidies Agreement dealing with non-actionable subsidies shall be expanded to include subsidies referred to in Article 3:1 of the Agreement when such subsidies are provided by developing country Members.

- Tiret 65
  Export credits given by developing countries shall not be considered as subsidies so long as the rates at which they are extended are above LIBOR.

- Tiret 66
  Any countervailing duties shall be restricted only to that amount by which the subsidy exceeds the de minimis level.

- Tiret 67
  Annex VII of the Agreement shall be modified to read as follows:
  The developing-country Members not subject to the provisions of paragraph 1(a) of Article 3 under the terms of paragraph 2(a) of Article 27 are:
  (i) The developing countries, including the least-developed countries, Members of the WTO that are included in the Low and Middle Income Category of the World Bank;
  (ii) Countries indicated in paragraph (i) above will be excluded from this Annex if their GNP per capita has exceeded the top level of the Middle Income Category of the World Bank. They will be automatically included in this Annex, if their GNP per capita falls at or under the top level of the Lower-Middle Income Category of the World Bank.

- Tiret 68
  The prohibition on using export subsidies under Article 27:6 shall be applicable to a developing country only after its export levels in a product have remained over 3.25 per cent of world trade continuously for a period of five years.

- Tiret 70
  Article 27.2 shall be amended so that the Article 3.1(a) prohibition does not apply to export subsidies granted by developing countries where they account for less than **5 per cent of the f.o.b. value of the product.**

- Tiret 71
  Countervailing measures shall not be imposed in the case of imports from developing countries where the total volume of imports is negligible, i.e. 7 per cent of total imports.

JOB(01)/152/Rev.1
Page 5

- Tiret 72
  Aggregate and generalized rates of duty rate remission should be allowed in case of developing countries even though the individual units may not be able to establish the source of their inputs.

- Tiret 73
  Developing countries should be allowed to neutralize the cost escalating effect of taxes.

- Tiret 74
  Article 11:9 should be modified to provide an additional dispensation for developing countries, in as much as that any subsidy investigation shall be immediately terminated in cases where the subsidy being provided by a developing country is less than 2.5 per cent *ad valorem*, instead of the existing de minimis of 1 per cent presently applicable to all Members.

- Tiret 75
  The present de minimis level of 3 per cent below which countervailing duties may not be imposed for developing countries, needs to be increased (Article 27:11).

- Tiret 76
  There should be a clarification in Article 27:3 that it is applicable notwithstanding the provisions of any other agreement.

- Tiret 77
  The definition of "inputs consumed in the production process" (footnote 61) needs to be expanded to include all inputs, not just physical inputs, which may have contributed to the determination of the final cost price of the exported product.

- Tiret 78
  Annex I of the Agreement shall be amended to provide developing countries the flexibility to finance their exporters, consistent with their developmental objectives.

- Tiret 79
  The provisions of Article 27 shall be re-evaluated so as to address, under a permanent and more adequate framework, the needs and specificities of developing countries concerning incentives and subsidies.

- Tiret 81
  The language of Annex I of the Agreement, particularly item 'k', shall be reviewed to permit developing countries to provide competitive export financing *vis-à-vis* the conditions found in the international market or those offered by the credit agencies of developed countries (controlled by and or acting under the authorities of the governments).

- Tiret 83
  The SCM Committee shall review the threshold of US$ 1000 in Annex VII (b) and examine the possibility of including in Annex VII, Members in the low and lower-middle income categories as classified by the World Bank. The SCM Committee shall examine additional possibilities for granting flexibility to developing countries such as threshold limits relating to percentage share of exports in import markets and in global trade.

JOB(01)/152/Rev.1
Page 6

Proposals by Least-Developed Countries, 22 October 2001

- The General Council agrees that subsidies required for development, diversification and upgrading infant industries including freight rebate schemes in developing countries shall be treated as non-actionable subsidy.

- The General Council agrees that LDCs shall be exempted from competitiveness thresholds of subsidies and the threshold for imports referred to Article 27.10 of the Agreement shall be increased from 4 per cent to 10 per cent in case of LDCs. LDCs shall be exempted from cumulation.

- The General Council agrees that financial resources shall be provided to LDCs to enable them to meet their special needs, in particular with respect to subsidies covered by Article 8.2 (c) (green subsidies).

9. Agreement on Safeguards

- Tiret 84
  Article 9.1 shall be amended so that safeguard measures are not applied to imports from developing countries which individually account for less than 7 per cent of total imports and 15 per cent collectively.

10. Agreement on Trade-Related Aspects of Intellectual Property Rights

- Tiret 87
  In the light of provisions contained in Articles 23 and 24 of the TRIPS Agreement, additional protection for geographical indications shall be extended for products other than wines and spirits.

- Tiret 88
  A clear understanding in the interim that patents inconsistent with Article 15 of the CBD shall not be granted.

- Tiret 91
  The period given for implementation of the provisions of Article 27.3(b) shall be five years from the date the review is completed.

- Tiret 93
  The transitional period for developing countries provided for in Article 65.2 shall be extended.

  Proposal by Least-Developed Countries, 22 October 2001

- The General Council agrees that the transition period for LDCs shall be extended so long as they retain the status of an LDC.

- Tiret 94
  Articles 7 and 8 of the TRIPS Agreement to be operationalized by providing for transfer of technology on fair and mutually advantageous terms.

- Tiret 95
  [Article 27.3(b) to be amended in light of the provisions of the Convention on Biological Diversity and the International Undertaking. Also, clarify artificial distinctions between biological and microbiological organisms and process; ensure the continuation of the traditional farming practices including the right to save,

exchange and save seeds, and sell their harvest; and prevent anti-competitive practices which will threaten food sovereignty of people in developing countries, as permitted by Article 31 of the TRIPS Agreement.] [Article 27.3(b) should be amended to take into account the Convention on Biological Diversity and the International Undertaking on Plant Genetic Resources. The amendments should clarify and satisfactorily resolve the analytical distinctions between biological and microbiological organisms and processed; that all living organisms and their parts cannot be patented; and those natural processes that produce living organisms should not be patentable. The amendments should ensure the protection of innovations of indigenous and local farming communities; the continuation of traditional farming processes including the right to use, exchange and save seeds, and promote food security.]

Proposal by Least-Developed Countries, 22 October 2001

- The General Council agrees that the review process should clarify that all living organisms, including plants, animals and parts of plants and animals, including gene sequences, and biological and other natural processes for the production of plants, animals and their parts, shall not be granted patents.

11. Cross-cutting issues

- Tiret 98
  Having regard to the significant role played by preferential trading agreements between developing and developed countries, Members agree to consider favourably, as appropriate, the granting or extension of waivers to Article I of GATT 1994 covering such agreements.

- Tiret 99
  The General Council shall adopt measures designed to secure a redistribution of negotiating rights in favour of small and medium-sized exporting Members in trade negotiations.

Appendix 8
Proposed Procedures for Extensions Under Article 27.4 for Certain Developing Country Members
G/SCM/39
(20 November 2001)

WORLD TRADE ORGANIZATION

G/SCM/39
20 November 2001

(01-5767)

Committee on Subsidies and Countervailing Measures

PROCEDURES FOR EXTENSIONS UNDER ARTICLE 27.4 FOR CERTAIN DEVELOPING COUNTRY MEMBERS

The Committee on Subsidies and Countervailing Measures ("SCM Committee") shall follow the procedures set forth below in respect of extensions of the transition period under Article 27.4 of the Agreement on Subsidies and Countervailing Measures ("SCM Agreement") for certain developing country Members. The programmes to which these procedures shall apply are those meeting the criteria set forth in 2.

1. Mechanism for extension

(a) A Member that maintains programmes meeting the criteria set forth in 2 and that wishes to make use of these procedures, shall initiate Article 27.4 consultations with the Committee in respect of an extension for its eligible subsidy programmes as referred to in 2, on the basis of documentation to be submitted to the Committee not later than 31 December 2001. This documentation shall consist of (i) an identification by the Member of those programmes for which it is seeking an extension under SCM Article 27.4 pursuant to these procedures; and (ii) a statement that the extension is necessary in the light of the Member's economic, financial and development needs.

(b) Not later than 28 February 2002, the Member seeking an extension shall submit to the SCM Committee an initial notification as referred to in 3(a) providing detailed information about the programmes for which extension is being sought.

(c) Following receipt of the notifications referred to in 1(b), the SCM Committee shall consider those notifications, with an opportunity for Members to seek clarification of the notified information and/or additional detail with a view to understanding the nature and operation of the notified programmes, and their scope, coverage and intensity of benefits, as referred to in 3(b). The purpose of this consideration by the SCM Committee shall be to verify that the programmes are of the type eligible under these procedures as referred to in 2, and that the transparency requirement referred to in 3(a) and 3(b) is fulfilled. Not later than 15 December 2002, Members of the SCM Committee shall grant extensions for calendar year 2003 for those programmes notified pursuant to these procedures, provided that the notified programmes meet the eligibility criteria in 2 and that the transparency requirement is fulfilled. The notified information on the basis of which the extensions are granted, including information provided in response to requests from Members as referred to above, shall form the frame of reference for the annual reviews of the extensions as referred to in 1(d) and 1(e).

(d) As provided for in SCM Article 27.4, the extensions granted by the SCM Committee pursuant to these procedures shall be subject to annual review in the form of consultations between the Committee and the Members receiving the extensions. These annual reviews shall be conducted on the basis of updating notifications from the Members in question, as referred to in 3(a) and 3(b). The purpose of the annual

G/SCM/39
Page 2

reviews shall be to ensure that the transparency and standstill requirements as set forth in 3 and 4 are being fulfilled.

(e) Through the end of calendar year 2007, subject to annual reviews during that period to verify that the transparency and standstill requirements set forth in 3 and 4 are being fulfilled, Members of the Committee shall agree to continue the extensions granted pursuant to 1(c).

(f) During the last year of the period referred to in 1(e), a Member that has received an extension under these procedures shall have the possibility to seek a continuation of the extension pursuant to SCM Article 27.4, for the programmes in question. The Committee shall consider any such requests at that year's annual review, on the basis of the provisions of SCM Article 27.4, i.e., outside the framework of these procedures.

(g) If a continuation of the extension pursuant to 1(f) is either not requested or not granted, the Member in question shall have the final two years referred to in the last sentence of SCM Article 27.4.

2. Eligible programmes

Programmes eligible for extension pursuant to these procedures, and for which Members shall therefore grant extensions for calendar year 2003 as referred to in 1(c), are export subsidy programmes (i) in the form of full or partial exemptions from import duties and internal taxes, (ii) which were in existence not later than 1 September 2001, and (iii) which are provided by developing country Members (iv) whose share of world merchandise export trade was not greater than 0.10 per cent[1], (v) whose total Gross National Income ("GNI") for the year 2000 as published by the World Bank was at or below US $ 20 billion,[2] (vi) and who are otherwise eligible to request an extension pursuant to Article 27.4,[3] and (vii) in respect of which these procedures are followed.

3. Transparency

(a) The initial notification referred to in 1(b), and the updating notifications referred to in 1(d), shall follow the agreed format for subsidy notifications under SCM Article 25 (found in G/SCM/6).

(b) During the SCM Committee's consideration/review of the notifications referred to in 1(c) and 1(d), notifying Members can be requested by other Members to provide additional detail and clarification, with a view to confirming that the programmes meet the criteria set forth in 2, and to establishing transparency in respect of the scope, coverage and intensity of benefits (the "favourability") of the programmes in question.[4] Any information provided in response to such requests shall be considered part of the notified information.

---

[1] According to the calculations performed by the WTO Secretariat as reflected in Appendix 3 to the Report of the Chairman (G/SCM/38).

[2] The SCM Committee shall consider other appropriate data sources in respect of Members for whom the World Bank does not publish total GNI data.

[3] The fact that a Member is listed in Annex VII(b) shall not be deemed to make that Member otherwise ineligible to request an extension pursuant to Article 27.4.

[4] The scope, coverage and intensity of the programmes in question will be determined on the basis of the legal instruments underlying the programmes.

4. Standstill

(a) The programmes for which an extension is granted shall not be modified during the period of extension referred to in 1(e) so as to make them more favourable than they were as at 1 September 2001. The continuation of an expiring programme without modification shall not be deemed to violate standstill.

(b) The scope, coverage and intensity of benefits (the "favourability") of the programmes as at 1 September 2001 shall be specified in the initial notification referred to in 1(b), and standstill as referred to in 4(a) shall be verified on the basis of the notified information referred to in 1(d) and 3(b).

5. Product graduation on the basis of export competitiveness

Notwithstanding these procedures, Articles 27.5 and 27.6 shall apply in respect of export subsidies for which extensions are granted pursuant to these procedures.

6. Members listed in Annex VII(b)

(a) A Member listed in Annex VII(b) whose GNP per capita has reached the level provided for in that Annex and whose programme(s) meet the criteria in 2 shall be eligible to make use of these procedures.

(b) A Member listed in Annex VII(b) whose GNP per capita has not reached the level provided for in that Annex and whose programme(s) meet the criteria in 2 may reserve its right to make use of these procedures, as referred to in 6(c), by submitting the documentation referred to in 1(a) not later than 31 December 2001.

(c) If the per capita GNP of a Member referred to in 6(b) reaches the level provided for in that Annex during the period referred to in 1(e), that Member shall be able to make use of these procedures as from the date at which its per capita GNP reaches that level and for the remainder of the period referred to in 1(e), as well as for any additional periods as referred to in 1(f) and 1(g), subject to the remaining provisions of these procedures.

(d) For a Member referred to in 6(b), the effective date for the standstill requirement referred to in 4(a) shall be the year in which that Member's GNP per capita reaches the level provided for in Annex VII(b).

7. Final provisions

(a) The decision by Ministers, these procedures, and the SCM Article 27.4 extensions granted thereunder, are without prejudice to any requests for extensions under Article 27.4 that are not made pursuant to these procedures.

(b) The decision by Ministers, these procedures, and the SCM Article 27.4 extensions granted thereunder, shall not affect any other existing rights and obligations under SCM Article 27.4 or under other provisions of the SCM Agreement.

(c) The criteria set forth in these procedures are solely and strictly for the purpose of determining whether Members are eligible to invoke these procedures. Members of the Committee agree that these criteria have no precedential value or relevance, direct or indirect, for any other purpose.

Appendix 9
Committee on Agriculture
Implementation Related Issues,
Report to the General Council by the Vice-Chairman
G/AG/11
(28 September 2001)

WORLD TRADE ORGANIZATION

G/AG/11
28 September 2001

(01-0000)

Committee on Agriculture

COMMITTEE ON AGRICULTURE (REGULAR MEETINGS)
IMPLEMENTATION-RELATED ISSUES

Report to the General Council by the Vice-Chairman

The present report on the outcome of the Committee's consideration of the three implementation-related issues which were referred to the Committee by the General Council is submitted on the responsibility of the Vice-Chairman, Minister Yoichi Suzuki, as agreed by the Committee at its meeting on 27 September 2001.

A. ARTICLE 10.2 OF THE AGREEMENT ON AGRICULTURE: THE DEVELOPMENT OF INTERNATIONALLY AGREED DISCIPLINES TO GOVERN THE PROVISION OF EXPORT CREDITS, EXPORT CREDIT GUARANTEES OR INSURANCE PROGRAMMES, TAKING ACCOUNT OF PARAGRAPH 4 OF THE MARRAKESH NFIDC DECISION

1. The question of the implementation of Article 10.2 of the Agreement on Agriculture was referred to the Committee on Agriculture by the Special Session of the General on 18 October 2000, it being understood that in pursuing their work on export credits, export credit guarantees or insurance programmes account would be taken of the provisions of paragraph 4 of the Marrakesh NFIDC Decision. This subject was taken up at the at the regular meetings of the Committee on Agriculture held in November 2000, March, June and September 2001, with progress reports being made to the General Council in documents G/AG/6, G/AG/8 and G/AG/9 and Corr.1).

2. As part of the overall results of the Uruguay Round negotiations WTO Members undertook, in terms of Article 10.2 of the Agreement on Agriculture, to work towards the development of internationally agreed disciplines to govern the provision of export credits, export credit guarantees or insurance programmes and, after agreement on such disciplines, to provide export credits, export credit guarantees or insurance programmes only in conformity therewith. In terms of paragraph 4 of the Marrakesh NFIDC Decision Ministers agreed to ensure that any agreement relating to agricultural export credits makes appropriate provision for differential treatment in favour of least-developed and net food-importing developing countries.

3. Negotiations on a proposed Sector Understanding on Export Credits for Agricultural Products amongst WTO Members which are participants to the OECD Export Credit Arrangement have been ongoing for a number of years. Members involved in these negotiations have informed the Committee that this work has reached an advanced stage, in the form of a proposed text which is acceptable to most but not all of the participants concerned, and which makes provision for differential treatment in favour of least-developed and net food-importing developing countries. At the same time work within the WTO on the question of agricultural export credits has been progressing in both the regular meetings of the Committee on Agriculture and in the Special Session Negotiations under Article 20 of the Agreement on Agriculture on the basis, *inter alia*, of the proposals that have been tabled and other inputs, including with respect to special and differential treatment in favour of developing countries.

G/AG/11
Page 2

4. In the light of their discussions and informal consultations on this matter Members are agreed and recommend that work in the regular meetings of the WTO Committee on Agriculture on the development of disciplines pursuant to Article 10.2 and the related provisions of the Marrakesh NFIDC Decision should continue in line with the following general understandings:

(a) that the focus of the work in the regular Committee meetings would be on the implementation of Article 10.2 and the disciplines foreseen therein, whereas the Special Session negotiations would focus on the proposals tabled or to be tabled on export credit practices;

(b) that, without prejudice to further work to be undertaken in the regular meetings of the Committee as provided for in subparagraph (i) above, in the event that a Sector Understanding on agricultural export credits is concluded at the OECD, the Committee would, as envisaged in the report of the Committee on Agriculture to the Singapore WTO Ministerial (G/L/131, paragraph 11), consider how any such understanding could be multilateralized within the framework of the Agreement on Agriculture and how the provisions of paragraph 4 of the Marrakesh NFIDC Decision have been taken into account; and

(c) that the Committee on Agriculture should submit a report to the General Council on this subject following its regular September 2002 meeting.

B. EXAMINATION OF POSSIBLE MEANS OF IMPROVING THE EFFECTIVENESS OF THE IMPLEMENTATION OF THE DECISION ON MEASURES CONCERNING THE POSSIBLE NEGATIVE EFFECTS OF THE REFORM PROGRAMME ON LEAST-DEVELOPED AND NET-FOOD-IMPORTING DEVELOPING COUNTRIES

1. At its meeting on 15 December 2000 (WT/L/384, paragraph 1.2, refers), the Special Session of the General Council instructed the Committee on Agriculture to examine possible means of improving the effectiveness of the implementation of the Decision on Measures Concerning the Possible Negative Effects of the Reform Programme on Least-Developed and Net-Food-Importing Developing Countries (a copy of the Decision is attached as Annex A). This examination was undertaken in the regular meetings of the Committee on Agriculture as well as through informal consultations. These consultations included an informal roundtable to examine detailed proposals by the net food-importing developing countries for the establishment of a revolving fund, as well as other measures for improving the effectiveness of the implementation of the Marrakesh NFIDC Decision (G/AG/W/49 and Add.1 and Corr.1 refer). Specialist representatives of the IMF, the World Bank and the FAO participated in this Roundtable.

2. Progress reports were made to the General Council on the Committee's work in this regard at its regular meetings in March and June this year in documents G/AG/7 and G/AG/10 respectively. Copies of these progress reports, which include the detailed proposals referred to above as well as the comments of the IMF and the World Bank on access to their facilities and on the proposed revolving fund, are attached hereto as Annexes B and C. A summary of the Committee's discussion on this subject at its meeting on 27 September will be included in the Secretariat report (G/AG/R/28) on that meeting.

3. In the light of the discussions and informal consultations in connection with the Committee's examination of possible means of improving the effectiveness of the implementation of the Marrakesh NFIDC Decision, the following recommendations are forwarded for approval by the General Council:

I. Food Aid (paragraph 3 (i) and (ii) of the Decision)

(a) that early action be taken within the framework of the Food Aid Convention 1999 (which unless extended, with or without a decision regarding its renegotiation, would expire on 30 June 2002) and of the UN World Food Programme by donors of food aid to review their food aid contributions with a view to better identifying and meeting the food aid needs of least-developed and WTO net food-importing developing countries;

(b) WTO Members which are donors of food aid shall, within the framework of their food aid policies, statutes, programmes and commitments, take appropriate measures aimed at ensuring: (i) that to the maximum extent possible their levels of food aid to developing countries are maintained during periods in which trends in world market prices of basic foodstuffs have been increasing; and (ii) that all food aid to least developed countries is provided in fully grant form and, to the maximum extent possible, to WTO net food-importing developing countries as well.

II. Technical and Financial Assistance in the Context of Aid Programmes to Improve Agricultural Productivity and Infrastructure (paragraph 3(iii) of the Decision)

(a) that developed country WTO Members should continue to give full and favourable consideration in the context of their aid programmes to requests for the provision of technical and financial assistance by least-developed and net food-importing developing countries to improve their agricultural productivity and infrastructure;

(b) that, in support of the priority accorded by least-developed and net food-importing developing countries to the development of their agricultural productivity and infrastructure, the WTO General Council call upon relevant international development organisations, including the World Bank, the FAO, IFAD, the UNDP and the Regional Development Banks to enhance their provision of, and access to, technical and financial assistance to least-developed and net food-importing developing countries, on terms and conditions conducive to the better use of such facilities and resources, in order to improve agricultural productivity and infrastructure in these countries under existing facilities and programmes, as well as under such facilities and programmes as may be introduced.

III. Financing Normal Levels of Commercial Imports of Basic Foodstuffs (paragraphs 4 and 5 of the Decision)

(a) that the provisions of paragraph 4 of the Marrakesh Ministerial Decision, which provide for differential treatment in favour of least-developed and WTO net food-importing developing countries, shall be taken fully into account in any agreement to be negotiated on disciplines on agricultural export credits pursuant to Article 10.2 of the Agreement on Agriculture;

(b) that an inter-agency panel of financial and commodity experts be established, with the requested participation of the World Bank, the IMF, the FAO, the International Grains Council and the UNCTAD, to explore ways and means for improving access by least-developed and WTO net food-importing developing countries to multilateral programs and facilities to assist with short term difficulties in financing normal levels of commercial imports of basic foodstuffs, as well as the concept and feasibility of the proposal for the establishment of a revolving fund in G/AG/W/49 and Add.1and Corr.1. The detailed terms of reference, drawing on the Marrakesh NFIDC Decision, should be submitted by the Vice-Chairman of the WTO Committee on Agriculture, following consultations with Members, to the General Council for approval by not later than 31 December 2001. The inter-agency panel shall submit its recommendations to the General Council by not later than 30 June 2002.

IV. Review of Follow-up

(a) that the Committee on Agriculture shall review and report to the General Council on the follow-up to these recommendations following its regular September 2002 meeting.

C. THE SUBMISSION BY MEMBERS ADMINISTERING TARIFF QUOTAS OF ADDENDA TO THEIR NOTIFICATIONS TO THE COMMITTEE ON AGRICULTURE (TABLE MA:1) IN ACCORDANCE WITH THE DECISION OF THE GENERAL COUNCIL IN WT/L/384 REGARDING THE ADMINISTRATION OF TARIFF RATE QUOTA REGIMES IN A TRANSPARENT, EQUITABLE AND NON-DISCRIMINATORY MANNER

1. Paragraph 1.1 of the General Council decision WT/L/384 provides that: "Members shall ensure that their tariff rate quotas regimes (TRQs) are administered in a transparent, equitable and non-discriminatory manner. In that context , they shall ensure that the notifications they provide to the Committee on Agriculture contain all the relevant information including details on guidelines and procedures on the allotment of TRQs. Members administering TRQs shall submit addenda to their notifications to the Committee on Agriculture (Table MA:1) by the time of the second regular meeting of the Committee in 2001." The understanding was that this decision should not place undue new burdens on developing countries (WT/GC/M/62, paragraph 14, refers).

2. So far the following Members administering tariff rate quotas have submitted the requisite Table MA:1 Addenda: Australia (G/AG/N/AUS/1/Add.1); Canada (G/AG/N/CAN/2/Add.2, 6/Add.1, 10/Add.1, 19/Add.1); European Communities (G/AG/N/EEC/1/Add.2, 3/Add.1, 14/Add.1, 15/Add.1); Japan (G/AG/N/JPN/1/Add.1, 8/Add.1, 23/Add.2, 57/Add.1); Latvia (G/AG/N/LVA/1/Add.1); New Zealand (G/AG/N/NZL/1/Add.1); Norway (G/AG/N/NOR/1/Add.1); and United States (G/AG/N/USA/2/Add.3 and 34/Add.1).

3. It is recommended that implementation of the General Council decision in paragraph 1.1 of WT/L/384 be kept under review by the Committee on Agriculture at its regular meetings.

* * * * *

As agreed by the Committee at its meeting on 27 September 2001 the General Council is accordingly invited to <u>approve</u> the recommendations in Sections A, B and C of this report.

ANNEX A

DECISION ON MEASURES CONCERNING THE POSSIBLE NEGATIVE EFFECTS OF THE REFORM PROGRAMME ON LEAST-DEVELOPED AND NET FOOD-IMPORTING DEVELOPING COUNTRIES

1. *Ministers recognize* that the progressive implementation of the results of the Uruguay Round as a whole will generate increasing opportunities for trade expansion and economic growth to the benefit of all participants.

2. *Ministers recognize* that during the reform programme leading to greater liberalization of trade in agriculture least-developed and net food-importing developing countries may experience negative effects in terms of the availability of adequate supplies of basic foodstuffs from external sources on reasonable terms and conditions, including short-term difficulties in financing normal levels of commercial imports of basic foodstuffs.

3. *Ministers* accordingly *agree* to establish appropriate mechanisms to ensure that the implementation of the results of the Uruguay Round on trade in agriculture does not adversely affect the availability of food aid at a level which is sufficient to continue to provide assistance in meeting the food needs of developing countries, especially least-developed and net food-importing developing countries. To this end *Ministers agree*:

(i) to review the level of food aid established periodically by the Committee on Food Aid under the Food Aid Convention 1986 and to initiate negotiations in the appropriate forum to establish a level of food aid commitments sufficient to meet the legitimate needs of developing countries during the reform programme;

(ii) to adopt guidelines to ensure that an increasing proportion of basic foodstuffs is provided to least-developed and net food-importing developing countries in fully grant form and/or on appropriate concessional terms in line with Article IV of the Food Aid Convention 1986;

(iii) to give full consideration in the context of their aid programmes to requests for the provision of technical and financial assistance to least-developed and net food-importing developing countries to improve their agricultural productivity and infrastructure.

4. *Ministers* further *agree* to ensure that any agreement relating to agricultural export credits makes appropriate provision for differential treatment in favour of least-developed and net food-importing developing countries.

5. *Ministers recognize* that as a result of the Uruguay Round certain developing countries may experience short-term difficulties in financing normal levels of commercial imports and that these countries may be eligible to draw on the resources of international financial institutions under existing facilities, or such facilities as may be established, in the context of adjustment programmes, in order to address such financing difficulties. In this regard Ministers take note of paragraph 37 of the report of the Director-General to the CONTRACTING PARTIES to GATT 1947 on his consultations with the Managing Director of the International Monetary Fund and the President of the World Bank (MTN.GNG/NG14/W/35).

6. The provisions of this Decision will be subject to regular review by the Ministerial Conference, and the follow-up to this Decision shall be monitored, as appropriate, by the Committee on Agriculture.

G/AG/11
Page 7

ANNEX B
(G/AG/7 dated 25 April 2001)

EXAMINATION OF POSSIBLE MEANS OF IMPROVING THE EFFECTIVENESS OF THE IMPLEMENTATION OF THE DECISION ON MEASURES CONCERNING THE POSSIBLE NEGATIVE EFFECTS OF THE REFORM PROGRAMME ON LEAST-DEVELOPED AND NET FOOD-IMPORTING DEVELOPING COUNTRIES

Report by the Vice-Chairman, Minister Yoichi Suzuki, to the General Council

5. At its meeting on 15 December 2000, the Special Session of the General Council referred to the relevant subsidiary bodies, including the Committee on Agriculture, a number of implementation related issues. The General Council decided, *inter alia*, that:

> "[t]he Committee on Agriculture shall examine possible means of improving the effectiveness of the implementation of the Decision on Measures Concerning the Possible Negative Effects of the Reform Programme on Least-Developed and Net Food-Importing Developing Countries and report to the General Council at the second regular meeting of the Council in 2001." (WT/L/384 refers).

6. In this context, a group of sixteen WTO net food-importing developing countries comprising Côte d'Ivoire, Cuba, Dominican Republic, Egypt, Honduras, Jamaica, Kenya, Mauritius, Morocco, Pakistan, Senegal, Sri Lanka, St. Lucia, Trinidad and Tobago, Tunisia and Venezuela has submitted to the Committee on Agriculture a "Proposal to Implement the Marrakesh Ministerial Decision in favour of LDCs and NFIDCs" (the text of the proposal is attached in Annex 2). The proposal was the subject of preliminary informal consultations as well as discussions at the regular meeting of the Committee on 30 March 2001. A detailed summary of the discussions at the regular Committee meeting is attached in Annex 1.

7. As part of the follow-up to these useful discussions, it has been agreed to take up in further informal meetings the issues of access to the financing facilities of the international financial institutions; food aid; and technical and financial assistance. These informal meetings will be held for the purpose of identifying specific problems regarding these issues. It has been indicated that the involvement of the relevant international organization would be appreciated and indeed necessary.

8. As agreed by the Committee on Agriculture at its meeting on 29-30 March 2001, this report is submitted to the General Council on my responsibility as Vice-Chairman of the Committee.

ANNEX 1

Examination of Possible Means of Improving the Effectiveness of the Implementation of the Decision on Measures Concerning the Possible Negative Effects of the Reform Programme on Least-Developed and Net Food-Importing Developing Countries Summary of the Discussion at the Meeting of the Committee on Agriculture on 30 March 2001

1. Pakistan introduced the "Proposal to Implement the Marrakesh Ministerial Decision in Favour of LDCs and NFIDCs" (attached in Annex 2) on behalf of sixteen WTO net food-importing developing countries. The main objective of the Agreement on Agriculture was to reduce through multilateral disciplines structural surpluses that were generated by production and trade-distorting policies in agriculture pursued by some Members. Such disciplines would normally result in increased food import bills for the LDCs and the net food-importers. Recognition that such price effects could create difficulties for the LDCs and the NFIDCs was reflected in the Marrakesh Ministerial Decision through response mechanisms in the areas of food aid, access to financing facilities, and technical and financial assistance to increase agricultural productivity. Having been concerned and disappointed with the lack of implementation of the Ministerial Decision, some Members had raised this issue under the rubric of Implementation Concerns under paragraph 9 of the Geneva Ministerial Declaration. Subsequently, this Committee had been instructed to examine the possible means of improving the effectiveness of the implementation of the Ministerial Decision under the specific directions of the General Council. The present proposal was aimed at helping the Committee to take the necessary positive steps to resolve this important implementation issue at an early date. The sponsors of the proposal were grateful to the Vice-Chairman for encouraging them to submit this concrete proposal on ways how the Ministerial Decision could be effectively implemented, which was a legal commitment of WTO Members under Article 16 of the Agreement. The sponsors were also encouraged by the manner in which the Vice-Chairman had conducted informal consultations on this issue and were confident that the deliberations in this Committee would result in concrete suggestions for adoption by the General Council, which should allay the genuine concerns of the NFIDCs and LDCs.

2. Pakistan continued that the proposal established, on the basis of factual data provided by FAO, the causality between policy reforms under the Uruguay Round and higher food import bills for the two groups of countries. It contained concrete suggestions to improve the effectiveness of the implementation of the Ministerial Decision in three areas referred to above. Furthermore, with the objective of ensuring that the commitments were binding and effectively monitored, the sponsors had proposed that:

(i) all major developed exporting countries should put aside supplies, under national food reserves, specifically earmarked to be released to the NFIDCs and LDCs under reasonable prices during years of high world prices;

(ii) developed countries and international development and financial institutions (World Bank, IMF, UNDP) should contribute to the financing of the two components of the Revolving Fund which, in turn, should be managed by an inter-agency arrangement with the full involvement of FAO;

(iii) the commitment of Members regarding volumes of food aid, volumes of physical reserves, contributions to the two components of the Revolving Fund would be inscribed in their country schedules as binding and legally enforceable;

(iv) Members should make regular annual notifications in respect of these commitments to the WTO Committee on Agriculture.

The sponsors of the proposal were willing to enter into discussions with Members in good faith and with a view to reaching effective solutions.

3. Egypt stated that the effects of agricultural trade liberalization resulting from the implementation of the Agreement on Agriculture were felt in the LDCs and NFIDCs through higher prices for basic foodstuffs, a decrease in food aid deliveries to NFIDCs, or a decline in agricultural production combined with a lack of technical and financial assistance to improve their agricultural productivity and infrastructure. These effects had a significant impact on family incomes, employment, rural development, food security as well as economic and social stability. The increase of the cereal import bill of LDCs and NFIDCs during the first three years of implementation was approximately 49 per cent although admittedly a small part of this increase was due to reasons other than the implementation of the Agreement on Agriculture. In the case of Egypt, the result of implementation in terms of net agricultural trade was negative. The average value of agricultural imports in 1995-98 was 37 per cent higher than in the period 1990-94, although Egypt had experienced a declining trend in food imports since 1985. There was now a history of six years to judge whether the reform programme had caused negative effects and not just "possible negative effects" in the future. There was clearly a causality between liberalization and higher prices, at least in the short and medium term. The sixteen countries including Egypt had submitted the proposal as part of the implementation exercise relating to the Uruguay Round commitments and the ongoing negotiations. It might be expected that LDCs and NFIDCs would call for a more extensive compensation mechanism with further trade liberalization.

4. Egypt noted further that one of the major deficiencies of the Decision was the definition or interpretation of certain terms, particularly what constituted "negative effects". With respect to food aid and the relationship between the Decision and the Food Aid Convention (FAC), there were differences in the way in which the beneficiaries were categorized. Unlike the Decision, the FAC also assigned priority to certain groups of countries. It was therefore doubtful whether the Convention fully reflected the concerns of the Decision. With respect to the issue of access to financing facilities, Egypt noted that the IMF Compensatory Financing Facility (CFF) was limited to cereals only and the conditions in accessing it were difficult to meet which meant that the CFF had no relevance to the Decision's objectives and coverage. More importantly, the Decision dealt with effects arising from international factors, while the IMF facility addressed or required domestic policy adjustment related mainly to balance of payments difficulties. Of course, the modalities of the management of the resources of the proposed Inter-Agency Revolving Fund needed to be agreed. In the view of Egypt, there was a need to combine shared functions or actions under one mechanism. Egypt expressed the hope that Members would lend their support to the proposal and the sponsors stood ready to have further discussions on the technicalities of operating the Revolving Fund.

5. Sri Lanka recalled that at the November 2000 meeting of the Committee Sri Lanka had stated its views on why the Marrakesh Decision had not been implemented. The reasons included ambiguity with respect to timing and mechanisms to operationalize the Decision. There was also a lack of clarity with respect to the meaning of "negative effects", "reasonable terms and conditions", "sufficient level of food aid" and "normal level of imports", and with respect to assigning precise rights and responsibilities to the relevant agencies. Furthermore, there were no binding WTO commitments on the main three elements of the decision, namely food aid, technical and financial assistance, and access to all basic foodstuffs and necessary concessional financing facilities. According to FAO data, these two groups of countries were facing higher cereal import bills than before. The NFIDCs should have access to basic foodstuffs when stocks were low and prices were high on the international market. Therefore, there was a linkage between access to food and the availability of finance to purchase food. The proposal envisaged establishment of a Revolving Fund with a view to ensuring access for LDCs and NFIDCs to concessionary financing when world prices were high with a link to a food reserve to ensure that these countries could purchase food at

reasonable prices in the international market. Sri Lanka agreed that the main objective of the Agreement was to create a fair and market-oriented agricultural trading system by removing trade-distorting policies which in the past had led to structural surpluses. If the fundamental objective of elimination or gradual reduction in export subsidies and reduction in domestic support was successful and structural surpluses were decreased there would be an increase in the cost of food imports of the LDCs and NFIDCs. In this connection, Sri Lanka recognised Japan's proposal at the Special Session for the establishment of an international food reserve.

6. In the view of Sri Lanka there were further reasons that justified the establishment of a Revolving Fund. The IMF compensatory financing facility (CFF) had not been used by many NFIDCs and LDCs due to its conditionality; the CFF covered only the cereal cost of food and did not cover all basic foodstuffs as envisaged in the Decision, and it was subject to standard interest rates. Furthermore, the IMF was in the process of reviewing the CFF in the context of an overall reform of the financial architecture with emphasis on the Poverty Reduction and Growth Facility. The IMF was not looking at cereal import bills separately but rather in the context of the balance of payment situation and other adjustment conditionalities. Moreover, the availability of financing under the CFF would be reduced as its operation was reviewed. Under the second window of the Revolving Fund, technical and financial assistance would be made available to improve agricultural productivity and related infrastructure so as to enable the LDCs and NFIDCs to increase their food production and be less dependent on food imports. On food aid, the philosophy of the Food Aid Convention had changed with the intention to encourage commercial purchases, decrease the availability of food aid and provide finance to purchase food on a commercial basis. There was an emphasis on encouraging commercial buying, hence the importance of a Revolving Fund. Sri Lanka also believed that there was a need for donor countries to commit greater commodity volumes under the Food Aid Convention and to make food aid available in fully grant form.

7. Sri Lanka expressed the hope that the proposal would receive positive consideration by developed country Members and donor countries as the reform process envisaged in Article 20 of Agreement on Agriculture should also take into account possible negative effects arising from the reforms. On this condition, these two groups of countries would be able to make further commitments in the reform process since this would impose additional burden of adjustment on these two groups of countries.

8. Honduras, on behalf of Cuba and the Dominican Republic, stated that after six years of implementation of the Agreement, there were no concrete measures in favour of the LDCs and NFIDCs. As the proposal indicated, the situation of the net food-importers had deteriorated as a result of the Uruguay Round. The Marrakesh Decision was only one of the many Uruguay Round benefits which developing countries were supposed to have received but which had not materialized. It was therefore difficult for these Members to consider the launching of a new round of negotiations since they were still waiting to obtain the benefits from the past round. These Members hoped that this proposal would be well received by Members and that it would result in concrete decisions to be adopted by the General Council in the implementation process before the fourth Ministerial Conference which would contribute to the process of strengthening confidence in the multilateral trading system.

9. Senegal stated that as one of the sponsors of the proposal it fully supported the specific ideas that had been put forward. Senegal considered that the proposal constituted an important step towards finding a solution to this priority issue. In Senegal food imports constituted approximately 45 per cent of total imports and this issue was therefore of utmost importance since it was directly linked to food security. Senegal called on Members to give the proposal their highest attention so as to make progress on this issue.

10. India supported the proposal made by the group of sixteen net food-importing developing countries. India noted with concern that food aid was lower when world market prices were high. If Members were serious about implementing the Marrakesh Decision in good faith, food aid should increase when it was most needed, that is when world market prices were high. India also supported steps for capacity enhancing in the long term so that dependence on food aid was reduced. Food production could be boosted in many of the current food-importing developing countries if trade-distorting support to agriculture provided in several other countries was meaningfully reduced.

11. Indonesia recognized the importance of the proposal submitted by the sixteen WTO net food-importing developing countries. Indonesia looked forward to constructive results in the consultations undertaken by the Vice-Chairman with a view to finding appropriate mechanisms to implement the NFIDC Decision.

12. New Zealand noted that it was one of those Members which had supported the decision in the General Council to bring this issue before the Committee on Agriculture with a view to finding ways of more effectively implementing the Marrakesh Ministerial Decision. New Zealand commended the proponents of the proposal for tabling this thoughtful paper. New Zealand already provided all of its food aid in fully grant form and would encourage others to do so as well. New Zealand agreed that donor countries should commit greater commodity volumes under the Food Aid Convention as the need dictated. New Zealand also agreed that it was essential that additional and more targeted technical and financial assistance be provided to NFIDCs and LDCs to increase their agricultural productivity and infrastructure. There were many other interesting suggestions in the proposal, including the inter-agency Revolving Fund concept, which New Zealand would need more time to reflect upon. New Zealand looked forward to take forward the discussion in a substantive manner and supported ongoing informal consultations by the Chair on the subject.

13. Thailand welcomed the constructive proposals by the sixteen developing countries. It could support the proposal that food aid should be provided in fully grant form. In addition, Thailand suggested that the purchase of food stocks for food aid should be made from developing countries only.

14. Australia welcomed the proposal for revising existing WTO provisions under the NFIDC Decision and the establishment of mechanisms to improve the implementation of that Decision. Australia was interested in further technical elaboration of the proposals in the paper. Australia noted that at a preliminary discussion between the sponsors of the proposal and donors, which was convened by the Vice-Chairman, it was agreed that as a first step it would be helpful if the IMF, the World Bank, the International Grains Council and the FAO could inform Members on their actions relevant to the proposals on access to financing facilities, food aid, and technical and financial assistance. Australia would welcome this approach.

15. Canada thanked the proponents for their efforts in preparing the proposal. Canada shared the interest in ensuring that the Decision was effectively implemented. While the submission alluded to a clear causality between Uruguay Round policy reforms and higher food import bills experienced by LDCs and NFIDCs, Canada was not convinced that the paper clearly established this causal link. In fact, the Table attached to the proposal seemed to show food import bills rising in 1995/96 and falling since. Per unit import costs had done likewise, and based on the further decline in prices for 1999/2000, it could be expected that they would decline still further when more recent data became available. This suggested there might be many other reasons for the changes in food import bills of the LDCs and NFIDCs than a link with the reform programme. The issue of causality was very important in the discussion of the implementation of a decision dealing with the effects of the reform. Canada recognised the legitimate concerns of the sponsors of the proposal regarding instability in food import bills and wanted to see the Decision work effectively. Canada also agreed with India that reduced distortions and a better functioning agricultural trading system would contribute to improved

food security in NFIDCs and LDCs. On food aid, Canada supported the call for all food aid to be provided in fully grant form. On the question of larger volume commitments under the Food Aid Convention, Canada had increased its volume commitments under the Food Aid Convention in 1999, and had consistently exceeded its Food Aid Convention commitment threshold. With regard to the idea of carrying forward and back food aid commitments, Canada wondered if this would run counter to the principle of providing assurances of the availability of minimum levels of food aid. In considering this proposal, Canada believed that the appropriate forum to consider food aid volume commitments was the Food Aid Convention and not the WTO. On the proposed new financing facilities, Canada would like to learn more about the reasons for the under-utilisation of existing facilities. Canada would encourage a detailed and specific discussion of what problems existed within existing mechanisms, and how they might be resolved, before considering the establishment of a new mechanism. Regarding technical and financial assistance, Canada was interested in examining how this assistance could be targeted more effectively. Canada had doubts, however, about whether the WTO was an appropriate forum for countries to make commitments on the level and direction of their development assistance activities.

16. The EC stated that it was fully committed to the Food Aid Convention and strongly supported the proposal that food aid should be provided in fully grant form. The EC also had noted that food aid had been lower when market prices were higher, and vice-versa. This illustrated another important issue, namely the abuse of food aid to enhance market penetration. With respect to increases on food aid, the EC believed that food aid should be given to those in need and when needed. Food aid should not create dependence, nor jeopardise local production of food. With respect to financial facilities, the EC's view at this stage was that they should be dealt with by the IMF and the World Bank.

17. The United States thanked the sponsors of the paper for their contribution to the discussion. The United States felt that the debate on whether or not the modest Uruguay Round reform process had a negative effect on the LDCs and NFIDCs had probably gone on long enough. Nonetheless, some countries might feel that their reliance on food imports left them vulnerable to the uncertainties of the market place and these concerns must be addressed if these countries were to participate in and benefit from further reform. While there were a number of points in the proposal with which the United States agreed, on some issues the United States had different views. In the view of the United States, the negotiations on food aid should remain with the Food Aid Convention and not be taken up by the WTO. The United States were thus reluctant to make binding commitments on food aid within the WTO schedule of commitments. The United States as the largest donor of food aid provided more than 85 per cent of food aid in grant form. The United States considered that there was an important role to play for concessional loan based food aid. The United States were also reluctant to commit to a new financing facility without first exploring the deficiencies of the current arrangements. Furthermore, a new financing mechanism could not be established quickly and a great deal of technical work would be required. In any event, the United States took the proposal seriously and were committed to working with interested members on the matter. The United States encouraged the Vice-Chairman to continue the informal technical discussions.

18. Japan welcomed the proposal by the sixteen developing countries. This proposal sought to address the problems which NFIDCs and LDCs were facing during the Uruguay Round implementation period. Japan supported the efforts to consider what should be done to solve these problems and to make the Marrakesh Decision effective. In the view of Japan, the specifics of the proposal should be examined carefully. Japan supported that FAO play an important role as a competent agency on food security issues in developing countries. Members should draw on FAO's expertise to examine the implementation experience of the Agreement on Agriculture, approaches towards food security, technical problems on food stockholding schemes and other issues. Japan felt that it could also be useful to have discussions among relevant international organizations, including FAO. Regarding food aid, Japan believed that the possibility to provide food aid on a loan basis should be maintained, taking into account the needs of recipient countries and financial conditions of

donor countries in the case when large-scale food shortages occurred. Regarding the proposal on stockholding, Japan had also proposed an international food stockholding system in its negotiating proposal. Japan would like to examine with the developing countries concerned what measures were effective for establishing such an international food stockholding scheme.

19. Uruguay welcomed the concrete proposals made by the sixteen Members. Uruguay supported a number of suggestions, in particular that food aid should be provided in fully grant form and be available when most needed. The proposals should be carefully studied and given priority attention. While Uruguay shared the doubts expressed by Canada concerning the causal link between the reform process and the problems faced by these countries, it agreed that work should be undertaken to identify problems within the framework of existing mechanisms before recommending new solutions. Uruguay supported the idea of seeking additional information from the relevant international organisations.

20. Argentina welcomed the proposal and was prepared to support it. Although Argentina had concerns regarding the justification of the proposal, Argentina considered the proposal to be a step in the right direction by suggesting aid for imports rather than subsidies for exports of agricultural products. Another merit of the proposal was to draw attention to the importance of technical assistance as a means to increase production in the countries concerned. Argentina noted that it might be complicated and possibly beyond the Committee's mandate to establish a new fund. Nevertheless, Argentina supported the suggestion of Australia to first proceed to an examination of the existing mechanisms and facilities, in the light of which the Committee could then make recommendations, as appropriate. Argentina considered, on the other hand, that the suggested causality between the Uruguay Round commitments and higher food import bills was far from clear since many factors were at play, including the financial crisis, natural disasters and civil wars. Argentina also considered that applications to be included on the WTO list of net food-importing developing countries (G/AG/5/Rev.4) should be considered with good will but cautioned against diluting the list if the Marrakesh Decision was to be implemented effectively.

21. Pakistan thanked Members for having positively engaged in these discussions. Their ideas and suggestions would be helpful in refining the proposal. With respect to the argument by certain Members that the causality between the reform progamme and international food prices was not established or rather weak, Pakistan observed that in the first two years of implementation, world market prices for food had increased as domestic support and other trade-distorting support was reduced; in subsequent years, prices had decreased since trade-distorting support to agriculture had been increased to levels of the base period. In the view of the sponsors of the proposal, there was thus a clear causal link between the "reform policies" and international food prices. In any event, the sponsors were willing to elaborate their proposal which reflected genuine concerns and difficulties.

22. Argentina took issue with Pakistan's statement concerning the issue of causality. In the view of Argentina, the situation was as follows: initially, when the commitments on domestic support and export subsidies were not constraining, international commodity prices had increased; subsequently, when the commitments became more constraining, world prices had declined – and not the other way round as might be expected. In other words, there could be a linkage between the WTO commitments in agriculture and world prices but the suggested causality was far from clear. For this and other reasons, Argentina would be concerned about statements to the effect that the results of the Uruguay Round were prejudicial to the interests of the NFIDCs and LDCs.

23. In summarizing the discussion, the Vice-Chairman noted that Members had held an interesting debate on the issue of causality between the Uruguay Round results in agriculture and world food prices and although different views had been expressed, there was a common view that it was important to ensure stable food supplies for LDCs and NFIDCs. There had also been different views on the question of which institutions should deal with the various elements of the Marrakesh

G/AG/11
Page 14

Decision. It would be his suggestion to continue the informal discussions with participation of experts from the relevant international organizations, with a view to identifying the specific problems in implementing the Decision. In such informal meetings, it would be his intention to take up the issues separately, that is access to the financing facilities of the international financial institutions; food aid; and technical and financial assistance.

G/AG/11
Page 15

ANNEX 2

PROPOSAL TO IMPLEMENT THE MARRAKESH MINISTERIAL DECISION IN FAVOUR OF LDCS AND NFIDCS

Submitted by Côte d'Ivoire, Cuba, Dominican Republic, Egypt, Honduras, Jamaica, Kenya, Mauritius, Morocco, Pakistan, Senegal, Sri Lanka, St. Lucia, Trinidad and Tobago, Tunisia and Venezuela *

We are grateful to the Vice-Chairman of the WTO Committee on Agriculture for inviting concrete proposals by the NFIDCs and the LDCs on the relevant points under paragraph 21 of the Draft Ministerial Declaration of 18 October 1999 related to the implementation of the Marrakesh Ministerial Decision on Measures Concerning the Possible Negative Effects of the Reform Process on Least-Developed and Net Food-Importing Developing Countries. We look forward to the following proposals being given immediate and favourable consideration to allay the genuine concerns of the NFIDCs and LDCs and effectively implement the relevant Ministerial Decision which is a legal commitment of WTO Members under Article 16 of the Agreement on Agriculture. We are confident that the discussions in the Committee on Agriculture on this issue will lead to the submission of positive suggestions to the General Council for adoption.

The main objective of the Agreement on Agriculture was to decrease the structural surpluses generated in the past by production and trade-distorting policies in agriculture. It is, therefore, obvious that if this fundamental objective of the AoA is successful, the effect for the NFIDCs and LDCs will be an increase in the cost of their food imports. The period since the UR came into being provides a good example for examining the experience of NFIDCs and LDCs as regards their food import bills.

According to the data provided by FAO (see Table I), these two groups of countries are facing much higher cereal import bills than before. Taking the two years prior to 1995 as a benchmark (i.e. the average of the two marketing years 1993/94 and 1994/95), the increase in the cereal import bills in 1995/96 to 1996/97 amounted to 36.6 per cent for the two groups of countries taken together. Nearly all of this increase (35.1 per cent) was due to increases in the per unit cost of imported cereals, as volumes changed only marginally. Moreover, even after the world prices returned to more normal levels since the 1997/98 marketing year, the cereal import bills of these two groups of countries remained at a much higher level than they were prior to 1995.

In view of the above, the causality between policy reforms under the Uruguay Round and higher food import bills for the LDCs and NFIDCs is clear.

Proposals for Implementation

The Ministerial Decision includes three mechanisms to respond to the difficulties faced by the LDCs and NFIDCs: food aid, access to financing facilities, and technical and financial assistance to increase agricultural productivity and infrastructure. We have the following proposals in respect of each of these three mechanisms.

*(G/AG/W/49, dated 19 March 2001.)

Food Aid

Unfortunately, it has been observed that food aid is lower when world market prices are high and hence more food aid is needed, and vice versa. Moreover, the new Food Aid Convention (FAC) approved in June 1999 has lesser volume of commodity commitments (4.895 million tonnes, in wheat equivalent) than under the previous 1995 FAC (5.35 million tonnes, in wheat equivalent) and 1986 FAC (7.5 million tonnes).

We therefore, propose that:

(i) all food aid should be fully in grant form;

(ii) donor countries should commit greater commodity volumes under the Food Aid Convention;

(iii) the donor countries commit that the food aid volumes will increase in years of high world market prices when such aid is most needed. This can be achieved by providing appropriate flexibility in the Convention, e.g. carry forwards from periods of low prices and hence of low demand for food aid and call forwards from next year(s) contributions under the FAC.

Access to Financing Facilities

The NFIDCs and LDCs need access to special financing facilities to maintain the normal volume of food imports during times of high market prices without further jeopardizing their balance-of-payments position. Experience has shown that the existing facilities under the Bretton Woods institutions, due to the conditionalities attached and other technicalities, have not been used by the countries in need of such financing. Moreover, the required financing facility should have some corresponding link with physical stocks of food grains. We therefore propose that:

(i) FAO, in the light of its experience and work in this area, should be asked to provide estimates of the volumes of normal annual food imports that are needed by individual NFIDCs and the LDCs to maintain consumption levels, and assess the assistance needed to import these quantities;

(ii) an inter-agency Revolving Fund should be set up with two components. The first, and variable component of this Fund (to comprise existing and/or new financing facilities as appropriate), will be to ensure that adequate financing at concessional terms is made available to the NFIDCs and LDCs in times of high world market prices;

(iii) the producing countries commit, in years of plentiful supplies as we are witnessing now, to put aside over and above volumes required for food aid, emergencies and essential nutritional assistance projects, sufficient national food reserves in accordance with the normal import requirements of the NFIDCs and LDCs as indicated by FAO;

(iv) these reserves should be released to the LDCs and NFIDCs at reasonable prices, in times of high world market prices, to help them, together with available food aid, meet their normal import requirements.

Technical and Financial Assistance

Further, we consider it essential that technical and financial assistance be provided to the NFIDCs and the LDCs to increase agricultural productivity and infrastructure. This will address directly the very problem responsible for the heavy dependence of LDCs and NFIDCs on the world market. We, therefore, propose that:

(i) the second, and fixed component of the above-mentioned Revolving Fund should provide technical and financial assistance to NFIDCs and LDCs for specific projects linked to improving agricultural productivity and related infrastructure;

(ii) this technical and financial assistance to be provided to the NFIDCs and the LDCs should be over and above the regular bilateral and multilateral activities of donors in this area.

Binding Commitments and Effective Monitoring

To ensure certainty and predictability in respect of food aid, financing, and technical and financial assistance, it is recommended:

(i) all major developed exporting countries should put aside supplies, under national food reserves, specifically earmarked to be released to the NFIDCs and LDCs under reasonable prices during years of high world prices;

(ii) developed countries and international development and financial institutions (World Bank IMF, UNDP) should contribute to the financing of the two components of the Revolving Fund which, in turn, should be managed by an inter-agency arrangement with the full involvement of FAO;

(iii) the commitment of WTO Members regarding volumes of food aid, volumes of physical reserves, contributions to the two components of the Revolving Fund are inscribed in their country schedules as binding and legally enforceable;

(iv) the WTO Members should make regular annual notifications in respect of these commitments to the Committee on Agriculture of the WTO.

We are willing to enter into discussions with our trading partners in good faith and with a view to reaching effective solutions. Depending on these discussions, we will be happy to provide further technical elaboration of the points made in this proposal.

Table I

Cereal Imports of LDCs and NFIDCs (1993/94 to 1999/00) - Information as of November 15, 1999

	1993/94	1994/95	1995/96	1996/97	1997/98	1998/99	1999/00
Import bill ($ million)							
LDCs	1,375	2,195	2,272	1,871	2,357	1,996	na
NFIDCs	3,775	4,559	6,265	5,857	5,397	4,617	na
LDCs+NFIDCs	**5,150**	**6,754**	**8,537**	**7,728**	**7,754**	**6,613**	na
% change over 1993/94-94/95	-13.5	13.5	43.4	29.8	30.3	11.1	na
Total volume imported (1000 tons)							
LDCs	11,167	13,310	12,273	10,753	14,390	15,380	13,108
NFIDCs	25,516	25,995	26,093	28,038	30,974	29,370	31,542
LDCs+NFIDCs	**36,683**	**39,305**	**38,366**	**38,791**	**45,364**	**44,750**	**44,650**
% change over 1993/94-94/95	-3.4	3.4	1.0	2.1	19.4	17.8	17.5
Food aid (1000 tons)							
LDCs	3,932	4,326	3,305	2,553	2,669	3,157	na
% of total imports	35.2	32.5	26.9	23.7	18.5	20.5	na
NFIDCs	1,857	1,325	641	495	622	616	na
% of total imports	7.3	5.1	2.5	1.8	2.0	2.1	na
LDCs+NFIDCs	**5,789**	**5,651**	**3,946**	**3,048**	**3,291**	**3,773**	na
% of total imports	15.8	14.4	10.3	7.9	7.3	8.4	na
Benefit from US EEP ($ million)							
LDCs	99	35	1	0	0	0	na
NFIDCs	355	88	21	0	0	0	na
LDCs+NFIDCs	**454**	**123**	**22**	**0**	**0**	**0**	na
% change over 1993/94-94/95	57.4	-57.4	-92.4	-100.0	-100.0	-100.0	na
Per unit import cost ($/ton)							
LDCs	123.1	164.9	185.1	174.0	163.8	129.8	na
NFIDCs	147.9	175.4	240.1	208.9	174.2	157.2	na
LDCs+NFIDCs	**140.4**	**171.8**	**222.5**	**199.2**	**170.9**	**147.8**	na
% change over 1993/94-94/95	-10.4	9.7	42.0	27.2	9.1	-5.7	na
Wheat export price							
US no 2 hard winter ($/ton)	143	157	216	181	142	120	110
% change over 1993/94-94/95	-4.7	4.7	44.0	20.7	-5.3	-20.0	-26.7

	1993/94-94/95	1995/96-96/97	1997/98-98/99
Averages (LDCs+NFIDCs)			
Import bill ($ million)	5,952.0	8,132.5	7,183.5
Total volume imported (1000 tons)	37,993.9	38,578.5	45,057.0
Food aid (1000 tons)	5,719.8	3,496.8	3,532.0
Benefit from US EEP ($ million)	288.5	11.0	0.0
Per unit import cost ($/ton)	156.7	210.8	159.4
Wheat export price ($/ton)	150.0	198.5	131.0
% change over 1993/94-94/95			
Import bill	0.0	36.6	20.7
Total volume imported	0.0	1.5	18.6
Food aid	0.0	-38.9	-38.2
Benefit from US EEP	0.0	-96.2	-100.0
Per unit import cost	0.0	34.6	1.8
Wheat export price	0.0	32.3	-12.7

Source: FAO. Figures for 1998/99 are provisional and for 1999/00 are estimates

ANNEX C
(G/AG/10 dated 6 July 2001)

EXAMINATION OF POSSIBLE MEANS OF IMPROVING THE EFFECTIVENESS OF THE IMPLEMENTATION OF THE DECISION ON MEASURES CONCERNING THE POSSIBLE NEGATIVE EFFECTS OF THE REFORM PROGRAMME ON LEAST-DEVELOPED AND NET FOOD-IMPORTING DEVELOPING COUNTRIES

Report by the Vice-Chairman, Minister Yoichi Suzuki, to the General Council

1. At its meeting on 15 December 2000, the Special Session of the General Council referred to the relevant subsidiary bodies, including the Committee on Agriculture, a number of implementation related issues. The General Council decided, inter alia, that:

> "[t]he Committee on Agriculture shall examine possible means of improving the effectiveness of the implementation of the Decision on Measures Concerning the Possible Negative Effects of the Reform Programme on Least-Developed and Net Food-Importing Developing Countries and report to the General Council at the second regular meeting of the Council in 2001." (WT/L/384 refers).

2. In this context, a group of sixteen WTO net food-importing developing countries comprising Côte d'Ivoire, Cuba, Dominican Republic, Egypt, Honduras, Jamaica, Kenya, Mauritius, Morocco, Pakistan, Senegal, Sri Lanka, St. Lucia, Trinidad and Tobago, Tunisia and Venezuela submitted to the Committee on Agriculture a "Proposal to Implement the Marrakesh Ministerial Decision in favour of LDCs and NFIDCs" (G/AG/W/49). The sponsors of this proposal have submitted an elaborated proposal which has been circulated as G/AG/W/49/Add. 1 (copy attached as Annex 3). The list of co-sponsors now includes Peru, bringing the number of co-sponsors up to 17. The proposals were the subject of continuing discussions, including at an Informal Roundtable Discussion with the IMF, the World Bank and the FAO as well as at the regular meeting of the Committee on 28-29 June 2001.

3. The IMF representative stressed that the IMF has sufficient financial resources but lending by the IMF had to be aimed at addressing balance-of-payments problems. The World Bank representative observed that World Bank lending for rural development had declined from about US$4 billion per annum a decade ago to US$1 billion last year, the lowest level ever. This decline was due not to lack of World Bank resources, but to a decline in demand for loans aimed at agricultural and rural development. The World Bank representative stated that the Bank was concerned that agricultural development was no longer being accorded a high priority in many developing countries in terms of the use being made of the Bank's resources. Frustrations were expressed by the proponents of the proposal that adequate financing facilities to meet the short-term difficulties of the NFIDCs and the LDCs were not existent. A detailed summary of the discussions at both meetings is attached in Annexes 1 and 2.

4. Regarding future work, I noted that there is support among Members to continue the consultation. I intend to organize more informal consultations. There will also be an opportunity to pursue the issue at the Special Session of the Committee on Agriculture in July in the context of the discussions on food security. This will contribute to define more clearly the scope of issues that need to be taken up in the context of implementation. The content of my consultations will include how to address short-term financial difficulties, whether present IMF and World Bank facilities are suited to address concerns, and the proposed revolving fund. I will also provide opportunities to consult in a wider context including the issues of food aid and technical and financial assistance to improve agricultural productivity and infrastructure.

G/AG/11
Page 20

5. As agreed by the Committee on Agriculture at its meeting on 28-29 June 2001, this report is submitted to the General Council on my responsibility as Vice-Chairman of the Committee.

G/AG/11
Page 21

ANNEX 1

Examination of Possible Means of Improving the Effectiveness of the Implementation of the Decision on Measures Concerning the Possible Negative Effects of the Reform Programme on Least-Developed and Net Food-Importing Developing Countries Summary of the Discussion at the Meeting of the Committee on Agriculture on 29 June 2001

6. Egypt noted that the participants in the Roundtable had reached the conclusion that the current financial facilities available under the aegis of the IMF and World Bank did not serve the purpose of the Marrakesh Decision. These facilities were anchored in balance-of-payments relief at the IMF, and in long-term agricultural production projects at the World Bank. Because of time constraints, there had not been a full discussion of the proposal for a new food financing facility. In view of the rising opposition of civil and other sections of society to further liberalization in agriculture, it was becoming increasingly difficult for the decision makers in various capitals to engage wholeheartedly in the work of the special negotiating sessions. Doha presented a unique opportunity to convince the doubters of the feasibility and desirability of further reform of the multilateral trade system. This would be impossible without a suitable sign of the international community's commitment to address the concerns of the weaker trading partners. NFIDCs and LDCs were frustrated and disappointed about the lack of constructive engagement and the slow pace of discussions, and reiterated a willingness to accelerate work on the issue with a view to presenting the Ministers at Doha with a pleasant surprise.

7. In Pakistan's view, it would be embarrassing for Ministers if the Marrakesh Decision was not operationalized before the Doha conference, six years after it had been taken; this issue should be one of the many deliverables at Doha. The NFIDCs and LDCs had tried to explain the rationale of their proposal, and put forward a solution. The existing facilities of the IMF and World Bank did not cater to the needs of the proponents. The Contingency Financing Facility (CFF) of the IMF was not used frequently because of the conditionality, and this conditionality had been further strengthened. The possibility of modifying the CFF criteria was remote. Since the existing facilities did not meet the needs, alternative institutions should be considered, for example the International Fund for Agricultural Development (IFAD). IFAD was an international financial institute, had logistic capacity, but lacked money. In response to those who failed to see the link between prices and the reform programme, Pakistan pointed out that according to the OECD, support to agriculture had risen, which naturally had led to falling prices. Especially Cairns Group countries should not be blind to this link between increased support and falling prices.

8. Venezuela noted that the concentration on short-term financing at the Roundtable should not mean that other topics, including food aid as well as technical and financial assistance, were not important. The discussions at the Roundtable had led to the conclusion that the existing financial facilities were not adequate for the needs addressed by the Marrakesh Decision. Unfortunately, at the Roundtable there had been no opportunity to discuss the proposal in detail. Venezuela emphasized in particular two aspects of this proposal: the self-financing character of the fund, and the possibility that IFAD could be a more appropriate framework for the administration of this fund given the lack of flexibility of the IMF and the World Bank.

9. Sri Lanka appreciated the opportunity to discuss this topic at the informal Roundtable, and clarified the overall purpose of the proposal. This proposal called for effective implementation of the Ministerial Decision, including three mechanisms: food aid, financing facilities, and technical and financial assistance to increase agricultural production and infrastructure. The co-sponsors of the proposal had highlighted the reasons why the Decision remained unimplemented at previous meetings. They proposed that all food aid should be fully in grant form, requested donor countries to

commit greater commodity volumes under the Food Aid Convention, and to make this aid available when it was most needed, during periods of high market prices. On access to financing facilities, they proposed the creation of a special facility to maintain the normal value of food imports during times of high market prices without further jeopardizing their balance-of-payments positions. The group proposed the establishment of an inter-agency fund with two components: one variable component to ensure that adequate financing was made available at concessional terms to NFIDCs and LDCs at times of high market prices; and a fixed component to provide technical and financial assistance to NFIDCs and LDCs for specific projects linked to improving agricultural productivity and related infrastructure. They also proposed to ensure the predictability of the operationalization of the Decision, and recommended that all stakeholders make commitments in different areas.

10. Sri Lanka then addressed the questions posed at the March formal meeting of the Agriculture Committee and at the Roundtable. The first set of questions was related to the causality between the Uruguay Round reforms and the higher import bills experienced by NFIDCs and LDCs. The group's paper had observed that in the first two years of implementation, world market prices for food had increased as trade-distorting support was reduced. In subsequent years, prices had decreased since trade-distorting support to agriculture had increased to levels of the base period. Sri Lanka stressed that the comparison should be between an outcome *with* the Uruguay Round and one *without* the Uruguay Round. There was a long-term downward trend in food prices since the beginning of the previous century, and this trend was likely to continue. Other primary commodities exported by developing countries experienced a similar downward trend. Hence, export earnings also had a downward trend, influencing the terms of trade. The argument that the reform process had not had any adverse effects on the capacity of NFIDCS and LDCs to purchase food contradicted the argument made by the same people who claimed beneficial effects of the reform process for developing countries stemming from agriculture.

11. A second set of questions concerned whether the food-aid component should remain within the Food Aid Convention, whether the WTO was the appropriate forum for countries to make commitments in the different areas, and whether the establishment of a new fund fell within the Committee's mandate. Sri Lanka believed that the Marrakesh Decision had emerged as a consequence of the liberalization process undertaken in the WTO context. Hence the implementation of the responsibilities attached to the Decision lay also within the WTO. Although the level of food aid was decided under the Food Aid Convention, it was morally and practically incorrect to claim that the issue of food aid should be dealt with outside the WTO because the Decision called for the adoption of guidelines to ensure that appropriate levels of food aid were made available to NFIDCs and LDCs in fully grant form. Under the Decision, the Ministers recognized that in order to address the short-term difficulties experienced by these countries in financing normal levels of commercial imports, they would be eligible to draw on the resources of international financial institutions under existing facilities or facilities to be established. In the absence of a Ministerial Conference, the General Council was empowered to review the Decision for its effective implementation. The General Council, in its decision of December 2000, had mandated the Agriculture Committee to examine possible means of improving the effectiveness of the implementation of the Marrakesh Decision. Therefore, the Committee had a mandate to examine such new schemes.

12. The last set of questions addressed by Sri Lanka was related to the proposed inter-agency revolving fund, and to technical clarifications on the existing financial facilities, how they functioned, and why they were under-utilised. The informal Roundtable had proved that the existing financial facilities under the Bretton Woods institutions could not be used by the NFIDCs and LDCs due to the conditionalities attached to such facilities, the limited product and country coverage, and their greater relevance to the policy decisions of beneficiary countries than to the needs of NFIDCs and LDCs. The group sponsoring the proposal intended to provide technical details at an appropriate time on the organization, implementation and monitoring of the inter-agency fund. Sri Lanka invited interested

G/AG/11
Page 23

delegations to submit alternative proposals while taking into account the weaknesses inherent in the existing mechanism.

13. Peru shared the previous speakers' view about the inadequacy of the existing financial mechanisms and supported the creation of a new fund for short-term financing of normal import levels of basic food products as an important contribution to food security. Increasing food import bills constituted an obstacle to development. The new proposal dealt only with one of the aspects of the Marrakesh Decision, but Peru continued to be interested in a full implementation of the Decision.

14. Trinidad and Tobago recalled that the first proposal had addressed the three elements of the Marrakesh Decision, namely food aid, access to financing facilities, and technical and financial assistance to increase agricultural productivity and infrastructure. The Roundtable, which had addressed the section of the proposal that dealt with short-term financing facilities, had not been encouraging. The existing facilities could not and did not respond to the needs of the NFIDCs and LDCs in implementing the Ministerial Decision. There was a need to be innovative in creating an instrument, i.e. the proposed revolving fund, which could facilitate implementation of the Decision. Consultations on all aspects of the Decision had to be pursued. Trinidad and Tobago pointed out that aside from the Bretton Woods institutions there was another international organization with experience in financing that was involved in the area of agricultural development and food security: IFAD. In light of the negative and rigid position adopted by the IMF and the World Bank at the Roundtable, WTO Members should examine whether IFAD might not be the ideal agency to manage an operationalized revolving fund.

15. The Dominican Republic, on behalf of Honduras, reminded the Committee that the Marrakesh Decision contained a long-term and a short-term component. The short-term component aimed to resolve difficulties in financing normal levels of commercial imports, while the long-term component was designed to improve agricultural productivity and infrastructure. The Roundtable had made it clear that the existing facilities were not designed to cover short-term needs as foreseen in the Decision. Therefore, a new self-financing fund of 1.2 billion dollars to be contributed by multi-lateral organisms and donors had been proposed. There had been a lack of political will to resolve this problem in the six years since the adoption of the Decision. Time before the Doha Conference was running short, and the lack of satisfactory solutions to this and other implementation problems would condition their acceptance of new elements for the future work programme of the WTO. The Dominican Republic and Honduras desired a more detailed discussion of the proposal, and asked their trading partners for the necessary flexibility to reach a solution.

16. Cuba noted that the proposal constituted a new effort to find a concrete solution to one part of the Marrakesh Decision. It was clear that the existing facilities could not be adapted to the needs of NFIDCs. Thus, a new fund had to be created in a multilateral framework. The fact that until now the WTO had not been able to correct this problem resulting from the Uruguay Round showed that there was a lack of political will. This resulted in considerable insecurity in developing countries when it came to accepting new commitments in the organization.

17. Jamaica recalled the importance for developing countries of resolving implementation issues. The operationalization of the Marrakesh Decision was one such issue. Jamaica had co-sponsored the proposal, but had also indicated that it remained open to other options. One example, IFAD, was a financial institution whose involvement could assist in effectively addressing Jamaica's concerns. As preparations for Doha intensified, Jamaica anticipated concrete positive responses to advance this discussion.

18. Nigeria stressed that the need to implement the Marrakesh Decision was ever more urgent in view of other problems facing LDCs, most of which were in Africa. These problems included heavy debt overhang, natural disasters, droughts, wars and the AIDS pandemic. In view of these problems it

was imperative that a way be found to implement this Decision in line with Article 16 of the Agreement on Agriculture. If the present proposal was not acceptable, Nigeria invited developed countries to make counterproposals that would lead to a resolution. Such a solution would increase confidence in the multilateral trading system.

19. Argentina questioned the link between international prices and the agricultural reform process, and recalled its statement at the March Committee meeting on this subject (G/AG/7 refers). Many factors had influenced prices, including the Asian crisis and technological progress. When the implementation period had started, prices had increased, but at the end of the implementation period for developed countries, prices had fallen. The proposal was interesting and should be analyzed, but it was based on the unjustified assumption that there was an obvious link to prices.

20. India reiterated that this was a real implementation problem arising from the Marrakesh Decision. India was concerned with the non-implementation of this decision affecting the most vulnerable developing countries, which would lead to a loss of these countries' faith in the WTO's responsiveness to their problems. India shared these concerns since it had graduated from being a net food importing country to self-sufficiency or even marginal exports. India urged the Vice-Chairman to develop a road map for the work leading up to Doha to find a solution to this problem. If food prices had decreased, and food aid had increased, India wondered why import bills had increased since the Uruguay Round. Through the Vice-Chairman, India requested FAO to analyze this problem and provide more information to the Committee.

21. New Zealand stressed that it had faithfully implemented the Marrakesh Decision and its follow-up at the Singapore Conference. LDCs wishing to trade with New Zealand had almost duty-free access, and starting on 1 July 2001 would have completely duty-free access for all products. New Zealand's food aid was guaranteed on a cash-only basis, and targeted assistance to agriculture was provided through its bilateral aid programme. New Zealand was neither for nor against the proposed short-term financing facility, but remained to be convinced of the need for a new fund. At the Roundtable, New Zealand had hoped to see an attempt to use the existing framework of the IMF and the World Bank since it saw significant barriers to the development of a new fund within the timeframe envisaged. New Zealand also saw difficulties in the notion of the WTO as a rules-based organization taking on this issue, and was struggling to find a way forward. Like India, New Zealand would endorse a road map, as well as further informal consultations and discussions at the July Special Session. If Ministers at Doha decided that the concept of a short-term financial facility should be pursued, then New Zealand would work faithfully to activate such a decision.

22. The European Communities noted that, similar to New Zealand, it had also opened its markets to LDCs. Regarding the proposal, the EC agreed that food aid should be in fully grant form, and should not be a means of surplus disposal. The EC was not convinced by the justifications given for the new fund. The Marrakesh Decision referred clearly to countries facing negative effects in terms of availability of food on reasonable terms and conditions, while the proposal referred to rising import bills, which might be caused by other factors, such as growing populations or higher incomes. While the Decision referred to the financial facilities of the current international organizations, the proposal suggested to create a new fund outside the umbrella of the current institutions. In addition, the EC was not convinced that the current financial facilities were inappropriate to meet the problems related to the availability of food. The EC remained open to further technical discussions to facilitate a better understanding of the issue. Food security would also be addressed in the negotiations under Article 20. Implementation of the Marrakesh Decision was important, and there was scope for significant improvements of conditions for the provision of food aid.

23. Venezuela replied that the Marrakesh Decision referred also to difficulties in financing normal levels of food imports. Regarding the link between the reform process and prices, the fact that there were many factors should not serve as an excuse to delay action. Paragraph 5 of the Marrakesh

Decision clearly referred to existing financial facilities and to possible new ones; thus the proposal aimed only at implementing something already contained in the Decision.

24. Egypt requested all delegates to concentrate on the proposal, which dealt with short-term financing requirements. Food aid did not replace these. Egypt was grateful for duty-free market access for LDCs, but this did not provide for food security. The new fund did not have to be outside the Bretton Woods organizations; the proposal mentioned that these organizations should be involved in its management. The fund was supposed to be commercially viable, and would constitute a safety net for bad times, which would help countries to go further in their liberalization efforts. Import bills of NFIDCs and LDCs for 2000/2001 were expected to rise by around 6 per cent. The Decision was meant to help NFIDCs and LDCs precisely in these situations, even if they did not reflect long-term market developments. Since it was to be expected that subsidies would be reduced through the ongoing negotiations, this would definitely result in price increases, probably about three to four years after the conclusion of an agreement. If nothing was done now, it would be very difficult to address that future situation, since it would take time to establish a new funding facility.

25. Canada recognized the concerns of some LDCs and NFIDCs over food security, particularly in the context of continuing agricultural trade liberalization. However, it reiterated the need to keep in mind the actual impact of the Uruguay Round on prices, which it believed to be slight. Canada looked forward to further consultations on the issue. If there were significant reductions in trade-distorting subsidies, this should normally result in rising prices, but the Uruguay Round results had not given a very good experiment to confirm this hypothesis since subsidies were still high. The Marrakesh Decision was about the impact of the Uruguay Round. In the future, further reduction in trade-distorting subsidies might actually result in rising prices. This suggested it would be appropriate to deal with the concerns of countries about the potential price impact of more significant reforms in the context of the negotiations. The discussion of food security in the July Special Session would be important in this regard.

26. Australia noted that it was interesting that according to the World Bank, the use of loans for agricultural development had declined. It would be useful to explore with the World Bank how this could be reversed. Agricultural development would be important to improve the food security situation of NFIDCs and LDCs. Other ways of improving the food security situation and address some of the concerns giving rise to the Marrakesh Decision were to work to eliminate export subsidies, reduce domestic support and increase market access. Australia looked forward to addressing these issues in more depth at the July Special Session in the context of the discussion of food security. Australia appreciated that these aspects addressed the longer-term issues, and that there also were short-term considerations. In this context Australia noted the proposal to establish a new fund, and looked forward to work with the IMF, the World Bank and the NFIDCs and LDCs on their concerns.

27. The United States also expressed concern at the decline in investment in agricultural and rural development noted by the World Bank. It was important to reverse this trend in order to address food security. Although they addressed very important issues, the United States had reservations about the specifics of the proposals, for example on the need for a new billion-dollar fund. The US considered fora other than the WTO more appropriate for making binding commitments on food aid.

28. As the biggest net food importer, Japan understood the necessity of making the Marrakesh Decision effective. Japan looked forward to participating in further informal meetings on the issue.

29. Switzerland believed that food aid should best be discussed in the Special Session of the Committee on Agriculture. Switzerland remained committed to the Food Aid Convention, strongly supported the proposal that food aid should be provided in fully grant form, and was ready to increase its commitments under the next Convention. However, food aid should not create dependence or

jeopardize local production. In this light, technical assistance, which was also part of the proposal, was of primary importance. With respect to financial facilities, the Swiss view was that they were best dealt with in the context of the Bretton Woods institutions. The Roundtable had shown that there were under-utilised facilities, and that both the World Bank and the IMF would welcome increased use of their facilities. Switzerland was not convinced that the existing facilities were not appropriate to accommodate the concerns, and looked forward to more informal consultations.

30. Norway agreed that the Marrakesh Decision needed to be operationalized. Norway thought that food aid should be given in fully grant form, and that there might be a need to increase the commodity volumes under the Food Aid Convention as well as technical and financial assistance. Starting on 1 July 2002, Norway would fully open its markets for imports from LDCs. As to short-term financing, Norway was not yet sure that the best solution was the creation of a new mechanism. First it should be analyzed what could be done to improve the existing mechanisms. Norway looked forward to a continued dialogue.

31. The Vice-Chairman summarized the discussions. Regarding future work, the Vice-Chairman planned to continue the informal consultations. There would also be an opportunity to pursue the issue at the Special Session in July in the context of the discussions on food security. The content of the consultations would include how to address short-term financial difficulties, whether present IMF and World Bank facilities were suited to address concerns, and the proposed revolving fund. He would also provide opportunities to consult in a wider context including the issues of food aid and technical and financial assistance to improve agricultural productivity and infrastructure.

G/AG/11
Page 27

ANNEX 2

Examination of Possible Means of Improving the Effectiveness of the Implementation of the Marrakesh NFIDC Decision Summary of the Interventions by the IMF, the World Bank and the FAO at the Informal Roundtable Discussion held on 18 June 2001

The International Monetary Fund

Item (i) **The issue of access to the financing facilities of the international financial institutions**

32. The IMF makes its financial resources available to member countries through a variety of lending, including through the following four "regular" facilities:

(a) Stand-By Arrangements (SBA): Designed to deal with any temporary balance-of-payments (BOP) problem. The typical SBA is for 12-18 months, but may be as long as three years and disbursement of financing is usually conditioned on the borrower meeting specified performance requirements. Loans must be repaid within 3 ¼-5 years. The expected repayment period is shortened to 2 ¼ - 4 years if the country' s external position allows it to repay earlier.

(b) Extended Fund Facility: Designed to provide medium-term assistance in particular to members with (a) an economy suffering serious payments imbalance relating to structural maladjustments in production and trade and where price and cost distortions have been widespread; or (b) an economy characterized by slow growth and an inherently weak balance-of-payments position which prevents the pursuit of an active development policy. The length of an EFF arrangement is typically three years and disbursement is conditioned on the borrower meeting specified performance requirements, including structural reforms. The facility has longer repayment periods than other facilities, 4 ½ - 10 years; the expected repayment period is shortened to 4 ½ - 7 years if the country' s external position allows it to repay earlier. If agriculture is targeted in a reform programme, countries can avail themselves of this facility. Some of the countries on the WTO NFIDC list would be eligible to use this facility.

(c) Compensatory Financing Facility (CFF): Provides financing for members experiencing temporary export shortfalls or excesses in cereal import costs, based on balance-of-payments situation. Interest rates are market-related, but are concessional in that the terms are better than would be available from commercial banks. Repayment in 3 ¼ – 5 years. The access limits have a range of up to 55 per cent of a country's IMF quota.

(d) Poverty Reduction and Growth Facility (PRGF): Highly concessional loans (0.5 per cent interest) with longer-term repayments (5 1/2-10 years). The PRGF could incorporate agricultural sector reform policies, as part of an overall strategy to reduce poverty. An eligible country may borrow up to a maximum of 140 percent of its IMF quota under a three-year arrangement; this limit (which is not an entitlement) may be increased under exceptional circumstances to a maximum of 185 percent of quota. Eligibility is based principally on a country' s per capita income and eligibility under the International Development Association (IDA), the World Bank' s concessional

G/AG/11
Page 28

window (the current cut-off point for IDA eligibility is a 1999 per capita GDP level of $885); accordingly, many of the countries on the WTO NFIDC/LDC list qualify. The PRGF is fully financed (i.e. available to meet the total theoretical demand).

33. According to its mandate, lending by the IMF must be aimed at addressing BOP problems. In the specific case of a loan request under the cereal component of the CFF, developments in cereal imports are examined from a BOP perspective, i.e., if import prices rise, the BOP situation has to indicate that there is a need. The CFF has been used infrequently. The most recent use of the cereals component was by Bulgaria in 1997. Conditionality is one of reasons for its infrequent use, the availability of other instruments is another. Infrequent use is not a problem of lack of financial resources.

Item (ii) **The scope for adapting the existing programmes and facilities of the international organizations in light of the Marrakesh NFIDC Decision**

34. The IMF is based on revolving resources. Thus, the notion of unused resources (mentioned by some participants in the roundtable) does not apply.

35. The CFF was recently reviewed as part of a process of refocusing the IMF. The decision taken in this regard has reduced access, strengthened conditionality, as well as established a stronger link to overall BOP conditions. There were also voices among IMF members to abolish the CFF. The IMF will review its decision concerning the CFF *not later than 30 August 2002.*

36. As an alternative to adapting existing IMF facilities, countries concerned could analyze their situation from a balance of payments perspective, to determine whether their perceived financing needs could be met through recourse to IMF financing.

Item (iii) **The Proposal to Implement the Marrakesh Ministerial Decision in Favour of LDCs and NFIDCs submitted by Côte d'Ivoire, Cuba, Dominican Republic, Egypt, Honduras, Jamaica, Kenya, Mauritius, Morocco, Pakistan, Peru, Senegal, Sri Lanka, St. Lucia, Trinidad and Tobago, Tunisia and Venezuela**

37. The IMF position remains that it is in a position to meet any anticipated balance-of-payments needs. In accordance with its mandate, the IMF could consider the proposal only if it was related BOP difficulties. Since the proposed new fund falls outside its authority, the IMF cannot make a contribution.

38. In theory, it would be easier to amend the CFF than establish a new fund.

The World Bank

Item (i) **<u>The issue of access to the financing facilities of the international financial institutions</u>**

39. World Bank lending for agriculture and rural development decreased from 30 per cent of its total in 1978-81 to 9.6 per cent in 2001 - the lowest level ever. It was US$ 3.5 billion a decade ago but only US$ 1 billion in 2000. As the World Bank's approach has become more demand-driven, requests for agricultural and rural development loans have declined. This development is alarming since 70 per cent of those living on less than a dollar a day live in rural areas and most are farmers. In view of this development, the Bank is currently conducting a review of its agricultural sector and rural development strategy.

40. Most client countries have under-performing agricultural sectors, partly as a result of under-investment in Green Box measures. In many cases, there is a pronounced urban bias, with most public investment flowing into the cities. In addition, the domestic policies in developing countries often depress the internal terms of trade against agriculture. Overvalued exchange rates and other government interventions in many client countries continue to adversely affect prices for agricultural products. Farmers in many developing countries remain net tax payers due to their own government's interventions. In such circumstances, conditionality is imposed to ensure that the client country's own policies do not make World Bank-financed projects less likely to succeed.

41. A number of reasons were responsible for the declining trend in loan disbursements, including the following. As the result of low commodity prices, it has been difficult to obtain a satisfactory internal rate of return. Commodity prices have declined over the past 150 years in real terms and, although the World Bank projects food demand to double by 2050, due to technological improvements in agriculture it does not expect prices to rise in the long term. Safeguards to address legitimate environmental and social concerns also add to the cost of borrowing. Furthermore, the political reality is that the rural poor have little political voice and their interests are not a priority to their own governments.

42. IDA terms for the lowest income countries are very favourable at 0.5 per cent interest and 30 years repayment. Loans on IBRD terms are on commercial terms, although the World Bank AAA rating provided some benefit.

43. With respect to short-term measures, the World Bank is committed to market-based instruments with a view to reducing the effects of price fluctuations on farmers. Since 1999 in a number of cases commodity swaps have been part of loan agreements, whereby the commodity price risk was transferred to, and hedged by, the World Bank. In addition, the World Bank has set up a task force to explore commodity risk management to allow farmers in developing countries, especially smallholders, to use options and futures contracts. Eight related case studies are underway and pilot projects are due to start in 2002. Market-based risk management instruments are amenable to both producers/exporters and importers of agricultural commodities. It might be noted that the Cotonou Agreement makes reference to, and encourages the use of, market-based instruments.

G/AG/11
Page 30

Item (ii) **The scope for adapting the existing programmes and facilities of the international organizations in light of the Marrakesh NFIDC Decision**

44. As noted above, the demand for loans related to agriculture and rural development has declined dramatically over the past decade. Had there been demand, the World Bank could have lent much more for agriculture and rural development. (This does not imply that the World Bank has unused financial resources since loans are financed from bond sales. The World Bank has additional borrowing capacity for client countries to request loans related to agriculture or rural infrastructure.)

Item (iii) **The Proposal to Implement the Marrakesh Ministerial Decision in Favour of LDCs and NFIDCs submitted by Côte d'Ivoire, Cuba, Dominican Republic, Egypt, Honduras, Jamaica, Kenya, Mauritius, Morocco, Pakistan, Peru, Senegal, Sri Lanka, St. Lucia, Trinidad and Tobago, Tunisia and Venezuela**

45. The World Bank provides loans for investment but its charter does not permit lending for consumption. Furthermore, the World Bank provides very little in terms of grants and thus would not be in a position to contribute to the proposed new fund.

46. The World Bank considers market-based instruments (as outlined above) to be preferable to the creation of a fund to compensate for unanticipated price shocks. With respect to market-based instruments, the World Bank would consider subsidising the premia for such price insurance policies.

The Food and Agriculture Organization

Item (iii) **The Proposal to Implement the Marrakesh Ministerial Decision in Favour of LDCs and NFIDCs submitted by Côte d'Ivoire, Cuba, Dominican Republic, Egypt, Honduras, Jamaica, Kenya, Mauritius, Morocco, Pakistan, Peru, Senegal, Sri Lanka, St. Lucia, Trinidad and Tobago, Tunisia and Venezuela**

47. The proposal is based on research undertaken by FAO and presented at a FAO roundtable at the Palais des Nations on 21 March 2001. If there is interest in pursuing this proposal, FAO stands ready to provide further information and assistance with respect to the needs assessment and the operation of the proposed fund.

48. As a preliminary idea, the fund could be set up by providing ex-post compensation to governments in times of import bills deviating significantly from the long-term trend. Governments may then use these resources by providing targeted assistance to those that are adversely affected by increase in prices. Also, these resources may be used to support food production and productivity increasing programmes. In order to avoid rapid drawing down of the fund's capital, the level of drawings could be capped.

WORLD TRADE ORGANIZATION

RESTRICTED
G/AG/W/49/Add.1
23 May 2001

(01-2663)

Committee on Agriculture

Original: English

PROPOSAL TO IMPLEMENT THE MARRAKESH MINISTERIAL DECISION IN FAVOUR OF LDCS AND NFIDCS

Submitted by Côte d'Ivoire, Cuba, Dominican Republic, Egypt, Honduras, Jamaica, Kenya, Mauritius, Morocco, Pakistan, Senegal, Sri Lanka, St. Lucia, Trinidad and Tobago, Tunisia and Venezuela

Addendum

The attached Addendum concerning the Proposal to Implement the Marrakesh Ministerial Decision in favour of LDCs and NFIDCs is being circulated at the request of the above-mentioned Members.

OPERATIONALIZING THE MARRAKESH DECISION:

A NEW APPROACH TO SHORT-TERM FINANCING REQUIREMENTS

Introduction

The aim of this paper is to serve as a background document for the Roundtable on Operationalizing the Ministerial Decision on Measures Concerning the Possible Negative Effects of the Reform Process on Least-Developed Countries and Net Food-Importing Developing Countries (hereinafter referred to as the Marrakesh Decision).

The Roundtable seeks to bring together all the parties concerned (LDCs, NFIDCs, donor countries, the WTO, FAO, IMF and World Bank), in an effort to discuss the operationalization of part of the proposals presented by a number of WTO Member states (document G/AG/W/49), namely to create a new fund whose purpose is to provide the 'safety net' promised by the Marrakesh Decision, under terms and conditions compatible with the latter. It is hoped that the Roundtable would produce an agreement on forging forward with ideas for financing LDC/NFIDCs, to be presented at both the autumn session of the IMF/World Bank and the WTO Ministerial in November 2001 for implementation.

Sincere thanks is hereby extended to Mr. Yoichi Suzuki, Minister Plenipotentiary at the Mission of Japan to the WTO, whose untiring efforts as Vice-Chair of the Committee on Agriculture at the WTO were instrumental in revitalising a subject long-thought dead and organising the

Roundtable. Special gratitude also goes to Frank Wolter and Thomas Friedheim, Director and Counsellor respectively of the Agriculture Division and their staff, for their help and cooperation with the current effort. Last, but most definitely not least, to all the men and women of the delegations of Member states who have, over the years, kept the flame burning. To them we owe our appreciation, gratitude and thanks. May the Almighty bless our efforts.

Why the Decision? And Why the Roundtable?

There is little argument that agriculture is - and will remain for the foreseeable future - the essential sector for the majority of LDCs and NFIDCs, whose impact spills over from the economic into the social and political arenas. Food security is also a major policy objective of these countries, particularly as they depend - to a smaller or larger extent - on importing a sizeable proportion of their populations' food requirements.

In order for LDCs and NFIDCs to sign onto the Agreement on Agriculture (AoA) in 1994, the Decision was taken by Ministers attending the launch of the WTO, with the express aim of providing a 'soft landing' for those Member states whose economies were most liable to be affected from the liberalisation of agriculture under the AoA. Particularly, the Decision focused on the concept of 'availability of **adequate** supplies of **basic foodstuffs** from external sources on **reasonable** terms and conditions'. Hence, the Decision proposed three short-to-medium term response mechanisms (more food aid in grant form, S&D treatment on export credits, short-term credit facilities), as well as a longer-term mechanism (technical and financial assistance to improve agricultural productivity and infrastructure).

In view of the fact that the Decision has been a subject for little more than 'discussion' and 'review' for the last six years, the Roundtable, therefore, aims to:

- Galvanise all concerned states and parties into adopting a more practical and pragmatic work programme aimed at moving from the 'discussion' phase to the 'doing' one; and

- Study the proposal presented herein to address the needs of LDCs and NFIDCs in their quest to satisfy their basic foodstuff requirements from the world market; under a mix of terms and conditions that may be considered reasonable, with a view to presenting a workable plan for implementation by the IV Ministerial Conference in Doha.

In order to visualise the urgency and importance of the issue at hand, a few figures would be needed. Drawing on figures published by FAO, the WTO[1] and other international sources, the following facts stand out:

1. The combined **populations** of the 49 LDCs and 20 NFIDCs broke through the 1 billion mark in 1998, representing over 22 per cent of the combined population of all developing countries. Meanwhile, undernourishment touched around 38% of LDC populations, and 17 per cent of those of NFIDCs.

2. **Per capita incomes** of LDCs in 1997 were 17 per cent of the average of developing countries, while the p.c.i. for the NFIDCs in the same year stood at about 70 per cent of the developing country average.

[1] 'Implementation of the Decision on Measures ', document no. G/AG/W/42/Rev.3, WTO, 31 October 2000; and 'Towards Improving the Operational Effectiveness of the Marrakesh Decision', Discussion Paper no.2, FAO, Rome 2001.

3. The combined **cereals import bills** for LDCs and NFIDCs rose by over 10 per cent from 1993-95 to 1998/99, with a peak rise of 42.6 per cent in 1995/96. It is forecast that the year 2000/01 will see a further rise of around 3 per cent ($800 million) in the value of cereal imports for these countries aver the figures for 1999/2000.
4. **Food aid** deliveries to LDCs and NFIDCs **fell** from 5.65 million MTs in 94/95 to an estimated 4.59 million MTs in 99/00; a drop of around 19 per cent. It is notable that the volume of food aid to LDCs in 1999 represented 99 per cent of the 90-99 ten-year average, while that for NFIDCs was only around 63 per cent of said average - compared to a 60 per cent rise in food aid deliveries to 'other' countries during the same period. As to the **concessionality** of food aid, there remains at least one donor country which does not yet provide such aid on a 100%-grant-basis.

5. The volume of **commercial imports** by LDCs and NFIDCs **rose** from 35.2 million MTs in 94/95 to an estimated 42.9 million MTs in 99/00 (a rise of over 21 per cent), with a further increase of 750,000 MTs forecast for 2000/01.

6. Although cereal **import bills** are now thankfully lower than the peaks reached in 1995/96, they still remain at a higher plateau than the period prior to 1994/95.

Scope and Magnitude of the problem

A recent FAO study[2] concluded that the inadequacy of physical supplies of basic foodstuffs on world markets are not currently an issue for reflection, and that the real problem lies in the conditions of access facing LDCs and NFIDCs in obtaining their food requirements. The study also concluded that, in view of the language used in formulating the Decision, the triggering mechanisms for 'operationalising' the Decision should be based on the totality of effects and factors, i.e. on unexpected levels of food import bills of LDCs and NFIDCs on an individual basis, rather than limiting them to individual factors that lead to the outcome (e.g. rises in world market prices, declines in food aid deliveries, and so on).

Based on these conclusions, the study went on to compute the magnitude of excess import bills for the period 1989-1998 based on 5 per cent and 10 per cent alternative thresholds. It concluded that, for all food items and 46 LDCs and 19 NFIDCs covered by the Decision, the aggregate "excess" food bill in the 'maximum' year (1995/96) over the mean of the period was $900 million (on the 5 per cent rule) and $605 million (based on the 10 per cent rule)[3].

Availability of Financial resources

The Decision foresees the need of LDCs and NFIDCs to address both short-term financing ('to cover difficulties in financing normal levels of commercial imports') and a longer-term financial need ('to improve their agricultural productivity and infrastructure').

On the short-term front, allusion has been made to the availability of financial resources under the **IMF**'s Compensatory Financial Facility (CFF). A recent evaluation undertaken by the IMF itself

[2] 'Towards improving the Operational Effectiveness .', FAO, op. cit, pg. 4.

[3] As shown in the FAO paper, the mean is the average for 1989-98 of the total "excess" import bills (i.e. the aggregate of all countries studied with import bills greater than 5 per cent or greater than 10 per cent above trend). Negative deviations from trend were not taken into account, since such deviations do not constitute a 'problem' to be addressed by the Decision.

points to the fact that 'there has been very little use of the CFF in recent years'[4]. In fact, reliable evaluative studies has come to the conclusion that, to make the CFF compatible with the terms of the Decision, the CFF would need 4 adjustments:

1. Extend its coverage to all basic food imports (rather than cereals only).

2. Relaxation of its general conditionalities and rules on eligibility.

3. Streamline eligibility requirements for both LDCs and NFIDCs.

4. 'Concessionalise' its resources, both in terms of repayment periods and interest levels.

It is to be noted that the same study concludes that 'the CFF is not the most suitable instrument for addressing the problem .. (sic. to be addressed through the Marrakesh Decision)'[5]. Meantime, the role and operations of the **World Bank** in the provision of short-term financing for emergency food imports are not clear.

The longer-term requirement for multilateral financial resources is **theoretically** available through the World Bank's contributions to the Consultative Group on International Agricultural Research (CGIAR), estimated at $ 50 million in 1998[6], and other World Bank projects in the field of agriculture. No clear figures are available to quantify the long-term technical assistance and capacity-building programmes for LDCs and NFIDCs, or a detailed evaluation of their effectiveness in raising productivity and production – a key component of the assistance foreseen in the Decision.

To sum up, the financing required to address the 'short-term difficulties' is practically non-existent from any multilateral source on the terms - and under the conditions – foreseen in the Decision; while the longer-term financing needed to upgrade physical and human resources in agriculture are partially available via the World Bank.

The New Fund

This dearth of suitably conditioned short-term (<24 months maturity) financial resources leads us to believe in the need for a totally new approach for the future, to be based on the philosophy and intent of the Decision. It is, in fact, neither inconceivable nor unreasonable to assume that the 1995/96 surges could happen repeatedly in the future. The idea is for the creation of a special Food Financing Facility (F^3), solely designed for the implementation of the Decision. The F^3 could be visualised as follows:

(a) In view if recent experience, its resource base is estimated at around $1,200 million[7]; to be drawn from a 'consortium' of multilateral financial organisations, G-7 and other donors, and major developed exporting Member states.

(b) The 'eligibility' of LDCs and NFIDCs to draw on the resources of the Fund would be decided on a country-by-country basis and in accordance with agreed-upon guidelines, and after a fair and factual computation/assessment was made of its requirements. Levels of each country's

[4] 'The Fund's Compensatory Financial Facility – Recent Developments', IMF Speaking points for the Geneva Roundtable on Selected Agricultural Issues, Geneva March 21st, 2001 pg.2.

[5] Ibid.

[6] WTO document G/AG/GEN/31 of 15 December 1998, pg 23.

[7] This figure was calculated on 2 years worth of credit facilities at the lower end level of $600 million, as per the FAO study.

compensation package could be capped in periods of surges in import bills, in order to avoid harming the Fund's long-term financial viability.

(c) The resources available to the Fund could be 'recycled' or repayable, so as not to unduly inflate the capital of said Fund. In fact, in the years when import bills are amenable, the resources could be earmarked by donors, but not disbursed, with a view to the optimal utilisation of such resources. Repayments of financial resources drawn-down by beneficiaries would be effected under a medium-term scheme on terms more favourable than current open market conditions.

(d) The responsibility for the administration and management of the Fund would need to be centralised in a small bureaucracy; said bureaucracy to be overseen by a Management Board comprising representations from the WTO, FAO, IMF, World Bank, donor states as well as the beneficiaries.

This Fund would, obviously, not cover the longer-term requirements of LDCs and NFIDCs to improve their basic infrastructures and enhance agricultural productivity. In this respect, a call is made out to all donor parties to earmark a greater proportion of any multi- and bi-lateral aid programmes for such use. It was the vision of the signatories to the Marrakesh Decision to 'wean' recipients away from their food-aid 'dependancy'. This can only be achieved through a serious, concerted and cooperative effort aimed at improving levels of self-sufficiency of LDCs and NFIDCs – while maintaining the gains achieved in the agricultural reform process under the AoA, and spurring these countries towards greater engagement in future reform processes under the current negotiations under Article 20 of the AoA.

Appendix 10
Decision on Implementation of Article 4 of the Agreement on the Application of Sanitary and Phytosanitary Measures
G/SPS/19
(16 October 2001)

WORLD TRADE ORGANIZATION

G/SPS/19
26 October 2001

(01-5267)

Committee on Sanitary and Phytosanitary Measures

DECISION ON THE IMPLEMENTATION OF ARTICLE 4 OF THE AGREEMENT ON THE APPLICATION OF SANITARY AND PHYTOSANITARY MEASURES

The Committee on Sanitary and Phytosanitary Measures,

Having regard to paragraph 1 of Article 12 of the Agreement on the Application of Sanitary and Phytosanitary Measures;

In response to the request from the General Council that the Committee examine the concerns of developing country Members regarding the equivalence of sanitary or phytosanitary measures and develop concrete options as to how to deal with them;

Reaffirming the right of Members to establish sanitary and phytosanitary measures necessary to ensure the protection of human, animal and plant life or health and the protection of their territory from other damage caused by the entry, establishment or spread of pests, in accordance with the Agreement on the Application of Sanitary and Phytosanitary Measures;

Desiring to make operational the provisions of Article 4 of the Agreement on the Application of Sanitary and Phytosanitary Measures;

Noting that equivalence of sanitary or phytosanitary measures does not require duplication or sameness of measures, but the acceptance of alternative measures that meet an importing Member's appropriate level of sanitary or phytosanitary protection;

Recognizing that equivalence can be applied between all Members, irrespective of their level of development;

Noting that Members have faced difficulties applying the provisions of Article 4 recognizing the equivalence of sanitary and phytosanitary measures;

Taking into account the specific concerns raised by developing country Members, and particularly the least developed among them, regarding their difficulties in having the equivalence of their sanitary or phytosanitary measures accepted by importing Members;

Recognizing the importance of minimizing possible negative effects of sanitary or phytosanitary measures on trade and of improving market access opportunities, particularly for products of interest to developing country Members;

Recognizing that transparency, exchange of information and confidence-building by both the importing and exporting Member are essential to achieving an agreement on equivalence;

Recognizing that there may be other less resource-intensive and time-consuming means for Members to enhance trade opportunities;

G/SPS/19
Page 2

Decides as follows:

1. Equivalence can be accepted for a specific measure or measures related to a certain product or categories of products, or on a systems-wide basis. Members shall, when so requested, seek to accept the equivalence of a measure related to a certain product or category of products. An evaluation of the product-related infrastructure and programmes within which the measure is being applied may also be necessary.[1] Members may further, where necessary and appropriate, seek more comprehensive and broad-ranging agreements on equivalence. The acceptance of the equivalence of a measure related to a single product may not require the development of a systems-wide equivalence agreement.

2. In the context of facilitating the implementation of Article 4, on request of the exporting Member, the importing Member should explain the objective and rationale of the sanitary or phytosanitary measure and identify clearly the risks that the relevant measure is intended to address. The importing Member should indicate the appropriate level of protection which its sanitary or phytosanitary measure is designed to achieve.[2] The explanation should be accompanied by a copy of the risk assessment on which the sanitary or phytosanitary measure is based or a technical justification based on a relevant international standard, guideline or recommendation. The importing Member should also provide any additional information which may assist the exporting Member to provide an objective demonstration of the equivalence of its own measure.

3. An importing Member shall respond in a timely manner to any request from an exporting Member for consideration of the equivalence of its measures, normally within a six-month period of time.

4. The exporting Member shall provide appropriate science-based and technical information to support its objective demonstration that its measure achieves the appropriate level of protection identified by the importing Member. This information may include, *inter alia*, reference to relevant international standards, or to relevant risk assessments undertaken by the importing Member or by another Member. In addition, the exporting Member shall provide reasonable access, upon request, to the importing Member for inspection, testing and other relevant procedures for the recognition of equivalence.

5. The importing Member should accelerate its procedure for determining equivalence in respect of those products which it has historically imported from the exporting Member.

6. The consideration by an importing Member of a request by an exporting Member for recognition of the equivalence of its measures with regard to a specific product shall not be in itself a reason to disrupt or suspend on-going imports from that Member of the product in question.

7. When considering a request for recognition of equivalence, the importing Member should analyze the science-based and technical information provided by the exporting Member on its sanitary or phytosanitary measures with a view to determining whether these measures achieve the level of protection provided by its own relevant sanitary or phytosanitary measures.

8. In accordance with Article 9 of the Agreement on the Application of Sanitary and Phytosanitary Measures, a Member shall give full consideration to requests by another Member, especially a developing country Member, for appropriate technical assistance to facilitate the implementation of Article 4. This assistance may, *inter alia*, be to help an exporting Member identify and implement measures which can be recognized as equivalent, or to otherwise enhance market access opportunities. Such assistance may also be

[1] Product-related infrastructure and programmes is in reference to testing, inspection and other relevant requirements specific to product safety.

[2] In doing so, Members should take into account the *Guidelines to Further the Practical Implementation of Article 5.5* adopted by the Committee on Sanitary and Phytosanitary Measures at its meeting of 21-22 June 2000 (document G/SPS/15, dated 18 July 2000).

with regard to the development and provision of the appropriate science-based and technical information referred to in paragraph 4, above.

9. Members should actively participate in the ongoing work in the Codex Alimentarius Commission on the issue of equivalence, and in any work related to equivalence undertaken by the Office International des Epizooties and in the framework of the International Plant Protection Convention. Bearing in mind the difficulties faced by developing country Members to participate in the work of these bodies, Members should consider providing assistance to facilitate their participation.

10. The Committee on Sanitary and Phytosanitary Measures recognizes the urgency for the development of guidance on the judgement of equivalence and shall formally encourage the Codex Alimentarius Commission to complete its work with regard to equivalence as expeditiously as possible. The Committee on Sanitary and Phytosanitary Measures shall also formally encourage the Office International des Epizooties and the Interim Commission on Phytosanitary Measures to elaborate guidelines, as appropriate, on equivalence of sanitary and phytosanitary measures and equivalence agreements in the animal health and plant protection areas. The Codex Alimentarius Commission, the Office International des Epizooties and the Interim Commission on Phytosanitary Measures shall be invited to keep the Committee on Sanitary and Phytosanitary Measures regularly informed regarding their activities relating to equivalence.

11. The Committee on Sanitary and Phytosanitary Measures shall revise its recommended notification procedures to provide for the notification of the conclusion of agreements between Members which recognize the equivalence of sanitary and phytosanitary measures.[3] Furthermore, the procedures shall reinforce the existing obligation in paragraph 3(d) of Annex B of the Agreement on the Application of Sanitary and Phytosanitary Measures for national Enquiry Points to provide information, upon request, on the participation in any bilateral or multilateral equivalence agreements of the Member concerned.

12. Members should regularly provide to the Committee on Sanitary and Phytosanitary Measures information on their experience regarding the implementation of Article 4 of the Agreement on the Application of Sanitary and Phytosanitary Measures. In particular, Members are encouraged to inform the Committee on Sanitary and Phytosanitary Measures of the successful conclusion of any bilateral equivalence agreement or arrangement. The Committee on Sanitary and Phytosanitary Measures shall consider establishing a standing agenda item for its regular meetings for this purpose.

13. The Committee on Sanitary and Phytosanitary Measures shall develop a specific programme to further the implementation of Article 4, with particular consideration of the problems encountered by developing country Members. In this respect, the Committee on Sanitary and Phytosanitary Measures shall review this decision in light of the relevant work undertaken by the Codex Alimentarius Commission, the Office International des Epizooties and the Interim Commission on Phytosanitary Measures, as well as the experience of Members.

14. The Committee on Sanitary and Phytosanitary Measures requests that the General Council take note of this decision.

---

[3] G/SPS/7/Rev.1